GW00480591

TOTAL STATE

TOTAL STATE

TOTALITARIANISM AND HOW WE CAN RESIST IT

Paul O'Brien

EASTWOOD BOOKS

First published 2023 by Eastwood Books
Dublin, Ireland
www.eastwoodbooks.com
www.wordwellbooks.com

1

Eastwood Books is an imprint of the Wordwell Group.

The Wordwell Group is a member of Publishing Ireland,
the Irish Publishers' Association.

Eastwood Books
The Wordwell Group
Unit 9, 78 Furze Road
Sandyford
Dublin, Ireland

© Paul O'Brien, 2023

ISBN: 978-1-913934-21-7 (Trade Paperback)
ISBN: 978-1-913934-50-7 (Ebook)

The right of Paul O'Brien to be identified as the Author
of this work has been asserted in accordance with the
Copyright, Designs and Patents Act 1988.

All rights reserved. No part of this book may be reprinted
or reproduced or utilised in any form or by any electronic,
mechanical or other means, now known or hereafter invented,
including photocopying and recording, or in any information
storage or retrieval system, without the permission in writing
from the Publishers.

British Library Cataloguing in Publication Data.
A catalogue record for this book is available from the National Library of Ireland and
the British Library.

Typesetting and design by the Wordwell Group
Copyediting by Myles McCionnaith
Printed in Ireland by Sprint Print, Dublin

CONTENTS

ACKNOWLEDGEMENTS

Gratitude is due to a number of people who read and commented on draft material. In particular I would like to thank Marion Kelly, who went out of her way to provide an ongoing and extremely helpful critique. Seanan Kerr offered valuable and extensive critical insights, and suggested some productive lines of enquiry. Thanks are due to Deirdre Coveney, Deirdre de Burca, Kenji Hayakawa, John Hutchinson, Daniel Lipstein, Mark Murphy, Laura Plunkett, Liam Ryan, Aoife Sheehan and Caroline Whyte. I wish to thank Ronan Colgan for his interest in, and support of, the project, and Myles McCionnaith for his careful and perceptive editing. Any mistakes are my own.

INTRODUCTION

Totalitarianism has been a bugbear of our collective consciousness in the modern age. This has been expressed particularly in literature (for example, in the writings of Yevgeny Zamyatin, George Orwell and Aldous Huxley) and film (*THX 1138*, *The Truman Show*, *The Matrix*, *Minority Report* and the recent *New Order*).

The danger seemed to have receded with the collapse of the Soviet Union towards the end of the twentieth century, but in more recent times it has raised its head again, with the rise of the far right at one end of the spectrum and the growing power and influence of China at the other. This is to say nothing of parallel technological developments, which threaten to turn our habitations into glass houses in which no one will be able to hide from the all-seeing eye of corporations or the state, or indeed their consolidation in the corporate state.

In the legal arena, there have been unsettling developments – such as in the United States, where the Patriot Act has greatly increased powers of surveillance[1] and the National Defence Authorisation Act[2] has provided for indefinite military detention. Elsewhere, we have seen the rolling back of protections against double jeopardy, the admissibility of hearsay evidence,[3] the threat to the ancient doctrine of *habeas corpus*,[4] the erosion of the right to silence[5] and the potential of laws against hate speech to infringe on free speech, and perhaps even on free thought.[6]

The United States is a nation founded on high-minded ideals; it is traditionally regarded as a bastion of liberty, despite the mistreatment of the native population and the institution of slavery that marred the first century of its existence. Nevertheless, it is there that we have seen the mainstreaming of discussions around the use of torture, as well as the already-established practices of mass (and racially biased) incarceration. There are the oppressive three-strikes-and-you're-out laws, the widespread use of the death penalty, the psychological torture of solitary confinement and the indefinite internment without trial in Guantanamo.

All of these raise issues about the role of the state and current related threats to freedom and democracy, not just in the United States but also worldwide. There is an urgent need for countermeasures in defence of cherished values and institutions.

Underlying these developments, it is argued here, is the problem of a basic over-extension of the state itself in two crucial areas.

The first is an out-of-control military–industrial complex that has sparked political destabilisation, particularly in the Islamic world. This is partly in an attempt to prop up the environmentally destructive oil industry, and partly in the service of its own self-perpetuation now that Soviet Communism has outlived its usefulness as a political threat – however exaggerated that threat may itself have been.

This, in turn, has fostered the growth of militant Islam, either directly or as a reaction to military interference, resulting in the expansion of terrorism and, consequently, repressive countermeasures to deal with it. An uncharitable view would be that the growth of militant Islam was not entirely unwelcome from the point of view of the preservation, and enhancement, of the 'defensive' (or rather offensive) military capabilities of the United States.

The second area in which the state has over-extended itself – one where it has no justifiable place – is in the domain of recreational drug use by individual citizens.[7] Drug prohibition, and its application in the 'war on drugs', has had many unfortunate results, not least of which is the counterproductive growth of the illicit drugs industry itself and the expansion of the wealth and power of criminal gangs. This, in turn, feeds into the enhanced status of the police and prison systems,[8] and the increasingly repressive laws to deal with the growth of organised crime – laws which have a negative effect on the liberties of the citizenry as a whole. There is also the growth of institutional corruption that the massive power and wealth of criminal gangs inevitably entails. In countries like Afghanistan, the issue of the drug trade and the issue of foreign military intervention are intertwined.

The underlying problem is that of an out-of-control, anti-environment industrial system, a rampant militarism, and a repressive corporate state that straddles the traditional left–right political divide. In the not-wholly-exaggerated terms of Zygmunt Bauman, 'Within certain limits set by political and military power considerations, the modern state may do anything it wishes to those under its control.'[9]

At the same time, as a kind of grotesque counterbalance, the neoliberal[10] or corporate state falls short in crucial areas where the contribution of the state could be of value – specifically, those of health, housing, the protection of workers and education.

This has had the negative effect – particularly in countries such as the United States, where neoliberalism is strongest – of exacerbating the recent Covid-19 pandemic, putting pressure on workers to earn a living rather than to prioritise keeping themselves, their families and the community safe from infection. To add insult to injury, in addressing the pandemic in recent times in the United States, much more emphasis was placed on supporting already-rich companies rather than assisting workers, families and students.[11] A deteriorating system of public education ensures the perpetuation of the political malaise, since a functioning democracy crucially needs an educated voting population.

Added to the above is the growth of a large-scale surveillance system, which in turn feeds the insatiable appetite of the corporate state.

In recent times, we have seen the institution of emergency legislation – on a global basis – as a countermeasure to the pandemic. The danger of repressive state responses to the pandemic challenge was illustrated by the signalling in the United Kingdom of possible ten-year prison terms for those in breach of pandemic-related travel restrictions.[12]

Overall, public responses to emergency measures ranged from support at one end of the scale, through reasoned concern for civil liberties, to out-and-out paranoia.

Distinct from the recent emergency measures, there has been the parallel – and largely unnoticed – imposition over the years of a stifling accountancy-law regime on the citizenry of developed countries, primarily through the tax, welfare, financial, legal and insurance systems. There is no escape from the Kafkaesque logic, or illogic, of an impenetrable web of rules and laws. The high school nightmare of information you don't understand – and which you can find no one to explain – extends throughout our adult lives, for business person and private citizen alike. The dominance of a quantitive mindset drives creativity to the margins of life.[13]

I began writing this book before the global health crisis, so it was fortuitous that the issue of the state's creeping control over citizens' lives took on a sharp urgency while I was well into the project. In the context of the pandemic, repressive measures – which only a few years ago would have been regarded as satire – became routinely discussed and implemented. A cartoon around the beginning of lockdown showed a picture of two inmates in prison. 'What are you in for?' asks one. 'I went for two walks,' was the reply. It was funny at the time.

In a dizzyingly short space of time, the unthinkable has become the norm, with the marginalisation of libertarians – and even conventional liberals – in public debate, and tight control of what is permissible, or not, in media discussion.

When the coronavirus hit, and the measures to contain it were activated, I had already planned to spend much of my time at my writing desk, so I wasn't affected as onerously as others may have been. One issue that has affected us all, though, is that the situation developed so quickly and in such unexpected ways that it was difficult to keep up with developments. Consequently, it has been hard to know what is ephemeral in terms of laws and regulations, and what will remain in the medium and long term.

In relation to the pandemic, therefore, I have attempted to steer clear of ever-changing, day-to-day legal issues and restrictions. These vary geographically, and may range from the prudent to the draconian. The arguments about the negative socioeconomic effects of lockdown measures vis-à-vis their necessity from a health point of view are familiar at this stage and I won't be pursuing them.

My main priority is to highlight the fragility of our liberties in the context of the state, the democratic system and corporate pressures. To that end I have tried to set out some basic ideas of key thinkers – past and present – in the area of political philosophy and to make them accessible to the interested reader. My main aim is not to pursue the political-philosophical issues themselves in any depth – for which there is neither the time nor the space – but to indicate some of the main concerns for the non-specialist reader, specifically the threat of totalitarianism to our hard-won freedoms. The principal idea is to assist in understanding, and perhaps helping in some way to counteract, such a development.

The current consensus is that the coronavirus originated in a wet market in Wuhan, rather than escaping from a laboratory. The pandemic is, at the moment, widely accepted as being an example of 'zoonotic spillover' (transfer from animals to humans in a natural context). If this theory of the coronavirus's origin is correct, the major factor behind this development is an unsustainable system of nature's exploitation. This system includes the destruction of animal living spaces, an unfettered trade in wildlife, deforestation, resource exploitation, intensified agriculture and the abuse of nature leading to climate change. These negative factors are made worse by poverty, urbanisation and globalisation.[14] Our relationship to nature is as unsustainable as our systems of corporate and state control are oppressive and destabilising.

If, on the other hand, the 'lab escape' theory turns out to be correct, the burden of blame shifts to the scientific establishment itself. Whichever explanation turns out to be true, we are presented with a deeply disturbing situation in terms of the operations of our society.

In the pages that follow, I have tried to make crucial theoretical approaches (such as those of Hannah Arendt, Giorgio Agamben, Karl Popper, Shoshana Zuboff, and Max Horkheimer and Theodor Adorno) accessible to the non-specialist reader, as well as critically linking the theoretical material to some recent and contemporary issues. While nothing can substitute for a study of the key authors themselves, I hope that the issues raised here may function as a critical guide to such further study.

This book is intended primarily as a political project in the public sphere rather than as a contribution to academic theory, though some academics may find it useful as an explanatory resource of key texts, or as a theoretically-based overview of the current political situation. The area is so wide that I have inevitably had to sacrifice depth for breadth, but the interested reader may find the book useful as a guide to further study in aspects of this vital area of political thought.

The idea for the book was sparked by a response to a general, and crucial, problem in our society: that of the gulf between academics operating in the sphere of political theory and related areas, and the widespread lack of public awareness, or understanding, of political issues that affect us all.

Feeding into the problem is the domination of a culture of managerialism in the academic world. To put it crudely, the contemporary university is inhabited by academics who, for the most part, don't have time to teach, let alone intervene in the political arena in terms of public debate. One reason is that they are overwhelmed by the need to produce publications in which quantity dominates over quality – publications that few people have the time, access or inclination to read.[15]

Furthermore, academics need to spend much of their time on unproductive administrative activities, reporting to their managers about the work they don't have time to do, partly because of the amount of time needed to account for the work in question.

In their intellectual work, academics are forced by a quantitative and analysis-dominated system, and an associated mindset, into focussing on ever-more-minute intellectual issues that may give them kudos from a career point of view. At the same time, however, their work may be of marginal concern to the wider society.

The authors I have discussed here are, by and large, exceptions to the above criticism; they have often made real attempts to have their work understood by the general public. It's important that the issues themselves become widely debated at a public level, not just an academic one.

On the other side of the academic–public divide is the thought-control of the public by the mainstream media[16] and the pervasive, and growing, phenomenon of infotainment.[17] This is paralleled, in the digital sphere, by the predominance of wild conspiracy theories, often manipulated by invisible interests. Deep knowledge on the part of the public of the minutiae of mass culture is often combined with a shattering ignorance of such key areas as history, geography and politics.

This gulf between arcane intellectual enquiry and widespread public unawareness represents a serious political danger. In order for democracy to function, it needs an informed electorate. If the split between the electorate and the intellectual world is such that the former doesn't have the capacity to make an informed political judgement – and perhaps isn't even aware of what the process of reaching such a judgement might involve – then that is a serious issue, with potential ill effects for everyone. The negative results in recent political experience – for example, in the United States and the United Kingdom – are so obvious as hardly to need mention.

The key issues touched on here include the menace to freedom and democracy from various sources, and the nature of threats to life and liberty such as fascism and totalitarianism. An attempt is made here to highlight issues such as the state of exception, dangers to liberty from the political left and right, populism, the widespread phenomenon of groupthink, and mass surveillance.

I have not attempted to pin down definitively such key concepts as those of the state, populism, freedom, democracy, liberalism, libertarianism, nationalism, authoritarianism, fascism, totalitarianism and so on. As will become evident, the terms in question tend to expand the more one tries to specify them; in some cases, even the possibility of definition is contentious. Any one of them could easily form the subject matter of a book in itself. Nevertheless, the reader who wishes to explore such basic concepts further may find assistance and relevant references in the endnotes.

Chapter 1

FREEDOM, DEMOCRACY AND THE STATE

The recent pandemic has brought into focus the issue of the relationship between the individual and the state. It has also raised the question of science's role as it interfaces with that relationship.

Like many things in Ireland, where I live, the process of restricting civil liberties under the pressure of the recent pandemic has, to date, been met with relative equanimity. Nevertheless, the emergency legislation was stringent, detailed and quickly adopted; it involved minimum debate around the potential future pitfalls in terms of civil liberties. There was also much initial confusion over the issue of where guidance ended and compulsion began – confusion the authorities did little to dispel.[1] As time went on and patience frayed, tensions between the imperatives of medical science and the practical realities of politics became evident; it is a process that has been ongoing in Ireland, and globally as well.

The theme of this book relates to the dangers as well as the benefits of the state particularly under the pressures of pandemics (present and future), as well as pressures of growing nationalism, protectionism and economic inequality, and the development of a surveillance culture.

The state can step in and co-ordinate emergency measures that individual citizens cannot organise on their own. On the other hand, and as history has shown, in extreme cases the state can annihilate democracy and freedom, often under the guise of protecting us from foes of one kind or another. The erosion of freedom and autonomy may take the guise of benevolence.

Theorists have had much difficulty in pinning down the nature of the state, in terms of both understanding the phenomenon throughout history and analysing it in the present. Some writers regard the state as being in the process of becoming obsolete, while some reject the whole notion of the state. From a poststructuralist point of view, the state is seen as an 'outcome of politics' rather than as an explanatory mechanism.[2] The state may be regarded as a collection of practices.[3]

The state is somewhat vague as an entity, a concept and a term. A key issue is the relationship between nation and state, the term 'nation state' being utilised to refer to a state with a strong element of cultural or ethnic homogeneity. In recent times, the idea of the nation state has been highlighted once more – in an attempt to resist the undermining of a traditional sense of identity under pressure from globalisation.[4]

The twentieth century had a love--hate relationship with the state. On the negative side, the state functioned as a means of implementing the most extreme horrors, from the Gulag in the Soviet Union to Auschwitz under the Nazis; from the terrors recounted by Aleksandr Solzhenitsyn to those described by Primo Levi. On the positive side, the state also operated as a means of softening the extreme effects of the capitalist system through the development of social resources and facilities – at its best facilitating (as in the Nordic countries, with their intersection of state and market) a comfortable and humane life for the citizenry. In social democratic countries, the downside is evident in high taxes and prices, an element of bureaucracy, and the complacency that security and safety tend to bring in their wake.

Marxists attack the state for its class-based nature, repressiveness and ideological function.[5] Conversely – from a prevalent perspective – they defend its possibilities of transformation in a socialist direction. The state has been worshipped by fascists; it has been derided by anarchists, such as Peter Kropotkin and Michael Bakunin. Nationalists and social democrats defend the state (though for different reasons: nationalists, because it strengthens a sense of national community; social democrats, because of its egalitarian potential, in terms of social services and the redistribution of wealth).

On the other hand, the state is often the object of suspicion on the part of conservatives and libertarians alike. (These two categories sometimes overlap with each other, particularly in the United States – for example, in the case of the veteran politician Ron Paul.)

Libertarians (Robert Nozick, for example[6]) often wish to minimise the role of the state, though not to abolish it completely. At its extreme, the libertarian position would accept the necessity for police and army but not much more. Conservatives have varying views on the role of the state, but they often believe in minimising it, particularly in the economic sector. Marxists, like anarchists, also desire (ultimately, in the case of the former) a stateless condition of society. Unlike anarchists, however, Marxists normally believe in seizing control of the state as a step on the road to that ostensibly desirable condition.

Nevertheless, things are much more complex than the above outline might suggest. In the United States, for example, there is sometimes an overlap between left and right – between the more enlightened progressives on the one hand (in Europe, we would call them leftists) and the more enlightened conservatives-libertarians on the other. Such an overlap might involve opposition to bank bailouts, to the criminalisation of recreational drugs or to foreign military adventurism.[7]

Nonetheless, there is often sharp opposition – between progressives and conservatives, in particular – on issues such as gun control, separation of church and state, and human reproduction. The possibilities of a crossover politics in the United States may exist, but such prospects are limited.

There is also a distinction to be made between different forms of nationalism. Nationalism may be conservative and right wing (as in contemporary Poland, Hungary, the United States and England) or socially liberal and economically left wing (for example, Sinn Féin in Ireland).

English nationalism is quite a different entity to Irish nationalism; Irish nationalism looks back to past victimisation and celebrates resistance, while English nationalism looks back with nostalgia – conscious or unconscious – to a colonial past, when Britain, and England in particular, told the world what to do.

BREXIT AND THE EU

In recent times, the exit of the United Kingdom from the European Union has brought into focus the issue of the state – specifically in the form of the nation state – as the process raises questions about national identity and its effect on political structures. In the case of Britain, the situation was influenced by historical echoes of the British Empire. This issue of the state arises particularly in regard to the question of whether the individual 'independent' nation state[8] (in this case, the United Kingdom) is to be preferred over national membership of a larger conglomeration (the EU) with aspirations to a federation of states. The former position seems to have won out in the United Kingdom, at least for the time being. At the same time, Brexit has highlighted a number of areas where the political issues have been obscured.

For a start, the handy term 'Brexit' (short for 'British Exit from the European Union') does not in fact sum up the project, either as it was envisaged or as it turned out. The simple reason is that describing Northern Ireland as 'British' is contentious – at least from an Irish nationalist perspective. ('Ukexit' would be less snappy though, which is presumably why it was not chosen.) Consequently, the very term 'Brexit' seems to raise questions about the relationship between Northern Ireland, the United Kingdom, the EU and the Irish Republic.

A further issue is that the United Kingdom does not comprise one nation but four: England, Scotland, Wales and Northern Ireland. The latter three may be described as ethnically Celtic, if indeed the term 'Celtic' means anything – apart from describing a subset of languages within the larger Indo-European context. Nevertheless, Wales is the only UK nation in which the native (Celtic) language is spoken, in everyday use, by a significant part of the population. In this, it implicitly points a finger at Ireland, where language revival has failed despite – or perhaps because of – political independence and autonomy, which engendered ham-fisted and counterproductive attempts at language revival.

The semantic problem raised by the term 'Brexit' is largely ignored (which serves to obscure the problematic nature of the Northern Ireland political entity, sometimes referred to as a 'statelet'). Complicating the issue further is the constitutional complexity of the United Kingdom itself, illustrated by the fact that the terms 'Britain', 'British Isles' and 'United Kingdom' all have separate, and sometimes contested, meanings.

Echoing this complexity is the nomenclature attached to the Irish state, which, with varying degrees of accuracy and inaccuracy, is referred to as 'Ireland', 'Eire', 'Éire', 'the Irish Republic', 'the Republic of Ireland' and, most piquantly, 'the Free State'. Since freedom is almost universally desired, the last term sounds as if it's a compliment, but it is really an insult. Northern Irish Catholic nationalists, for historical reasons, sometimes use the term disparagingly, in reference to the incomplete nature of the post-Rising Irish state: not yet a republic (until 1949), and still subject to partition from the North.

Blind spots are particularly characteristic of Irish politics. These include the forcible displacement of the native Irish population by British planters in the sixteenth and seventeenth centuries, a historical phenomenon often ignored, or unseen, by Northern Irish loyalists. On the other hand, Catholic atrocities against Protestants in England and on the Continent – which provided a handy rationale for the British plantations in Ireland – are often ignored, or unseen, as well.

To complicate the matter further, some Irish plantations actually took place under the reign of Queen Mary, a Catholic notorious for her persecution of English Protestants. Irish children are taught a lot about the historical misdeeds of the British, and specifically the English, but not much about their rationale. That rationale developed partly from fear of

Spain and of the Catholic Inquisition – as well as, more censurably, from British economic opportunism and rapaciousness.

The prevailing ideology often runs counter to the historical reality. There is the further fact that King William, victor at the Battle of the Boyne and the hero of Northern Protestants, was actually supported by the Pope of the time.[9] The original Irish republicans of the eighteenth century – the United Irishmen – comprised many Presbyterians who were disadvantaged by the same laws that victimised Catholics. There is the strange historical reality - confounding the caricature of the recent Irish Troubles as a Protestant–Catholic struggle – that monarchies are actually a Catholic institution and republics a Protestant one; the political theorist Montesquieu pointed to this fact centuries ago.[10] The nationalist–unionist polarity in Ireland, whereby nationalists identify as republicans and unionists as royalists, is an exact mirror-opposite of this.

To make things even more complicated, Irish Catholics in the seventeenth century made common cause with the English monarchy against the plebeian Protestant Roundheads. (The Roundheads were so-called because of their short hair, in contrast to the long-haired, monarchist Cavaliers.) The most reviled individual in Irish political memory was actually a republican of sorts: the king killer, Oliver Cromwell. Indeed, the term 'Tory', of Irish origin, originally meant a displaced Irish Catholic ally of English royalists. But facts, particularly in Northern Ireland, are seldom allowed to get in the way of political persuasion – something that features on both sides of the loyalist–nationalist divide.

There is also the – seldom-remarked – parallel between Northern anti-Catholicism and Southern (post-Catholic) secularism. Northern Protestants and Southern secularists often criticise the Roman Catholic Church in very similar ways, though usually without any acknowledgement of each other, or of the resemblances between the two positions – and often with complete mutual dismissal.

On the other hand, there has been the recent convergence in Northern Ireland of conservative, right-wing views around – for example – abortion and gay marriage, from both sides of the sectarian divide.

Somewhat ironically, the influence of church on state, to which Northern Protestants previously objected so vehemently, now seems to characterise the North rather than the South. Such developments may, in fact, indicate a growing political modernisation on the island, where a new secular–religious dichotomy replaces older sectarian tensions between the two mainstream Christian traditions.

The baffling complexity of (Northern) Irish politics is illustrated by the role played by the Irish–UK border in terms of the relationship between the United Kingdom and the EU. The two nation states (Ireland and the United Kingdom) embody formidable cultural complexities that potentially challenge the project of European integration, not to mention the long-term stability and continuity of the United Kingdom itself.

A related area of obscurity involves the intended shape of the EU – that is, whether its future is envisaged in terms of a tight federation of states (a kind of United States of Europe) or a loose confederation of otherwise-autonomous entities. The difference between the two is, perhaps, largely one of degree: a federation involves more central control than a confederation. For all kinds of reasons, including those of vested interests, the pressure towards federalism, or federation, is usually strong.

BREXIT, FREEDOM AND DEMOCRACY

Brexit illustrates some ways in which issues around the role of the state have functioned in our lives in the recent past – often without deep reflection by the populace on the conflicting elements and values involved – and indeed continue to do so in the present.

Brexit has also highlighted a key concern: the relationship between democracy and freedom in the contemporary state. It was taken for granted, by many on both sides of the Brexit debate, that the will of the majority in the Brexit referendum should be respected, and consequently that another referendum was out of the question. The question could be raised, though, as to whether that was an appropriate response. One can think of all kinds of absurd and oppressive decisions taken by majorities that would have to be overturned as quickly as possible – in the interest of freedom[11] and other desirable values, such as privacy,[12] dignity and autonomy.

Consequently, the statement that 'the will of the people is always right' is questionable. To take some examples, we could imagine some dire situation where a majority of the population voted in favour of laws to institute slavery, torture or genocide. Such a situation would be difficult – indeed, impossible – to justify, even as a result of a majority decision. As former Irish Taoiseach Éamon de Valera is reputed to have said, 'The majority have no right to do wrong.' There is an argument, in the very least, that the will of the majority has no obvious mandate once it exceeds a certain destructive threshold.

Apart from such extreme impositions as those mentioned above, what about a law that would seriously restrict foreign travel? It's arguable that Brexit impedes travel, since it places severe limits on the right to mobility within Europe – a right that the British people formerly benefitted from. It seems clear that the knee-jerk appeal to 'the will of the people', when it encroaches on human freedom, is at least questionable as a justification. This observation is given added weight when one remembers that the Brexit referendum was actually advisory in nature and not legally binding.[13]

Alexis de Tocqueville, one of the most trenchant defenders of democracy, pointed out that the concept of 'the will of the nation' has been abused throughout history by those of a despotic mindset.[14] In an important sense, though, the argument about the legitimacy of the Brexit referendum is academic. If the referendum had any claim, it was a moral one, not a legal one – and its moral claim was highly dubious. Apart from the non-binding nature of the Brexit referendum, there is also the issue of the slim majority in favour of leaving the EU and the tenuous role that facts often played in the debate.

Democracy is a means of maintaining important political values (including, crucially, freedom itself). Often, democracy works quite well to that end. Occasionally, however, there is a clash between the will of the people and the good of the population as a whole. When that happens, we have a situation that may be described as 'the tyranny of the majority', and a question arises of whether such tyranny should be accepted or rejected.[15] In the case of a legally-binding decision, this would raise considerable political difficulties, to say the least; in the case of a non-binding result, the issue seems much more clear-cut.

The fudge about the referendum result's moral weight was only one area where lack of intellectual clarity prevailed. And the blind spots weren't all on the side of the Brexit supporters. Largely unexamined factors on the pro-EU side included the effect of open borders on keeping down the price of labour (to the disadvantage of workers)[16] and the difficulties that EU membership might involve for the socialist project – supported by those on the left of the Labour Party – of the nationalisation of key industries, such as transport.[17] There has also been the EU's heavy-handed treatment of countries like Ireland and Greece during the recent economic crisis (not to mention, in the Irish context, issues regarding the EU's pressure on the Irish corporation tax structure). These examples of blurred vision occur when political preference overcomes rationality; they are not confined to the left or the right, to nationalists or internationalists, or to one kind of globalist or another.

BREXIT AND GLOBALISM

In respect of the role of the nation state, the phenomenon of globalism involves a further area of contention.[18] Prior to the present millennium (and 9/11), anti-globalism was largely a left-wing phenomenon – a fact that seems almost forgotten now. In the United States, President Donald Trump operated as the focus of right-wing anti-globalism, which adhered to economic protectionism and the defence of the national economy against foreign competition. His rule also involved anti-progressivism, curbs on immigration, opposition to environmental politics, and authoritarian nationalism. Much of the left-wing negativity towards the effects of globalism (sometimes justified) has been co-opted by the right, feeding into the success of the form of protectionist capitalism championed by Trump and his supporters.

In the United Kingdom, both sides of the Brexit debate seemed to see themselves as globalists, albeit of different kinds. On the one hand, the Brexiteers reached out to the English-speaking countries of the former British Empire ('Oceania', in George Orwell's terms). Their opponents, however, condemned Brexit as a piece of nationalist folly, and looked to the EU as a cosmopolitan saviour from the inward-looking 'Little Englanders'. In similar fashion, Irish cultural modernists have seen the EU as a resource against inward-looking Irish nationalism.

Globalism (or transnationalism) of whatever kind has been challenged recently by the Covid-19 pandemic, though global trade carried on despite the public health emergency. Nevertheless, stronger national border controls on people's movement may be necessary to contain future viral outbreaks, and there may be a perceived need for ongoing clampdowns on personal freedoms that are normally taken for granted.

On the face of it, developments such as Covid-19 seem to add credence to the arguments for strong borders, made by nationalists and authoritarians of one kind or another. Ironically, though, strongman leaders like Trump, Jair Bolsonaro of Brazil and Alexander Lukashenko of Belarus have been among the weakest when it comes to taking the problem seriously and implementing anti-pandemic controls. This perhaps signals a crucial vulnerability in their claim to power. In the case of Trump's support base, it involves a potential tension between libertarianism and authoritarianism, as well as a widespread ignorance of the science involved in analysing and reacting to the pandemic. Strength is weakness, to turn Orwell on his head.

At the same time, the pandemic also highlighted the potential for state authoritarianism underlying the democratic system: when the chips are down, citizens tend to do what the state tells them, including submitting to compulsory quarantine when necessary. The safeguard here is the inclusion of sunset clauses in emergency legislation, to ensure that the legislation ceases when the emergency does – something that, unfortunately, does not always happen.[19]

BREXIT, IMMIGRATION AND NATIONALISM

From an Irish perspective, it is easy to see the Brexit phenomenon in postcolonial terms. The Irish feel comfortable in the EU because it gives them a sense of equality with other European nations; the English felt uncomfortable in it, for more or less the same reason. As has often been observed, membership of the EU and its predecessors helped the Irish to move beyond a postcolonial mindset in which the former colonial power was simultaneously admired and resented.

Despite the EU's rough treatment in the context of the financial crisis more than a decade ago – and the corporation tax issues – Irish support for EU membership is overwhelming.[20] This is, in part, a response to the dog's dinner that the United Kingdom has made of its exit from the EU.

Yet the Irish should not be too glib about the situation. England, which is about twice the size of the Republic of Ireland in geographical terms, has nearly eleven times its population.[21] If there were a similar population level in the Republic, it would contain nearly thirty million people, instead of the present number of around five and a quarter million. It is not difficult to imagine the political stresses such a situation would involve.

In Ireland, where immigration has had considerable economic and cultural benefits, we congratulate ourselves on our cosmopolitan liberalism, in contrast to what we sometimes perceive as the benighted, insular English. To take an example, within a short walking distance of my home in the centre of Dublin, I have – in normal times, at least – access to dozens of excellent ethnic restaurants. Schoolchildren (when the schools are open) learn in multicultural environments – a huge cultural boon, at least potentially. With passers-by who look and sound so different from one another and from the native population, Ireland has been rescued from a dreary, insular demographic sameness. All that is needed to complete the picture is some Mediterranean weather.

Dublin, at least in times of normality, often feels like a mini London or New York: tolerant, prosperous, multi-ethnic and culturally enriched, though with some racist criminality on the margins. Insularity is a thing of the past: interracial relationships result, in due course, in children who may be bilingual or multilingual. Nor does this have a negative effect on traditional Irish culture. Irish-language schools are thriving, despite successive political establishments' cack-handed, counterproductive attempts at preserving the native tongue. Anti-immigration agitation in Ireland receives little support.[22]

Yet we in Ireland should ask ourselves the uncomfortable question as to whether our tolerant mindset would survive similar population pressures to those that exist in England. Irish people, as demonstrated by the result of the 2020 general election, do not normally make a connection between immigration and the pressures on health and housing – and this is no doubt correct. For one thing, immigrants normally pay taxes, just like the indigenous population. It is anyone's guess, however, whether this tolerance would continue with a greatly increased population and concomitant political, social, cultural and environmental pressures. Rational concerns about the general issue of overpopulation may easily slide into less rational anxieties about the ethnic composition of the population.

On the European continent, authoritarian nationalism – notably in France, Poland and Hungary – is the resort of those who regard the EU as part of a federalist, centralising movement. They see the EU's goal as being to undermine the nation state, together with European society and culture as a whole (particularly by encouraging mass immigration of people from non-European countries).

An overriding problem is the prevalence of unasked questions. For example, do we in Europe want to live in largely independent autonomous states, or under the umbrella of a supranational entity like the EU?

Or, asking a somewhat different question, do we wish to break down state barriers in favour of globalism, cosmopolitanism, internationalism – or, indeed, in favour of ecologically specific bioregions? These questions are seldom asked, and it often seems as if the lack of asking is a deliberate policy.

The rush to form a coherent European political entity as a hedge against a repetition of fascism and war, which disfigured the first part of the twentieth century in Europe, led to unintended consequences. The most significant of these, ironically, was the rise of authoritarian nationalism, with its destabilising implications, as a reaction against supranationalism. However enlightened and commendable the EU project may be, if you don't bring the population with you to a sufficient extent, you risk the future sabotage of the project through reaction. Electorates, as noted already, don't always get it right.

Circumstances are not helped by the closet federalism of the EU elite, which promotes 'ever-closer union' without adequately checking whether this is something that their electorates actually want.[23] The drive towards economic integration before political integration, epitomised by the adoption of the Euro as a common currency, may in hindsight be seen as a mistake. Indeed, the forging of European cultural links should probably have been at the foundation of the European project, rather than being an add-on or afterthought. The major issue here is the tacit assumption that the process of integration which worked in the United States, with its (more or less) homogeneous language and culture, would also work in Europe.

BREXIT AND THE STATE

The foregoing discussion illustrates some ways in which unspoken, and largely untheorised, issues around the role of the state have functioned in our lives in the recent past, and continue to do so in the present. This has political as well as theoretical implications: threatening nationalistic clouds seem to gather where the nation state encounters attempts, real or imagined, to supersede its powers.

In the United Kingdom, population pressures, along with tabloid manipulation and distortion, function to intensify nationalist (and specifically English) resistance against the EU. The EU is by no means faultless, but it has functioned – both in its present and previous incarnations – as a means of maintaining peace and social stability on a continent racked by war for centuries; a continent in which the most horrific events, including the attempt to exterminate the Jewish people, have taken place within living memory. By rationalising its trade structure, the EU largely lifts the burden of bureaucracy from individual firms, a benefit hitherto taken for granted.

The EU has recently come under threat, though, due to the inaction of the northern states in helping out countries, such as Italy, whose economies were endangered by Covid-19 and the socioeconomic consequences of the response to the pandemic. If the EU were to collapse, authoritarian nationalists are waiting in the wings. To take one example, Hungary gave Prime Minister Viktor Orbán the right to rule by decree for an indefinite period, though this was later rescinded.[24]

The UK populace was affected ideologically, over a period of decades, by distortion and displacement. Resentment was deflected from its rightful target (the inequity of the neoliberal capitalist system) towards fake or overstated targets, such as immigrants, the EU and the exaggerated phenomenon of anti-Semitism in the Labour Party. The economic ill-effects of Conservative austerity were real enough, but were glossed over by most of the media. The (entirely justifiable) indignation against austerity, with its policy of 'socialism for the rich, capitalism for everyone else', was instead projected onto immigration and the EU. In turn, the EU was blamed, largely incorrectly, for the effects of immigration. (The United Kingdom could have limited immigration even within the structure of the EU, but chose not to do so.[25])

This negativity was intensified by the disturbingly low level of political consciousness in the English population as a whole, which is arguably tied to the educational imbalance in the country. England has the distinction of containing some of the world's top universities, while Ireland's universities score much less impressively[26] (to the extent that quantitative measurement means much in this context). Nonetheless, any casual vox pop on television will illustrate the huge gap between ordinary people's levels of political consciousness in the respective countries. It is as though economic inequality in the United Kingdom (or at least England) is mirrored by its educational system: world-beating excellence for those who can afford it, unquestioning passivity and incomprehension for those who can't. One might say the same about the United States – a factor that has, arguably, fed into the Trump phenomenon.

This is not to say that, in regard to the Brexit phenomenon, the educated elite in England have covered themselves in glory. Debates in the House of Commons often seem to descend to the level of a spat between rowdy teenagers, to the dismay of their neighbours in the EU. The result of this political infantilism, in the major Anglo-Saxon-Celtic countries of the United Kingdom and the United States, has been a danger to democracy itself.

If, or more likely when, the nostalgia for a pre-Brexit never-never land fades in the cold light of reality, the result may be considerable political dislocation in Britain, never mind on the island of Ireland. Ironically, support for Brexit by the loyalist Democratic Unionist Party in Northern Ireland helped to hasten the DUP's worst nightmare: the heightened prospect of a united Ireland as a result of the weakening of the United Kingdom as a whole, in addition to the intensification of border issues on the island of Ireland. Added to this is Northern Ireland's problematic status in terms of trade – with the rest of the United Kingdom, with the Republic, and with the EU.

In the Irish Republic, the prayer of Saint Augustine has often been cited to illustrate attitudes to the idea of a united Ireland, 'Give me the gift of chastity, but not yet.' In other words, it's something to which most Irish people would aspire, and which would look vaguely neater on the map, but the obstacles in the way are considerable. These include the spectre of rationalisation and redundancy in the civil service on both sides of the border; the subvention cost of the Northern Ireland economy, hitherto borne by the UK taxpayer; and the necessity to extend the already creaking National Health Service in Northern Ireland to the island as a whole, or else to construct a workable all-island alternative. (This alternative would, presumably, be in the face of resistance from the medical and insurance establishments in the South, who may take the view that they have much to lose through the nationalisation of the health service.)

In this context, it's worth noting that the economic dislocation caused by the reunification of Germany lasted for decades – and is indeed ongoing – despite the fact that there was negligible opposition to the project at the time. However, the impetus towards a united Ireland has been increasing in recent times, spurred on by Brexit and by the rise of Sinn Féin as a political force in the South.

To sum up, Brexit has highlighted the uncertain future of the UK state, of Ireland, and perhaps of the EU itself as a collection or union of states. Scotland, which voted against Brexit, may attempt (again) to secede from the United Kingdom, partially motivated by a desire to remain in – or rather, rejoin – the EU. (Such an aspiration may be resisted by Spain, which wants to avoid a precedent being set for independence-minded Catalonia.) Northern Ireland, which often looked to Scotland for a cultural and ethnic connection, may be set (further) mentally adrift by that development, and the pressure for a united Ireland may become unstoppable.

In the long term – no doubt after much turmoil and dislocation – a closer alliance might evolve between a unified Ireland and an independent Scotland, which would perhaps help to resolve uneasiness within the unionist and loyalist population of Northern Ireland in regard to their position within a united Ireland. A Scottish–Irish alliance, of whatever nature, within the EU would have linguistic and historical credibility (bearing in mind the similarity between the Irish language and Scots Gaelic, and the political connections between the two countries – achieving their zenith, or perhaps nadir, in the Jacobite movement of the eighteenth century). It would also reflect the desire of progressive elements within both nations to develop their socioeconomic systems along the lines of the other countries of northern Europe, specifically the Nordic ones.[27]

Whether the religious differences between Ireland and Scotland would function to hinder such a development would remain to be seen. Ireland (or at least the Republic) has become increasingly secular in the recent past, and Presbyterian–Catholic political alliances on the island have occurred in the more distant past. In religious terms, a Scottish secession from the United Kingdom, and eventual closer links between Ireland and Scotland, would mean a more or less secularised Anglo-Catholic England and a more or less secularised mix of Roman Catholics and Presbyterians in Scotland and Ireland.

In this scenario, England and Wales would echo the respective roles of Serbia and Montenegro in rump Yugoslavia, while trying, with an aging population and an ever-receding memory of empire, to operate like Singapore on the fringe of Europe. To wonder whether Wales would eventually, as a consequence, join a future fringe alliance of the Celtic countries is to enter crystal ball territory.[28]

To sum up, the future in Europe – sharply illustrated by the Brexit controversy – looks like an intensified struggle between the exaltation of the nation state and a liberal, supranational EU federation (or, less likely, confederation). This dichotomy is represented by the choices taken by Britain (or England, at least) on the one hand and Ireland on the other. The key questions around the role of the state are in regard to the implications for the hard-won values of human freedom, dignity, privacy and autonomy.

POLITICS, DEMOCRACY AND THE UNITED STATES

Around the time of the Soviet Union's collapse, Georgi Arbatov of the Soviet Cabinet of Sciences stated that 'Our major secret weapon is to

17

deprive you of an enemy.'[29] Of course, that could not be allowed to happen; new enemies of the West duly appeared with the alacrity of Emmanuel Goldstein in George Orwell's *Nineteen Eighty-Four*: Saddam Hussein, Muammar Gaddafi, Osama bin Laden and a host of more minor characters. The military–industrial complex and the corporate party (in the United States, the Democrats and the Republicans) always need to ensure that there is an adequate enemy to justify military expenditure. Lone voices that speak out against this political stitch-up – for that is what it essentially is – are marginalised.

This is to by no means to indulge in anti-Americanism, or to ignore the positive political contributions of the United States, for example the separation of church and state and freedom of expression. In political and social terms, the First Amendment to the US Constitution, preventing the establishment of religion and guaranteeing freedom of expression, is a shining example of such contributions. In economic terms, it is hard to imagine life-revolutionising entities like Google, Facebook or Apple emerging in any environment other than that of the United States, with its ample resource of venture capitalists – however unsustainable capitalism as a system may be in the long term. It is too easy to highlight the negative aspects of the United States.

The United States gave us neoconservatism and neoliberalism, but it also gave us Henry David Thoreau, whose nature-loving philosophy has had such a powerful influence on the environmental movement; Rachel Carson, with her significant defence of nature; and such environmentally-influential figures as the landscape architect Frederick Law Olmsted. This is not to mention incisive political critics such as Noam Chomsky, Sheldon Wolin and Ralph Nader.

The US people's commitment to liberty is surely to be admired, despite the constant right-wing denigration of the term 'liberal' (which in fact has the same Latin origin as 'liberty'). While liberals may sometimes take on the illiberal aspects of statism (the belief that centralised state power is optimal), mental conformity and military aggression, in the social sphere liberalism itself is as defensible as liberty, and perhaps indistinguishable from it.[30] Nonetheless, those of us who do not identify with the statism, bureaucracy, military adventurism and ideological conformity sometimes associated with liberalism may identify instead as libertarian, with the qualification that one can be either a right-leaning or a left-leaning libertarian.

At its best, the US mindset is permeated by love of liberty. Indeed, the sentiment seems to have a certain longitudinal correlation. Arriving in Dublin or London after a flight from central or eastern Europe, my sense of freedom expands, though my sense of order may diminish. When I alight in Boston or New York after flying from Dublin, I feel a similar sense of expansion: introversion drops away, and I experience few qualms about chatting to someone in a queue (or rather line). A further trip to the west coast will immerse one in an intensified culture of extrovert friendliness, albeit – from a European perspective, at least – with a certain lack of emotional depth or historical rootedness. You aren't constantly wondering, as you are in Europe, if your cordiality will be rejected or misinterpreted. A culture of chatting to strangers is prevalent in the United States. This takes a while to shake off when you return to the more subdued, formal, introverted and perhaps even morose ambience of Europe.

But of course there is a downside to life in America too: examples include high crime levels, a fraught relationship between police and citizenry, lack of social mobility, a dearth of social and even personal security, and a fragmented and atomised society. The United States, is a great country if you are young, bright, extroverted, healthy, highly educated, ambitious and the beneficiary of some family capital. It is not so great if you are none of these things. In particular, the recent pandemic has painfully exposed the inadequacy of its privatised health system and lack of workers' rights.

The broader issue, though – highlighted by the Trump phenomenon, media control and manipulation, and ideological intolerance on both left and right – is that freedom and democracy seem under serious threat in the United States, specifically from a reactionary form of nationalism.

Democracy as we know it is only a couple of hundred years old. It is by no means certain that it will not collapse into a new barbarism, with the assistance of one demagogue or another.

SOME ANCIENT RESONANCES

In ancient Greece, Aristotle argued that the tyrant originally arises from the people as a demagogue, opposing the notables in defence of the people.[31] He pointed out that tyranny favoured the lower kind of human being, since freedom-loving individuals do not give him the flattery he craves.[32]

In his *Republic*, Plato argued that democracy inevitably leads to tyranny. While he wrote in the context of ancient Greece, his insights have implications for the present as well. He described how, in a democracy, a class of idlers develops; this class manages everything. A further class of money-makers arises, whose money is extracted by the idlers, like honey by drones. The idlers (i.e. the leaders) take wealth from the rich and distribute it to the workers, keeping the bulk of the wealth for themselves. The workers, who create wealth, are not involved in politics, but are in fact the most powerful group in a democracy. The rich money-makers object to having their money taken away, and are accused by the idlers of being opposed to the people. Thus, the money-makers become oligarchs. Plato points out that none of this is wilful; it happens because of the way the system is structured. Legal developments ensue, including impeachment.

The people then, as is their habit, exalt one man as the champion of their interests. This is how tyrants arise – their well-known request, for a bodyguard to keep them safe. Tyrants maintain their dominance through instigating war. For Plato, however, the tyrant's problem is that he has to do away with his friends as well as his enemies, since he cannot tolerate the truth if it criticises his actions. In contrast to how a doctor purges the body, the tyrant draws off the good and leaves the bad.[33]

An extreme version of this was seen graphically in the twentieth century, with Hitler and Stalin. Hitler, for example, did not normally liquidate his own military critics (as long as they weren't suspected of involvement in assassination plots), but his tyrant-minded failure to follow their advice, as well as a culture of toadyism among the top brass, helped to ensure his ultimate military defeat. Stalin notoriously presided over a post-revolutionary system that systematically eliminated its own supporters.

From a contemporary perspective, there are some limitations to Plato's views. Plato was, it should be said, no friend of democracy,[34] and the flaws that we might see as serious, he saw as fatal. He also conflates democracy and freedom, which as we have seen, is not always a legitimate thing to do – democracy can, and sometimes does, clash with freedom, through the tyranny of the majority. Furthermore, capitalism did not exist in ancient Greece, so – if critiquing our own systems – the drawbacks that he ascribes to democracy, we might ascribe to capitalism.

Nevertheless, there are unsettling parallels between Plato's thesis and developments in contemporary societies. In the United States, for example, the money-makers (i.e. capitalists), or at least a section of them, blame an idle, parasitical bureaucracy for wasting their money. An alliance develops between capitalists and workers in the emergence of an oligarchy, and a single individual claims to represent the interests of both.

Of course Plato, no matter how suggestive his ideas sound, was not a prophet. In our time, the corporate state, particularly in the United States, involves as much of an alliance of capitalists and bureaucrats as it does an antagonism between them. There is a stronger alignment between money-makers and workers in present-day society, in terms of authoritarian politics, than Plato might have conceived of in his. Nevertheless, it is quite a feat for him to have foreseen – no matter how roughly – a situation that would arise two and a half millennia after his time.

There are extreme versions of the emergence of authoritarianism (as in various fascist and Communist systems) as well as milder ones. The latter have come about in Britain and the United States. As in Britain with Brexit, Trumpism in the United States seemed to appeal to the lowest kind of populism. Online comments by Trump supporters may be identified by their poor grammar and spelling, before their substance (if any) is even considered. Neo-fascists and neo-Nazis, whose politics is barely disguised – or not disguised at all – count themselves among Trump supporters.

The negative issues around Trump are familiar. The combination of boorishness, ignorance, male aggression, domination, self-centredness and self-righteousness, of which he has functioned as a channel, is the exact opposite of the values that both mainstream Christian and secular elements in society claim to represent. Yet Trump, and in particular his anti-immigrant stance, has enjoyed support from a wide social spectrum. (This includes a disturbingly large number of people of Irish origin, as if the surest way to cast off the cloak of past victimhood is to force someone else – in this case Muslims or immigrants from Latin America – to wear it.[35])

Trump's support is sometimes viewed as being confined to older, deluded, gun-toting rust-belt males with opioid addictions, looking desperately for someone to return them, through economic protectionism, to a world that never existed in the first place. This is, though, a kind of caricature. That element is certainly there, together with an educational deficit arising from the mediocrity of the public educational system in the United States. Nevertheless, Trump's support has been broader in terms of voter background than one might think from the appearance and behaviour of his most vocal supporters.[36]

Trump's supporters have an arguably legitimate suspicion of the recondite and detached-from-reality mindset of the educated middle classes. An anti-intellectual revolt on the part of the public is the result of extreme academic specialisation (focusing on minutiae at the expense of trying to grasp the overall picture), the decline of the public intellectual, a pervasive culture of politically correct groupthink, and disdain for ordinary people by an educated elite; this has taken the form of derision towards detached academics, intellectuals and 'experts' who neither know what ordinary people think, nor could communicate with them if they did. Such a negative view of the detached intellectual elite is not without substance or accuracy.

Trump's genius – for that is what it is – was to plug into the prevailing exasperated populism. As Tocqueville pointed out as far back as 1835, the richer citizens are careful to stay on familiar terms with people below them on the social scale – a person's manner is more important than any material benefits that are imparted.[37] It is unlikely that Trump has read Tocqueville, but he learned that lesson well.

To stretch charity somewhat, it is possible that Trump's motivations were not wholly negative or destructive. He may have had a genuine desire to curb US military interventionism and to diminish the legacy of the Cold War with Russia. These wishes, if they existed, were thwarted to a considerable extent – unlike his much less admirable goals in the spheres of, for example, immigration and the environment. And his stated opposition to military adventurism and the deep state was not matched by a curb on US military spending.[38]

In the United States, the phenomenon of ideological displacement has predominated. Trump's taxation policies helped US corporations and the stock market, but did little for ordinary workers. Corporations used tax savings to buy back their shares, thus inflating the stock market. Meanwhile, public services suffered due to declining revenues from corporate taxes. The tax burden shifted from corporations to workers, and protectionism and trade wars damaged manufacturing and agriculture. Costs of health care and third-level education in the United States have remained prohibitive for large sections of the population.[39] Insecurity of employment, the threat of health-related bankruptcy and the burden of lifelong student debt weigh down the minds and lives of ordinary US citizens, who are also convinced by media repetition and right-wing cultural groupthink that the alternative would be the dreaded 'socialism'.

Saving for health care and their children's education, with all the stress and red tape involved, is a constant worry for US citizens. At the same time, citizens of more 'socialist' European countries are blissfully unaware of the stresses, including bureaucracy and insecurity, imposed by the dominance of the free market as a means of the fulfilment of basic needs. Far from always leading to more bureaucracy, European-style 'socialism' (or rather social democracy) may in some cases be a means of channelling bureaucratic tasks from the individual to the servants of the state, who – unlike the ordinary citizen – are paid to undertake them.

Instead of identifying the sources of social and economic woes in corporate welfare, the maldistribution of wealth, a bloated military budget and a dysfunctional private health system, taxpayers blamed immigrants and looked to Trump's protectionism as their saviour from the perils of globalisation. The oppositional political energy was used to fuel a supposed adversarial force – which was really just another version of the socioeconomic system already in place, in some ways intensifying its negative aspects.

Something similar happened in the United Kingdom, where the triumph of Brexit mirrored the political success of Trump in the United States. A dysfunctional educational system, and consequent lack of political consciousness on the part of broad masses of the population, together with a political system that was less than fit for purpose, intensified the problem. In place of a search for progressive, egalitarian solutions to the problems posed by contemporary capitalism, the public mind was misdirected against easier targets – for example, immigrants.[40]

'PROGRESSIVE' OPPOSITION AND ITS WEAKNESS

Trumpism and, more widely, authoritarianism are almost completely negative political developments, but the opposition has often seemed ill-prepared. While neo-Nazis openly strut on the streets of the United States – a country, it should be remembered, that acted as an example to Nazism itself, in historical and legislative terms – a large section of the left is, in the view of its critics, preoccupied with pronouns and bathroom access.[41] Internecine struggles take place between left defenders of class politics and identity politics: the predominance of alienating rhetoric is blamed in particular for the defeat of US presidential candidate Bernie Sanders.[42]

But it's not all about style and rhetoric. The problem is not confined to the right, or to the extreme wing of the 'profit before people' Republican Party. From one perspective, the two parties in the United States are in a polarised death struggle that is tearing the country apart;[43] from an alternative perspective, however, they are actually two sides of the same coin, or two branches of the corporate party that has essentially pursued a united policy of favouring, and being swayed by, the ultra-rich. The corporate party, from such a perspective, would be seen as the single party of foreign military interventionism, and of the persecution of ethnic minorities through the pursuit of the failed war on drugs.

Americans have witnessed the imposition of monstrous forms of bureaucracy, in the form of governmental complexity and overreach in the case of the left, and the support of a bewildering and obstructive health-care system in the case of the right – the limitations of the latter having been pitilessly exposed by the recent pandemic. This is not to mention the militarism endorsed by both sides of the supposed political divide, the continued erosion of freedom and privacy as a result of modern technological developments, and co-option by both private and state interests.

In mitigation, and as mentioned already, there is also the possibility in the United States of a more enlightened crossover politics, combining the few – but significant – areas where progressives and conservatives have something in common. Even in such a contested area as gun control, it is possible to understand the rationale behind libertarian and conservative desires to defend the right to citizen gun ownership.[44] This is, after all, in the face of a state system that increasingly resembles the more dystopian reaches of science fiction, with the police armed to the teeth with sophisticated Robo cop-style weaponry and equipment – such that the imposition of a permanent state of martial law, under whatever pretext, becomes a real possibility.

The forces that threaten to tear apart the United States, and consequently destabilise world peace and security, are the result of a complicated conflict between capitalism and democracy. There are two dominant versions of capitalism; currently, they seem to be at each other's throats. Version A is liberal, globalist, statist, cosmopolitan, bureaucratic, politically correct, militarily aggressive and paternalistically progressive; it is manifest in the Democratic Party. Its counterpart in the United Kingdom is, more or less, the Labour Party. Version B is nationalist, anti-globalist, isolationist, embodies a weird conglomeration of economic libertarianism and authoritarianism, and draws on the right wing of the Republican Party. Its counterpart in the United Kingdom – to an extent, at least – is the pro-Brexit element within the Conservative Party.

In the United States, defenders of freedom and democracy have been pushed to the margins by the struggle between these two capitalist mammoths; such defenders may be found at the political extremes.

These extremes comprise some elements of anti-interventionist paleoconservatism and social libertarianism on the right, and a 'socialism' (or rather social democracy) of the Bernie Sanders variety on the left. There are also Green Party figures, like Jill Stein and Ralph Nader, who overlap to some extent with the social democratic left and (in the case of Nader) attempt to forge a crossover politics with elements on the libertarian and conservative right.

Bizarrely, a left-wing public figure like Noam Chomsky in the United States sometimes seems – at least when it comes to issues like opposition to military adventurism – to be singing from the same hymn sheet as a conservative like Ron Paul.[45] The overall political situation involves the marginalisation of freedom and democracy, so that anyone who questions the dominant political mindset – not to mention the prevalent political mind-control – is seen as a maverick and effectively ostracised and neutralised.

The struggle between capitalism's Versions A and B can be seen as a struggle between the left and the right of what might be termed 'the corporate party'. This party formally manifests itself as the Democratic and Republican Parties, but, for practical purposes, represents the interests of capitalism – or at least the deformation of capitalism that arose when business took over the state. The routine insults the two flanks of capitalism throw at each other are not always misdirected, and the hesitant attempts to build bridges between freedom-lovers on opposite ends of the political spectrum may be paralleled by the self-destructive tendencies within corporate capitalism itself. Whether freedom and democracy can survive the process is another matter.

EUROPE

On the European mainland, the rise of authoritarian nationalism is of concern to those who cherish the value of freedom. A major contributor to the unsettled state of Europe has been the immigration from countries in North Africa and the Middle East, which have been destabilised largely as a result of Western military interventionism and political meddling. One key example is Libya, whose stability was subverted by the West to prevent the weakening of the dollar – a feared consequence of African moves towards financial independence.[46] US Democrats ('liberal hawks') and Republicans alike have engaged in such meddling.

The National Rally in France, the AfD in Germany, and authoritarian regimes in Poland and Hungary are examples of the new authoritarian nationalism, bolstered (particularly in Poland) by religious conservatism and opposition to foreign immigration.

In the nineteenth century, Tocqueville pointed out that European governments with absolutist tendencies were those least likely to concede to the decisive power of the normal course of justice.[47] Poland, a pre-eminent victim of both Nazism and Stalinism due to its geographical location, has turned not to the defence of liberty but to a strengthening of authoritarian state power – and in particular, to the undermining of judicial independence.[48]

27

National groups at times seem to exhibit a certain pathology, echoing the unfortunate phenomenon, at the level of the individual, that abused children sometimes grow up to become abusers themselves. Rationally, one would imagine – and hope – that the victim of abuse would grow up to become caring, freedom-loving and compassionate, to compensate for the abuse that was suffered in the past. That is, sadly, not always the case. The quickest, easiest and most destructive way to repress the memory of past mistreatment seems, unfortunately, to be to inflict such mistreatment on others.

Hungary also seems to be developing in the direction of right-wing authoritarian nationalism. Historically, Hungary aligned with Nazi Germany during the Second World War, though Hungarians did not even qualify as Aryan under Hitler's benighted taxonomy. That classification derived, in a garbled form, from a linguistic categorisation: whether or not a national language was of Indo-European origin.[49]

One might speculate that, on the part of the Hungarians, a historical combination of guilt and vulnerability, combined with a sense of victimhood vis-à-vis Stalinism, led to a turning inwards against the encroachment of the Western values of freedom and democracy. In countries, like Hungary, with a recent history of oppression by others, these values are sometimes met with fear rather than the welcome they might be expected to receive.

In France, authoritarian nationalism feeds off a reactionary mindset that predates the French Revolution – and that fed into the collaborationist Vichy regime and the post-war repression in Algeria.[50] Nonetheless, it sometimes exploits the weaknesses of its opponents on the left by incorporating worker-friendly policies, to the extent that it is questionable whether the National Rally is really a right-wing party at all. Opposition to the EU in France has roots in the historical traditions of both right and left.[51]

In Germany, authoritarian nationalism derives its energy largely from opposition to Islamic immigration. Attempts to link this opposition to Nazism, however – either by its proponents or adversaries – may be problematic. Hitler, while he disparaged Arabs in racial terms, was an admirer of Islam,[52] which the contemporary European far right regards as its main enemy, at least for the moment.

It would seem that an effective divide-and-conquer weapon against neo-Nazism, as the latter attempts to draw support from anti-Islamists, would be to highlight the fact that its hero, Hitler, believed that an Islamised Western society would have been a good thing. However, there is already a significant influence of anti-Semitic and Nazi ideology in some Islamic countries;[53] to highlight the Führer's admiration for Islam too much might actually encourage that influence further.

SOME KEY ISSUES

The discussion above may help to situate some significant questions in regard to the contemporary role of the state, by touching on some crucial ways in which it has impacted on our lives in the present and recent past, particularly under the pressure of resurgent nationalism. These include questions such as: What, if anything, do we owe the state? What moral authority does it have? What are the principal dangers of the institution of the state?

The notion of the 'social contract' is often mentioned as a way of describing how we owe something to the state.[54] It is a fictional concept in a sense; most people are born into citizenship and would, at that early post-natal stage of their lives, have been unable to give informed consent to a contract. The position of people adopting citizenship later in life – for example, through naturalisation – is somewhat different. Nevertheless, there is the widespread notion that we owe allegiance to the state through birth (or whatever other status is the legal norm), regardless of whether or not we have formally agreed to such an allegiance.

Aristotle argued that people develop a 'political association' (the state) and keep it going with the goal not just of the good life, but of life itself.[55] The state, then, functions to maintain not just enjoyment but survival. For Aristotle, the state is naturally prior to the household and the individual.[56] For Montesquieu, the state of equality into which we are born cannot prevail in the 'state of nature': laws are needed to enforce equality.[57] Tocqueville believed that the consent of citizens to be governed is more visceral than voluntary, resulting from common feelings and beliefs.[58] People may be more or less unconscious of the motivations that draw them together, or indeed of those that divide them, though such motivations may nevertheless be considerable.

The state, through its monopoly on violence, defends us from enemies both internal and external, real or imaginary. Without the awe inspired by a common power, in the oft-cited words of the English philosopher Thomas Hobbes, life would be 'solitary, poore, nasty, brutish and short'.[59] For Hobbes, the only way for people to establish internal and external security is to give power, by mutual agreement, to one individual or group who is to act for them all.[60] Nonetheless, the duty of subjects to the sovereign lasts only as long as the latter has power to protect them.[61] According to Hobbes, laws are there to place limitations on the freedom of particular individuals, so that they might help each other and defend against a common foe.[62]

These issues, including the relationship between the state and violence, have come to the fore in recent times. The role of the military in defending the state exemplifies the matter. This is distinct from pre-emptively attacking other states or groups with the ostensible purpose of heading off future danger. Such actions sometimes have the opposite effect – as can be seen from recent US military adventurism in the Middle East and North Africa.

John Locke observed that the only reason an individual is a member of a commonwealth (i.e. a state) is the danger of violence: without the fear of violence, there would be no need of government.[63] In Locke's terms, the function of law is to foster freedom.[64] Interestingly – and with relevance for our own times, where issues around drug-taking have been at the fore – Locke draws a key distinction between sin (moral wrongdoing) and crime: it is the function of the 'magistrate' (the state) to punish the latter, not the former. This is also the central message of John Stuart Mill's classic text, *On Liberty*.[65]

Had the wisdom of such thinkers as Locke and Mill permeated politics in recent times, it is arguable that much time, money, energy and grief might have been saved on the disastrous war on drugs, to take one notorious example.

The logical extension of criminalising sin is the concept of thought crime. This was presciently described by Orwell in *Nineteen Eighty-Four* and anticipated by Montesquieu, who recalls Dionysius's execution of Marsyas in ancient times. Marsyas had dreamed of killing Dionysius; Dionysius's justification for his response was that Marsyas only dreamed about the deed at night because he had thought about it during the day.[66]

For Montesquieu, speech is, similarly, unfairly criminalised, and is criminal only when it is associated with a criminal act. To treat speech itself as a capital crime is to invert the proper order of things.[67] Such insights have obvious current relevance, where the debate around hate speech potentially pits freedom-lovers against peace-lovers.

While there is considerable disagreement among thinkers regarding the correct scope of the state's power, there is broad implicit acceptance of the moral authority of the state. This is shown, in the present day, in the numbers of people who take their duty to vote seriously, even when their individual vote will, under normal circumstances, make virtually no difference.

The state is buttressed by the fact of its mass acceptance as an institution. The acceptance of given political, social and economic systems is partly the result of media and other manipulation on the part of vested interests; however, in respect of the continuance of the state as an institution, there is arguably an essential element of free choice on the part of the people as a whole. Even if the population are in bondage to the influence of the mass media, they have, if only unconsciously, made that choice. In principle, they are free to do otherwise – to construct alternative political and economic systems to the ones that prevail.

The argument could be made that the social contract is invalid (at least in a moral sense) insofar as the individual did not explicitly sign up to citizenship. Nevertheless, one does not normally come across people who have renounced their citizenship with the aim of becoming stateless. This is distinct, of course, from those who have become citizens of another country and do not wish, or are not permitted, to retain their original citizenship.

Even citizens of the United States who live abroad but are still subject to onerous US tax obligations would not normally renounce their citizenship without adopting that of another country. This is not just because, for US citizens, the process of renouncing one's citizenship is itself burdensome and expensive (not to mention whatever patriotic qualms, if any, the thought of renunciation might induce) but also because being stateless is a condition that few, if any, desire for themselves.

Even anarchists do not normally take the step of renouncing their status as citizens of one state or another. Stateless people I have met, regardless of their position on the political spectrum, usually have one overriding ambition, and that is to cease being stateless. There are very good reasons for this, since citizenship may confer rights of residency, education, property ownership, work and travel. It can impart legal, social and (perhaps) health protection. Such rights – or privileges, as the case may be – may be difficult or even impossible to enjoy without being a citizen of one state or another. Consequently, even the most strident opponents of the state seldom take the ultimate step of giving up their citizenship, unless such a step is related to the process of gaining citizenship of another country.

But the argument about the legitimacy of the state does not end there. For the question might then be raised as to the origin of the moral right of the state to constrain the ability of people to cross its borders and to live and work within its domain.[68] History offers a record of invasion and subjugation, whether it was the incursion of the Celts, Romans, Angles, Saxons, Vikings and Normans in Britain; the British, French and Spanish in the Americas; or the Celts, Vikings, Normans, and British in Ireland. As part of an ongoing tradition, the modern state, with its already-established population, is founded on the brutal principle that 'might is right'. The state has, or at least claims, a monopoly on violence, and this monopoly is often based on past terror and the invasion and subjugation of populations – a questionable basis, at least in moral terms.

Perhaps the paranoia that infused Brexit derived, in part, from the unconscious realisation (and resultant insecurity) that the British state itself – indeed, any state – is of questionable legitimacy in moral terms.

The EU has also faced such issues – for example, the crisis of immigration in the Mediterranean, a result of Western meddling in Libya[69] that led to an influx of migrants into Europe, with negative consequences for the political dynamics of the EU. The pressure of Syrian immigration has comparable causes. The Western priority is to protect oil resources at a time when reliance on oil itself is becoming the source of a major environmental threat. This fosters the instability of target nations and associated regimes, with the inevitable consequence of making bad situations worse.

In the era of climate change, an added issue has arisen in regard to the role of the state. Ecological problems tend to ignore state boundaries, which can then generate somewhat conflicting arguments for world government to replace the power of individual states, for powerful supranational organisations or for decentralisation of power.[70] The last-mentioned may be understood either as decentralisation 'downwards', towards more power at lower level, or decentralisation 'upwards', towards more power for supranational institutions.

One concept is that of the 'hollowing out' of the state, whereby the state, in a kind of automatic operation, is seen as ceding power upwards in a supranational process, sideways to the private realm, and downwards in terms of local control and devolution.[71] There is surprisingly little political debate, at least in the public sphere, on dominant issues such as nationalism versus supranationalism. The impetus towards supranational centralisation on the one hand, or state autonomy on the other – or some interaction of the two – is taken as a given by the proponents of each side, often without conscious debate or even the encouragement of such debate.

GREEN THOUGHT AND THE STATE

For Greens, state institutions develop in a self-serving direction under the influence of 'instrumental rationality': the separation of humanity from nature, of facts from values, focusing on analysis rather than connectivity. Echoing the sociologist Max Weber, Green thinking argues that states develop to become ends in themselves.[72] The state is seen as an instrument of domination founded on militarism.[73]

The analysis of the state in Green thought is full of tensions and contradictions. From one perspective, the state may be seen as an instrument of violence and repression, focused on its own perpetuation to the exclusion of ecological values. From another point of view, it may be seen as a means of implementing progressive environmental policies, as well as alternative, fairer means of wealth distribution – for example, universal basic income.[74] Nonetheless, insofar as such forms of wealth distribution are limited to the state, they may be seen as exclusionary vis-à-vis the rest of the world. By focusing on its own institutional interests, the state can be considered (from an anarchist perspective) as over-centralised, and (from a globalist perspective) as enjoying an unwarranted autonomy. These often-unformulated critiques permeate the Green response to the state.[75]

My own involvement in Green politics in Ireland, going back to the 1980s, has led me to the somewhat bleak conclusion that the choice facing political parties – at least small, radical ones – is between pure-minded impotence, as long as you stay outside of power, and hopeless political compromise, once you take on the mantle. On the other hand, 'canvassing' – talking to people on doorsteps about their concerns, environmental and otherwise – can be both humbling and enlightening. This is particularly so for those of us (like myself) who are easily seduced by visions of the way things could, and should, be done if only the right people (like oneself, for example) were in power.

There is no obvious answer to the dilemma facing small, radical political parties. If you stay out of power, you may remain pure but risk remaining impotent. If you take on power in combination with larger parties, you risk compromising your principles – and will be seen as having done so, whether deservedly or otherwise. For people who choose principle over self-interest, involvement in party politics is a no-win situation, which is one reason why some people eschew such involvement and may choose extra-parliamentary means, whether within the law or otherwise.

THE SPECTRE OF *NINETEEN EIGHTY-FOUR*

The foregoing overview of some issues around the state may serve to situate the discussion of the state's tendency to take over the lives of its citizens, whether under the pressure of the politics of nationalism, race or class, a burgeoning technocracy, or some combination of these.

The spectre of state domination has been a recurring nightmare for more than a century – explored, for example, in Yevgeny Zamyatin's novel *We*,[76] and exemplified most famously by George Orwell's *Nineteen Eighty-Four*.[77] Like many people, I first read *Nineteen Eighty-Four* as a teenager and was appropriately horrified at the potential of the state to become the monstrous entity that Orwell describes so chillingly. My dismay was intensified, given that the surname of the hero's tormentor (O'Brien) was the same as my own.

Orwell's book has weaknesses, most glaringly in the awkward love scenes and the less-than-believable naivety of the two central characters (Winston and Julia) as they walk blindly into a trap that should, surely, have been obvious from the start. Sexual psychology is not Orwell's forte. His dystopian state is characterised by an impetus to total power (weirdly combined with an extreme form of sexual puritanism). However, the motivation behind this phenomenon is not clarified. Is it an unfortunate result of the triumph of means over ends, an inevitable consequence of bureaucratic systems? Or simply a form of institutionalised lunacy. Or both. It is not made clear.

There is a strong suggestion that the underlying rationale, or irrationality, of the world of *Nineteen Eighty-Four* consists in simple craziness. Why go to all that trouble to 'cure' dissidents of their supposed insanity, only in order to liquidate them at the end? There is no clear logic to such a course of action, but perhaps that's the point.

The Party, as the book outlines it, persecutes sexual expression because such expression (naturally and healthily) channels the energy that would otherwise go into the exaltation of power itself. But is not the fetishism of power itself a misdirection of sexual energy? Orwell, perhaps understandably, does not explore such psychological issues. If power is all about sex, then the tendency to totalitarianism could be eradicated through psychological intervention.

There are implicit references to the totalitarian history of religion, and indeed it's entirely possible that religious elements (unconsciously) permeated historical forms of totalitarianism. This may have been particularly true of Stalinism, with its combination of brutality and sexual prudishness – notwithstanding the sexual depredations of the odious Lavrentiy Beria, the head of the Soviet Union's secret police. Orwell may have (somewhat astutely) plugged into this aspect of Soviet society, albeit sex (and love) are themselves the most problematic parts of the book.

This is not to say that the novel is a direct attack on the Stalinist version (or perhaps perversion) of Marxism. The ideology of Oceania is not dialectical or historical materialism – the official ideology of the Soviet Union - but a form of subjective idealism, which is the opposite of that ideology. The Party in Orwell's work creates reality: reality does not precede ideological intervention.

Perhaps, however, Orwell's description of the inversion of materialism and even of realism is a fair criticism of the practical implementation of Marxist–Leninist politics towards the goal of Communism. If everything is subservient to the revolution (which is viewed as both inevitable and desirable), then that includes truth itself. Reality becomes infinitely malleable. It does not exist outside of the revolution – it is created by the revolution. In our own time, the search for the origin of the coronavirus has been obstructed by Communist China – the inquiry after truth takes second place to political convenience.

In Orwell's version of totalitarianism, though, the Party no longer even pretends, at least to itself, that it is committed to freedom or justice – the goal is power for its own sake.

There are echoes in present-day society, in a quite different context, whereby truth is subjugated in the interests of one goal or another – the goal of libertarian fascism (another impossible oxymoron) in the case of the right, or that of ideological conformity and right-on 'wokeness' in the case of the left. It is not just the remit of Communist China: both sides of the political divide obscure truth in favour of ideological orthodoxy – whether the conformity of outlandish conspiracy theories at one end of the scale, or of an ideological comfort zone on the other.

Despite its flaws, *Nineteen Eighty-Four* was, and remains, a compelling account of the dangers of a state system that exists for its own sake; it exhibits the consequent evils of oppression, universal surveillance and the creation of reality through the systematic alteration of the past – and, in turn, the alteration of the present (and the future) as well. Orwell's honesty is evident in the fact that he is writing not from the perspective of someone hostile to socialism; the perspective is that of a committed socialist who yet fears its transformation into the perversion of English socialism (or 'Ingsoc') that he describes. In that system, the interests of party and state ride roughshod over those of the individual.

As has often been pointed out, there are uncomfortable and widely-acknowledged echoes of Orwell in the present era of fake news and the widespread policing not just of words but also of thoughts (a phenomenon that exists at least as much on the left as on the right, if not indeed more so).

Orwell's demarcation of the three competing world powers as Oceania (roughly the English-speaking world), Eurasia (the European continent, including Russia), and Eastasia (presumably dominated by China) seems remarkably prescient. Nonetheless – lacking the gift of clairvoyance – he overlooked the potential for the eventual collapse of the Soviet Union and the rise of militant Islam. Orwell also overestimated the danger of European domination by the USSR (a danger that, to some extent, was perhaps diminished by the pervasive influence of *Nineteen Eighty-Four* itself[78]). This influence operated through the book's highlighting of the negative potential of socialism – a highlighting process that, no doubt against Orwell's wishes, may have acted as an ideological buttress of capitalism.

Winston's world, Oceania, is dominated by what was formerly the United States (its currency is the dollar). The form of socialism that prevails in it is, in fact, weirdly suggestive of the present-day US corporate state. The latter is characterised by perpetual warfare, war hysteria, massive waste of economic resources, media manipulation, the creation of a false reality through the more-or-less conscious perpetration of lies, and a creeping surveillance of the lives of citizens.

Another issue that one might have with the book is the dismissive attitude (a mixture of exasperation and vague hope) towards the 'proles'. This, together with a barely-disguised cultural contempt, is found surprisingly often in left-wing intellectuals' regard for people of a lower social background than they, as if a 'progressive' political analysis gives them an excuse to indulge in some barely-repressed class prejudice.

In spite of its weaknesses, *Nineteen Eighty Four* stands as a chilling reminder of the danger of the triumph of means over ends, of the state over the individual, and of lies over truth. It sums up, in one volume, the perils of an institution that most of us accept, more or less reluctantly, as essential to our lives: the state.

Orwell's vision was prescient. The mechanically-composed songs in the novel prefigure today's automatic creation of journalistic text.[79] The artificial creation of war hysteria has been a feature of Western society since his time. But in some ways our own future, and even our present, is more chilling than even Orwell could have imagined. Winston and Julia manage a romantic escape to the countryside, where the danger from hidden microphones is remote. We, on the other hand, can be tracked at all times, anywhere we go, through our mobile phones – which, while at the moment voluntary, are increasingly becoming indispensable, and may in due course be superseded by implants of one kind or another. There are eyes in the sky as well as in the 'telescreen'. The Party was puzzled at the intractable problem of how to find out what people think without their knowing it. We may be on the verge of cracking it.

Chapter 2

WHAT IS
TOTALITARIANISM?

A virus of unknown origin has been unloosed on the world, raising crucial issues about public health, freedom and the role of the state vis-à-vis the individual citizen. There is the possibility it was the result of a lab leak, but the consensus at the time of writing seems to be that it arose in a natural context. Nonetheless, political constraints – particularly lack of openness by the Chinese government – may ultimately make it difficult or impossible to establish the truth.

Apart from its health implications, the virus threatens to destabilise the world's economies through business failure, unemployment and debt, as a result of countervailing measures.[1] Assuming that the current consensus as to its origin is correct, the underlying socioeconomic factors behind the current health crisis – or contributing to its intensity – are a combination of issues. These include agribusiness, deforestation, animal exploitation and globalisation, including mass trade and tourism.[2]

Unfortunately, the emergence of this and other viruses seems to be largely taken as a given; they are not habitually considered to be as a result of an unsustainable and destructive socioeconomic system, based on the exploitation of animals and nature as a whole.

Many countries have, on medical advice, resorted to lockdown in one form or another as a means of dealing with the threat. Views greatly diverge as to the inherent severity of the virus, how reliable the related statistics actually are, and to what extent government negligence has been a contributory factor in the spread of the virus.

The virus has caused much grief and many deaths that would not otherwise have occurred (or at least would have occurred somewhat later). This has been particularly the case in the older segment of the population. At the same time, there has been death and suffering – perhaps an ultimately unquantifiable amount – as a consequence of the drastic measures taken to counteract the pandemic, resulting in unemployment, economic precarity, starvation, mental illness, domestic violence and suicide. Political and economic exigencies have often conflicted with health requirements – not surprisingly, as governments are aware of the need to be re-elected, which does not always coincide with the necessity to do the right thing.

Combined with the shock fall in oil prices, Covid-19 had an initially unsettling effect on the stock market. At the time of writing, however, the market is booming, reflecting the growth of the virtual economy at a time when so many – as a result of pandemic-related limitations on normal activity – are working from home, and shopping and being entertained online. Furthermore, President Joe Biden's social democratic economic reforms, including support for infrastructure, skills development and research, and subsidies for manufacturing, may impart a new stimulus to the US economy.[3]

Post Trump, the disconnection between the real and the virtual economies (and more broadly, between Main Street and Wall Street) has been notable. Tech stocks, in particular, boomed – largely as a result of the above-mentioned migration online. The long-term effect of the virus – both directly and in terms of the effects of anti-virus measures – on the real economy (as distinct from the realm of finance) and society as a whole, remains unknown.

It will presumably be severe, despite the fact that governments, including that in the United States, have intervened in unprecedented ways to foster the direct distribution of wealth, now that the work–income model (clunky as a means of distribution at the best of times) is sputtering to a halt. The radical solution, a universal basic income for all citizens that might cushion them from the economic effects of the current pandemic and its future counterparts, remains unimplemented.[4]

The threat of a dramatic fall in economic activity, consequent on mass unemployment, initially seemed to threaten the entire capitalist system. Nevertheless, the threat seemed to recede as time went by. Many financially-secure people have saved money on goods and services that they might otherwise have paid for – and, as a result of working from home, have enjoyed a reduction in stress from constant commuting to work.

This has been counterbalanced, though, by the increased stresses of family life. Partners and children have been forced together for much of the time, whether they like it or not – a factor intensified by economic constraints the lower down you look on the socioeconomic scale. The pandemic has increased social inequality: in Ireland at least, many people will have accumulated a comfortable nest egg due to lack of opportunity to spend, which has helped to drive up house prices. Others, driven to the margins of homelessness and unemployment, will be less fortunate.

Traditional economic measurements count the sale of goods and services rather than human well-being (for example health, security, quality of life and overall happiness). These factors, difficult to quantify, may be enhanced or diminished in accordance with one's situation and mindset. Depending on a person's home circumstances, working from home may be a blessing or a curse, but for some people at least, it eases the daily pressure of normal life. The pandemic may have increased stress for some, and alleviated it for others.

Social supports in wealthier regions mean little to people living hand-to-mouth in southern Italy or South Africa – not to mention those subsisting in refugee camps scattered throughout the world, or refugees reliant on direct provision in Ireland. And stress reduction for the financially secure, who live in houses with large gardens, has its counterpart – intensified stress – for those living alone in small flats or apartments, whose only garden is a local park. During the severest forms of lockdown, such local parks may not even be accessible.

The imposition of a lockdown, a form of medical martial law, over wide swathes of the world's population received a mixed response. Conspiracy theories, often from a right-wing perspective, see such measures as a means of implementing the medical control of society through compulsory vaccination, tracing and screening. Studies have pinpointed the role of conservative ideology and media in resistance to preventative measures, including vaccination.[5]

From a more positive perspective, it seems remarkable how easily health and welfare systems can be adjusted by the state – when it really wants to act – in favour of the well-being of people as a whole. This may be a positive foretaste of a more human-friendly society in the future – though economic pressures may kick in to reverse any tendency in that direction.

Some on the left will take heart at the possibilities for socialised health care and a more human-friendly system for the redistribution of wealth. It is, though, remarkable how easily and quickly the state has moved to institutionalise lockdown (a term normally applied to a procedure used in prisons, which may illustrate the fundamentally coercive nature of the state itself). Negative responses to effectively draconian measures – however temporary they may be – range from reasoned concern at one end of the scale, to paranoia at the other.

The outbreak will undoubtedly operate as pressure, on those in a position to instigate change, to bring about widespread social and economic alterations that would otherwise have happened more slowly, or not at all.

Klaus Schwab and Thierry Malleret foresee, and largely endorse, widespread structural changes in terms of the widely discussed 'Great Reset' consequent on Covid-19. This, they believe, will involve enhanced interdependence, velocity and complexity.

The pandemic is, in their view, likely to intensify automation and deepen concerns about such issues as surveillance and immigration. They envisage far-reaching changes in the economic, societal, geopolitical, environmental and technological spheres, as well as in terms of industry.[6] The authors argue that we should take advantage of the changed situation to improve our society.[7]

Schwab and Malleret foresee a re-emphasis on the role of the state and of the public realm – the pandemic has shown the limitations of a market-based approach.[8] They favour a (moderately) Green and social democratic perspective, which perhaps explains the storm that has been stirred in conspiratorial circles around the notion of the Great Reset; their analysis threatens the hitherto-dominant policy of neoliberalism, highlighting the flaws in its vaunted ideology.

At the same time, the authors flag the danger of a surveillance society,[9] and the possible role of contact tracing in contributing to such a situation.[10] In particular, they cite concerns about the installation of surveillance technology in the workplace – technology that will have a tendency towards self-perpetuation, since employers will have no incentive to remove it. Indeed, employers will have an economic motivation to retain it as a means of checking on productivity.[11]

They cite the prospect of the reversal of globalisation[12] and the immense pressure that social distancing will place on air travel.[13] Virtualisation will affect housing, education and the price of real estate.[14]

The authors acknowledge that the human destruction of biodiversity is the origin of new viruses such as Covid-19.[15] Population growth, intensive farming and air pollution, in their mind, contribute to the problem.[16]

Despite signalling problems, Schwab and Malleret have a fundamentally optimistic outlook: that the pandemic may help to push the capitalist system in a desirable direction, in terms of how we may rethink our social, economic and individual goals and aims.

Other commentators are less sanguine. In the words of Naomi Klein, 'Far more hi-tech than anything we have seen during previous disasters, the future that is being rushed into being as bodies still pile up treats our [...] physical isolation not as a painful necessity to save lives, but as a living laboratory for a permanent – and highly profitable – no-touch future.'[17]

Klein paints a bleak picture of a future where we are virtually prisoners in our homes, traditional forms of employment have greatly diminished, and high-tech society is maintained by hordes of largely invisible exploited workers. There is institutionalised surveillance of the whole society. The impetus to develop the partnership between state and business in the rush to build a high-tech brave new world is under pressure of competition with China, which – it is feared – is set to outpace the United States. The question for Klein is whether technology will develop under democratic supervision, or whether it will be 'rolled out in state-of-exception frenzy', where key questions regarding its influence are overlooked. In the negative scenario, money is poured into a 'screen new deal' (a parody of the phrase 'green new deal') rather than invested in people and the environment.[18]

The quick and widespread implementation of drastic social restrictions stands in stark contrast to the foot-dragging that has persisted for decades in regard, for example, to the carnage on roads and motorways. One might also cite heel-dragging in regard to imposing limits on global warming.

The spectre of the pandemic is more immediate than that of global warming, which may be why it has gained more political attention, but the threat posed by climate change potentially involves an extinction-level event, and thus endangers the human species as a whole. This is distinct from the loss of individual members of the species who may be at risk of mortality – or at least somewhat earlier mortality than might normally have occurred – as a result of the pandemic.[19]

In the current atmosphere, fears of authoritarianism vie with anxieties about social anarchy at one end of the scale, and creeping socialism at the other. Strangely, concerns regarding the limitation of freedom (for example, the compulsory wearing of masks, social distancing, constraints on movement and the possibility of mandatory vaccination) seem to feature more on the conservative and libertarian right than on the left.

We have the bizarre phenomenon of fascists and neo-Nazis infiltrating, influencing and taking advantage of social movements that ostensibly exist to protest against the state's incursions on freedom. It hardly needs to be pointed out that, historically, the most egregious excesses of state control have occurred under fascism of one kind or another. At the same time, the left and liberals seem comparatively silent on the issue of state encroachment on everyday liberties that people have hitherto taken for granted.

The control of the media by state and corporate interests functions to mute whatever concerns the majority of the population may have regarding incursions on their freedom. It ensures that such opposition is largely confined to those depicted, whether correctly or not, as political extremists or hyper-libertarian cranks.

Behind all this lurks the ever-present spectre of totalitarianism, with the left and right threatening its imposition. Or perhaps some combination of the two – as nationalists, in time-honoured fashion, steal the political clothes of socialists, and socialists, in turn, try to paint nationalism red. Heavy-handed responses to the pandemic are only one possible source of a future dystopian state without freedom. Others, as will be explored later, include groupthink, racism, authoritarian nationalism (with the support of an uninformed electorate) and the prospect of universal surveillance. The threat of totalitarianism does not come merely from the authoritarian right or the Stalinist left; it may develop as a feature of the interaction of corporate and state interests.

HANNAH ARENDT AND TOTALITARIANISM

Totalitarianism is a distinct category from, for example, military dictatorship or some forms of authoritarian nationalism. The situation of an individual caught up in a totalitarian system is comparable to the traditional notion of a child's relationship to Santa Claus: you'd better be good if you know what's good for you.[20] The difference, of course, is that Santa only has the negative power of withholding good things; the totalitarian state has this negative power, along with the positive power of imposing bad – very bad – things if the citizens don't behave.

It may also reward them well, if they do behave. For example, artists – at least those willing to toe the line – in some cases do better under totalitarian regimes than in liberal democracies. To take one example, it is hard to imagine the enormous success of the film director Leni Riefenstahl without the backing of the totalitarian Nazi regime, despite her prodigious energy, talent and creativity.

In theological terms, totalitarianism offers a direct parallel with the traditional notion of the individual's relationship to the divine. In that concept, God is everywhere, all knowing, and all powerful. Totalitarianism's key difference from traditional theology is that if you flout God's law (by committing sin, or neglecting to make a religious commitment), your punishment – while perhaps severe in terms of intensity or duration – is not immediate. It is deferred to the end of your life, and may be subject to cancellation if you fulfil certain conditions. And, of course, there is always the possibility that God never existed in the first place, in which case you are off the hook.[21]

No such comfort is available to the individual subjected to the workings of the totalitarian state. Such a situation is evoked in the labyrinthine complexities of Giovanni Piranesi's images of prisons, or in the writings of George Orwell or Franz Kafka.

In Orwell's *Nineteen Eighty-Four*, the anti-hero Winston Smith is helpless in the face of a system that approximates to the theological condition of divine omniscience, omnipotence and omnipresence.

In Kafka's novels *The Trial* and *The Castle*, nothing the anti-hero does can prevent his descent into the bureaucratic nightmare of the total state. This is a scenario whose outlines we can already perceive in the corridors of the pre-totalitarian state, in the form of legal and regulatory labyrinths: a state characterised by the oppressive complexities of tax, welfare and insurance systems, a rampant technocracy and burgeoning surveillance regime.

Particularly in the United States, the state features an out-of-control police and prison system that functions on an industrial scale and prioritises law (and the interests of police and prison officers through their unions) over the people whom laws are supposed to serve. In the case of the military, it operates to destabilise national and global security, and seems to exist – to a great extent – for the purpose of its own proliferation. Anti-statists have a blind spot in regard to the military: burgeoning military expenditure is as much a feature of an out-of-control state as expenditure on bureaucracy, though this factor remains essentially invisible.

Ernst Nolte, the historian and philosopher, points out that German and American authors developed the term 'totalitarian' as a response to Nazism and bolshevism. Politically, totalitarianism is anti-liberty and ter-roristic. Metaphysically, it supplants the obligations of individuals to one another, as well as to their religious principles.[22] The recent curtailing of religious activities under the pressure of the pandemic,[23] and large-scale public acquiescence to such restrictions, may be a source of related con-cerns, as the right of people to practise their religion becomes subservient to public health and the priorities of its administrators. However, such concerns do not, for obvious reasons, feature prominently on the agenda of secularists.

The legal theorist Carl Schmitt, one of the most prominent intellec-tuals of the Third Reich, formulated the concept of the 'total state' – a power that has the potential to encompass every sphere of life, cultural and economic. In Schmitt's terms, 'This results in the identity of state and society.'[24] In the total state, there is nothing outside of politics.[25]

In regard to the concept of totalitarianism however, recent commen-tators Roger Eatwell and Matthew Goodwin point out that the term 'totalitarian' was first used by its adversaries, then endorsed by Italian Fascists. Nonetheless, Italian Fascism, unlike Nazism, never developed into full-scale totalitarianism. Eatwell and Goodwin note the later pop-ularity of the term among liberal academics, as a means of emphasising similarities between Communism and Nazism.[26]

Richard Shorten argues that totalitarianism comprises three strands, which he characterises as utopianism, scientism, and revolutionary vio-lence.[27] These three overlap in the practices of both Nazism and Stalinism, though biological racism is specific to the first, and Marxism to the second. Shorten describes how, in his view, the 'shared ideological space' between Nazism and Stalinism has been manifest in four ways: a reliance on emotional attraction; a rejection of liberalism and individualism; the striving for technological modernity; and the goal of producing a new kind of human being.[28] Shorten believes that mass murder, rather than state control, is the key defining feature of totalitarianism; he excludes Italian Fascism from the totalitarian category due to the absence of genocide.[29] (However, this seems to ignore the complicity, albeit delayed, of the Italian Fascists in terms of co-operation with Nazi genocide.) Shorten also omits Italian Fascism from the totalitarian classification because of its emphasis on the state – the state cannot compete in the totalitarian stakes with class or race as 'constructions of social identity'.[30] There are limits to how much emotional investment can be made in an abstract concept, or entity, like the state, compared to more concrete identifiers, such as class or race.

Shorten argues that political violence is due to some secular thought-currents coming together.[31] He discusses key figures in the history of thought, such as Jean-Jacques Rousseau, Charles Darwin, Friedrich Nietzsche and Johann Gottlieb Fichte, and how they contributed to the mindset that produced Nazism in particular. In making this connection, Shorten cites Nietzsche's endorsement of the will to power.[32] He highlights differences in these historical figures' level of guilt – in his terms, 'Darwin is more remote from blame than are either Rousseau or Nietzsche.' Nevertheless, Darwin did produce two concepts that were influential on totalitarianism: the ideas of evolutionary progress and strife for existence.[33]

Shorten argues that an understanding of totalitarianism in terms of 'intellectual trajectory' is more important than a 'structural' analysis. In other words, an analysis of the underlying ideas is crucial to understanding the phenomenon. The aim of totalitarianism was to achieve the utopia of human authenticity through the application of scientism (an overemphasis on science) and revolutionary violence.[34]

Tzvetan Todorov writes that totalitarianism involves abolishing the division between private sphere and public regulation: individual life is subsumed under a public standard. The individual and their relationships are downgraded in favour of the totalitarian state's requirements.[35] Totalitarianism denies the right of individuals to choose the guidelines for their lives, whether theological, natural or philosophical.[36]

Totalitarianism, in Todorov's terms, involves revolution in its commencing phase, the morphing of collective determination into a veneer, and the suppression of personal freedom. Key to totalitarianism is terror, collectivisation, the cult of war, the physical elimination of difference and the repudiation of pluralism.[37]

In regard to our own times, Todorov argues that there are three main threats to our democracy: an 'excess of identity politics', moral correctness, and what he terms 'overinstrumentalisation'[38] – which might also be termed instrumental rationality, or the tendency to focus on means rather than ends. These issues will surface later in the course of this book.

It is not possible here to cover the (minute and prolific) academic discussions around totalitarianism in any detail. Instead, the focus will be on one important contributor, Hannah Arendt, as a means of highlighting some of the basic issues – issues that have been discussed at length since her time.

In her key text, *The Origins of Totalitarianism*,[39] Arendt relates the danger of a police state to the growth in the numbers of stateless people, which increases the control of the police over the population. In Arendt's terms, the temptations of totalitarianism for the police derive from the fact that they have an enhanced social status in totalitarian countries.[40]

Arendt's remarks have resonances in our own time, where the self-interest of police forces combines with institutionalised forms of racism to intensify injustice and the oppression of one ethnic group by another. The fact of mass immigration into Western society, and the threat of its increase in the future – particularly under the pressure of global warming and military interventionism – give added weight to Arendt's warnings.[41]

Arendt had a unique perspective on totalitarianism – a former student of the Nazi-associated philosopher Martin Heidegger, she was herself a Jewish refugee from Nazism,[42] though her personal experience of totalitarianism was limited.[43] *The Origins of Totalitarianism* originally appeared at a time – the early 1950s – when the threat of Nazism had receded, though that of Stalinism was still to the fore. To what extent the forms of totalitarianism she described as manifest in Nazism and Stalinism resembled each other, has been a matter of contention ever since.[44]

Her book also conveniently fitted into the Cold War mindset of the time, since it emphasised the similarities between Soviet and Nazi totalitarianism. The fact that Stalinist oppression was largely confined to the Soviet Union and its sphere of influence, and tended to draw its victims from within the Communist movement rather than from without, perhaps makes it a somewhat less terrifying form of totalitarianism than its rival Nazism – at least to the ordinary, apolitical person in the street.

For Arendt, political life itself embodies a profound suspicion of the sphere of private life. The latter is regarded as a threat to the public sphere, which elevates equality over difference.[45] Spontaneity is the greatest impediment to total domination.[46] Totalitarianism aims towards a situation where individuals are superfluous, where humans are replaced by puppets.[47] For Arendt, totalitarian movements are mass organisations of individuals whose condition is one of isolation and social fragmentation.[48]

In the light of Arendt's analysis, we can see unsettling portents of totalitarianism in our own time, where social media, the corporate interests of advertisers, the all-seeing eye of the state and various forms of enforced groupthink combine to erode whatever private life we may have left. The pandemic has exacerbated this situation, however persuasive the arguments for some of its related constraints may be. The pressure on media to toe the party line – always present to some extent in a controlled system – is intensified under pandemic conditions.

In Arendt's terms, totalitarian governments change classes into masses, the mobilisation of which replaces the party system. The police replace the army as the centre of power, and world domination is the overt goal.[49]

The question might be raised, though – particularly in regard to Nazism – as to whether Hitler actually wanted to dominate the world. Or whether he would, at least initially, have been content with controlling Europe while sharing world power with the British Empire, Japan and the United States. We must leave that question unanswered, together with the query as to how much the motivations of dictators are of explanatory use in understanding the development of various forms of totalitarianism.

Arendt describes how the (assumed) law of history, in the case of Stalinism, and of nature, in the case of Nazism, becomes the overriding impetus.[50] Terror serves the goal of nature or history.[51]

The law of history, in the case of Stalinism, represents the idea (supposedly both correct and inevitable) that the working class is destined to triumph on the stage of history. The law of nature, in the case of Nazism, represents the Social Darwinist idea of the survival of the fittest – in the case of Nazi ideology, this is represented by the Aryan-Nordic race.

We might observe here the flaw in the logic of both Stalinism and Nazism. In the case of Stalinism, even if the proletariat (or their self-appointed representatives) are destined to triumph, it does not mean we should necessarily support that process. It might turn out to be a bad thing – perhaps through social chaos, bourgeois reaction or extreme forms of repression. In historical terms, the last of these transpired – the counter-productive result of a political impetus that was regarded as both natural and desirable.

Similarly, in regard to Nazi ideology with its notion of the survival of the fittest, there is a key incoherence. Endogamy is not a recipe for the health of the species[52] any more than technologised war is an effective means of preserving the national breeding stock. For one thing, the notorious warlike tendency of the 'Nordic people', at least as celebrated by the Nazis, does not provide a reliable basis for a stable society, particularly in the era of nuclear, chemical and biological weapons. The ritual sacrifice, through war, of the supposed cream of humanity, blond and blue-eyed, is not an obviously useful means of securing triumph for the Aryans or Nordics. War is no longer a means of national purification. (Indeed, it never was, and its futility has been exposed by the very technology that has contributed to the fury of warfare in recent years.)

Furthermore, if the Nazi ideology of Germanic supremacy were a testable theory, the downfall of the Hitler regime – particularly in the face of Slavic victory – proved its falsity. This is something that Hitler himself may have realised in the bunker in 1945, as he laid the blame on the German people for their defeat.[53]

In Arendt's view, in her outline of the development of totalitarianism, the masses believed in the infinity of possibility and that there was no such thing as truth. They had no real objection to being lied to, because everything was believed to be a lie.[54] For her, the 'ideal subject' of totalitarianism is one for whom there is no longer any difference between fact and fiction in the experiential realm, and between true and false in the mental.[55]

There are obvious parallels with our own time, where the concept of truth itself is under attack not only in the academy – where it has been besieged for decades by postmodernism – but also in society as a whole, where fantasies, baseless conspiracy theories and outright lies vie for dominance of the public mind. The diminution of the importance of truth, summed up in the contemporary phrase 'truth decay', is alarming.[56]

On the one hand, there is the echo chamber of conspiracy theorists, with their fixation on the existence of all-compassing plots (though a combination of incompetence and opportunism on the part of the establishment may be a more likely explanation); on the other, there is an echo chamber of intellectual orthodoxy, which automatically rubbishes anything that deviates from whatever happens to be the accepted narrative at any given time. Consensus does not necessarily equal truth.

Propaganda and media replace news; lies and distortions proliferate in the political sphere. The groupthink of conspiracy theories predominates on the right, while that of right-on woke ideology prevails on the left.

In the centre, a prevalent orthodoxy – which mistakes consensus for truth – automatically tends to marginalise anything that deviates from the accepted norm. The ideological struggle between the various forms of groupthink bodes ill for political freedom – and for any attempt to resist the slide into totalitarianism, whether mental, physical or both.

Arendt points out that totalitarianism (the paradigm examples for her are Nazism and Stalinism) rules and terrorises human beings from within. The totalitarian leader acts as an operative of the masses. The masses and the leader depend on each other.[57] She argues that the failure of the totalitarian leaders prior to their political triumph, far from being an obstacle, was the strongest element in their appeal to the masses, intensifying their solidarity from the perspective of the latter.[58] Totalitarianism for Arendt, when it achieves power, replaces people of talent with 'crackpots and fools' whose negative mental attributes ensure their loyalty.[59]

While we have not (yet) reached a state of totalitarianism in the modern West, the resonance of Arendt's analysis with recent political events hardly needs to be laboured. The deplorable behavioural qualities manifest by former President Trump, insofar as they reflect comparable qualities in his support base, are surely an indictment of the US educational system, with its underpaid teachers and emphasis on factual learning rather than creativity. This is not to mention the unyielding pressures on child-rearing, resulting from the parental stress of relentless work commitments, crippling and lifelong student debt, and the terror of getting sick without adequate health insurance. Added to this is the fear of losing health insurance if you become unemployed (under the pressure of the pandemic or otherwise).

Less than half of adults questioned in a recent US survey were aware that it took a year for the earth to orbit the sun.[60] A multitude of embarrassing YouTube videos involving the impromptu quizzing of (often young) passers-by – on their knowledge, or lack thereof, of history, geography and politics – make the problem plain. While interviewees often display a comprehensive knowledge of the particulars of mass culture, that is hardly a substitute for geographical, historical or political awareness.

Shawn Rosenberg argues that the pandemic is contributing to a structural shift in American life; according to him, it threatens to destabilise democracy in favour of populism and authoritarianism. This is exacerbated by the incoherence, and constantly changing nature, of the official narrative. Rosenberg contends that people do not have the cognitive ability to deal with the challenge. Most people's thinking is 'unself-conscious, partial and concrete'. Their mindset is specific rather than systematic, conventional rather than creative. As a consequence, most do not have the mental ability to deal with the coronavirus threat, with its multitude of uncertainties and constraints. As science and government lose their credibility, a resentful population looks for political alternatives. In Rosenberg's view, democracy itself is under threat.[61]

For Arendt, totalitarianism involves a somewhat equivocal relationship between party and state. In totalitarian states, the party and state vie for authority.[62] In the terms of Hitler himself, 'the total state must not know any difference between law and ethics.'[63] As Arendt explains it, the assumption is that valid legislation is undifferentiated from common ethics rooted in the conscience of the people.[64] In the Nazi system, the 'will of the Führer' trumped the formal ordinances of the law.[65]

The idea seems to be that the leader plugs in to the instinctive, righteous feelings of the masses, functioning as their mouthpiece. The parallels with recent events in the United States are clear, though the latter have in no way equalled the horror of their global totalitarian predecessors. Indeed, they have looked more like farce than tragedy. Nevertheless, President Trump's constant appeal to mass sentiment – as distinct from notions of truth, democratic norms or the opinions of 'experts' – suggested an attempt to bypass traditional democratic modes of behaviour in favour of the direct enactment of popular opinion. The populist rejection of experts in the United States is paralleled by the rejection of experts in the United Kingdom – which in the case of the latter may have something to do with the generalist educational background of many who end up in positions of political influence.[66]

For Hitler, in Arendt's analysis, the state was a means towards the conservation of racial values; for Stalin, the intensification of state power was to prepare the conditions for its own demise, in a Communist society.[67]

Arendt's analysis gives rise to an interesting question. Were individuals like Hitler and Stalin consciously motivated by power-lust, or was the development of the totalitarian system a by-product of their devotion to other ideals – ideals based on race and class respectively? But such a question is perhaps mainly of psychological interest, since politics comes down, in the end, to what people do rather than their reasons for doing it. Nevertheless, the psychological analysis of leaders may be important in estimating to what extent their mindset, tending towards domination, may infringe on the freedoms we take for granted.

Whether or not the impetus towards total control is a by-product of other impulses, the devastating consequences of the intensification of state control are clear from recent history. The state, with its bureaucratic structures and limitations on human freedom, is at best a necessary evil, at worst the means of facilitating a slide into hell.

In Arendt's view, human beings in totalitarian societies are automatically suspects, merely by virtue of their ability to think. As a consequence, mutual suspicion pervades all social relationships, even beyond the direct surveillance of the secret police.[68] Arendt points out that while arbitrariness, the untrammelled exercise of state power, efficiently destroys freedom,[69] arbitrary arrest and disappearance are not enough: it is also important that the victim should disappear both from memory and history.[70]

The resonances with *Nineteen Eighty-Four* are haunting. In Nazi terminology, this process of disappearance was described as Nacht und Nebel, or 'night and fog'.

The ideal of the totalitarian police, Arendt asserts, is that a giant map should display all human relationships and their level of intimacy. Such a goal, she admits, was technically challenging in her time, but its realisation would make it possible to liquidate people without leaving a trace.[71] Post Arendt, we may observe that technology seems to be making such a goal increasingly feasible.

For Arendt, the epitome of totalitarianism is the concentration camp.[72] Since no one could know whether a prisoner was alive or dead, the concentration camp took even death away from the individual; in effect, the individual had never really existed.[73] In fictional terms, though with a disturbing anticipation of possible future events, Orwell's *Nineteen Eighty-Four* examines, in pitiless detail, the totalitarian project of obliterating the past.

The camps, Arendt points out, displayed the possibility of reducing humans to their animal nature, thereby eradicating the human element.[74] In her terms, totalitarian terror gets rid of individuals for the sake of the species.[75]

Zygmunt Bauman, a philosopher, suggests that the Holocaust emerged from the removal of social control from the political state, with the state's monopoly on violence and its desire to remake the world.[76] In Bauman's penetrating criticism of the dominance of practical reason in politics, under the pressure of instrumental rationality the state becomes a gardener, fostering acceptable plants and discarding weeds.[77] With the Holocaust, in Bauman's terms, 'Europe's inner demons were to be exorcised with the sophisticated products of technology and the concentrated power of the state – all modernity's supreme achievements.'[78] The Holocaust is the offshoot of a modern, out-of-control impetus towards a fully controlled environment.[79] Artifice is substituted for nature, a process that facilitates inhumanity.[80] Science became morally blind: the end justified the means.[81] In Bauman's terms, what was specifically characteristic of modern cruelty was the wilful use of means to create a specific order – making possible the Holocaust and other horrors.[82]

In the contemporary world, however, Bauman sees the main threat as arising from the negative aspects, the downside of technology rather than from utopian aspirations.[83]

Our recent travails are in no way comparable with the Holocaust, but there are perhaps some uneasy resonances. In the time of pandemic, we have already become familiar with the lonely, comfortless deaths of elderly relatives and the enhanced grief of depersonalised funerals. While such a situation falls short of the worst dystopian scenarios, it is perhaps a portent of a future where, with the passive acquiescence of the citizenry, the priorities of public health and physical well-being increasingly encroach on those of personal autonomy and happiness.

Arendt's analysis is a terrifying, and unparalleled, exposition of the possibilities of totalitarianism that underlie the bland surface of our (supposedly) free societies. In times of dislocation, particularly in regard to the recent state of emergency consequent on the pandemic, it seems vital to be aware of how easily society can slide into the abyss of the total state. In our own time, the possibilities indicated by visionaries like Orwell and Arendt seem intensified by sometimes-unprecedented developments. These include the threat of mass surveillance and state control, domination of the media, the erosion of freedom under the pressure of 'groupthink' in universities, the convergence of corporate and state interests, and the development of ideological 'silos', or segregated thought-systems, whether on the left, the right or the political centre.

Against this, and on the positive side, we should not forget the oppositional possibilities offered by digital media's availability to the populace, the space opened up by alternative digital platforms, and the courageous, often unpopular stands against the various forms of consensus and ideological conformity taken by public intellectuals, journalists, artists and whistle-blowers of one kind or another. Whether such forms of opposition will suffice to resist the paralysing forms of groupthink and intellectual domination that threaten our culture, only time will tell.

There remains the stubborn fact of the pandemic and its future counterparts – the direct products of an out-of-control socioeconomic system. From this arises the consequent, inevitable clash between biopolitics (the intersection of biology and politics) and the ideal of social freedom. How to manage that clash is the demand of the present, and this demand will persist into the future.

I have focused on Arendt's contribution to the debate on totalitarianism not because it is the last word on the subject but because of its influence on our understanding of this historically vital topic. David D. Roberts, an authority on the area, describes *The Origins of Totalitarianism* as 'certainly the most influential book on totalitarianism ever written, achieving something like canonical status'.[84] Nonetheless, he criticises Arendt for failing to explain the embrace of the ideology of totalism; she seems to rely on some implicit concept of a 'fear of freedom', which Roberts characterises as a form of reductionism.[85] He also criticises Arendt's notion of Soviet terror as being simplistic: it was also a reaction to their own propaganda, a response to the fear of sabotage.[86]

Roberts insists on the importance of research subsequent to Arendt's influential though 'seductive' contribution.[87] A subsequent, more empirical study of totalitarianism was that by Carl J. Friedrich and Zbigniew Brzezinski, *Totalitarian Dictatorship and Autocracy*,[88] which analysed totalitarianism as involving a totalist ideology, a single party, a monopoly on weapons and communications, terroristic police control, and a centrally planned economy.[89] Nevertheless, Roberts notes the critical response to this work – that it was overly 'static and mechanical'.[90]

One influential left-wing theorist, Slavoj Žižek, rejects the very notion of totalitarianism; in his view, the idea 'relieves us from the duty to think', and involves a neoliberal claim that the impetus towards emancipation inevitably leads to domination.[91] Žižek's point echoes a traditional critique: that the notion of totalitarianism was used as a Cold War weapon.

FREEDOM OR LIFE?

The prospect of totalitarianism has been to the fore in our society in recent times, when, under the pressure of Covid-19, many countries seemed to become quasi-police states almost overnight. Homes turned into places of incarceration – luxurious prisons for the privileged, a nightmare of sunless confinement for the lower orders. This has been facilitated, in most cases, by the acquiescence of the citizenry, coupled with various degrees of media control.

On the upside, it may be hoped that the emergency measures will be lifted when the immediate threat is over – though such a sunlit outlook is tempered by the spectre of recurring pandemics, consequent on an unsustainable socioeconomic system. On the downside, the prospect of compulsory testing, screening, vaccination, tracking and tracing rings alarm bells for civil libertarians.

The choice between freedom and life is not an easy one, particularly when the actions of individuals may threaten the lives of others. There are arguments in favour of draconian measures to counter pandemics; there are also arguments against them, particularly in regard to the social, economic and psychological damage – and the related morbidity and mortality – that such measures may entail. Finding a balance between physical health on the one hand, and social, economic and psychological well-being on the other, is a challenging task.

In purely practical terms, the pandemic has highlighted some practices in our society that may be unsustainable. These include the custom of going to school or work, or socialising, when you're suffering from an infectious illness. There is also the somewhat strange ritual (at least in the northern hemisphere) of scheduling convivial celebrations to mark such festivals as Thanksgiving, Christmas and New Year's at a time of the year when seasonal illnesses tend to prevail.

Unease about the erosion of civil liberties existed long before the latest health alarm, and civil control of the population in a time of health emergency is nothing new, as Daniel Defoe's (albeit semi-fictional) *A Journal of the Plague Year* indicates.[92] In his book *Discipline and Punish: The Birth of the Prison*, Michel Foucault describes anti-plague measures at the end of the seventeenth century, which included partitioning, closure, prohibition on travel, strict surveillance, quarantine and the avoidance of congregation.[93] Social distancing is nothing new.

Nonetheless, with the installation of systems of mass surveillance, technology seems to be in danger of outstripping the power of law and democratic systems to rein it in. Preventative measures have involved an increase in surveillance, which is unlikely to cease once the current health scare is over. This leads to what has been termed the 'pandemic surveillance state'. The threat is that surveillance technologies may erode the right to privacy in favour of the right to public health. The advice of public health experts may swamp the voice of the defenders of civil liberties.[94]

At the same time, hyper-capitalism combines with the state in the social sphere to erode individual freedom and autonomy. Even under the consensual view of its causation, the pandemic threat itself owes its origin and effect to a combination of agribusiness, deforestation, globalised travel and trade, and animal exploitation – again, by-products of hyper-capitalism or neoliberalism.

The increase in the dangers of zoonotic diseases is linked to the threat to the planet, involving the destruction of nature and the loss of biodiversity. Covid-19 is the latest in a series of zoonotic diseases spread from animals to humans. Predecessors included Ebola, MERS, SARS, West Nile virus, dengue fever and bird flu. Neoliberalism has led to greatly increased incursions into the natural abode of animals. Deforestation, intensive farming, trade and large-scale transportation of animals, forced cohabitation with other species in markets, and the uncontrolled gathering of wild species are all part of the problem. Behind it all is the neoliberal dogma of unrestrained trade and competition. In particular, buffer zones between humanity and animals are urgently needed.[95]

The socioeconomic effects of neoliberalism have made things worse than they might otherwise have been. Health care is undermined by the impetus towards profit maximisation; cohesion, likewise, is eroded by competition. Workers are devalued, and the most vulnerable are disregarded.[96]

Neoliberalism, or unrestrained capitalism, causes – or at the very least facilitates – our pressing global health problems. This, in turn, leads to pressure for increased surveillance of the citizenry as a countermeasure. Unrestrained economic freedom for corporations contributes to the erosion of the freedom and autonomy of the citizen. The ready facility of invoking the emergency suspension of civil liberties reveals the fragility of our present systems of law and government; freedom is often appealed to as a primary value, but may be eroded under the threat to life itself.

The implicit argument is that life is more basic than freedom: you can have life without freedom, but not vice versa.

Against such an argument, however, it could be pointed out that many people have sacrificed their lives for the freedom of others – 'Give me liberty, or give me death', in the popular US catchphrase attributed to Patrick Henry. This undermines the argument that the necessity of avoiding death necessarily entails the erosion of freedom; some things, such as a life without freedom, may be considered worse than death, and resisted accordingly.

Since everyone dies anyway (science fiction visions of future techno-immortality aside), the best we can hope for is the postponement of mortality, or at least the avoidance of unnecessary suffering in the process of leaving this plane of existence.

THE STATE OF EXCEPTION

Long before the Covid-19 development, the Italian theorist Giorgio Agamben considered the concept of the 'state of exception': the situation in democratic systems whereby civil liberties are suspended in the interest – at least officially – of preserving stability, safety and security.[97] This phenomenon of suspension in turn raises the issue as to whether – or to what extent – our democratic norms and the rule of law are merely a façade covering an authoritarian, or even potentially totalitarian, reality.

More recently, Agamben criticised the 'techno-medical despotism' that, in his view, has developed in response to the pandemic.[98] Agamben, citing the writings of Patrick Zylberman, refers to the development of a novel model of government in which health security became a basic element of strategy, involving the creation of a kind of 'sanitary terror' whereby the right of the citizen to health is replaced by a health obligation (biosecurity).[99] The duty to maintain the health of the population is paramount.

Agamben notes what he terms the paradox of the left in accepting limitations on freedom – limitations that in fact went beyond anything envisaged by fascism. The virtualisation of human relationships has, in his view, a rationale in the goal of political control. Human needs are sacrificed to those of biosecurity, with its economic rationale.[100] We are all familiar with the way in which virtual meetings have replaced face-to-face encounters, though the latter are already problematised in 'real life' by mask-wearing.

In his earlier book *State of Exception*, Agamben discusses the tricky issue of what happens at the border between politics and law.[101] Historically, he refers to Hitler's 1933 Decree for the Protection of the People and the State, which suspended the personal liberties of the Weimar Constitution and was never repealed. Agamben argues that, consequently, the Third Reich can be viewed as a twelve-year-long state of exception.[102] Hitler's rise to power was facilitated, crucially, by an already-existing presidential dictatorship and a non-functioning parliament.[103] The seeds of totalitarianism were already present in the political system, before the establishment of the Third Reich.

As noted by Robert Paxton, the 1933 decree suspended freedom of speech and other liberties, allowed the arrest of political suspects, and facilitated the centralisation of police power.[104] It was followed by the Enabling Act of 1933, or the 'Law to Relieve the Distress of the People and Reich', facilitated by the arrest of Communist deputies and by the support of the Catholics. This, in turn, enabled the establishment of a single-party dictatorship. The Enabling Act was subsequently renewed every five years – even Hitler wanted a veneer of law for his actions.[105]

This historical reference may be food for thought when we consider the contemporary imposition of supposedly temporary restrictions on human freedom. There are a number of reasons for such caution: that such restrictions may become permanent; that a less benign government than the one that imposed them may inherit them, and be less scrupulous in regard to their application.

In the terms of the legal theorist Carl Schmitt, the Weimar Constitution enabled a coup d'état more easily than any other.[106] The lesson is that democratic republics need to be aware of the uses to which less scrupulous political successors may put their laws and legal principles.

According to Agamben, constitutional dictatorship inevitably results in totalitarianism, as displayed by the fate of the Weimar Republic.[107] Totalitarianism in our times, he believes, may be defined as the facilitation, through the state of exception, of the liquidation both of political opponents and entire sections of the citizenry. He argues that the establishment of an ongoing state of emergency has become a key factor of contemporary states, including democracies.[108]

Agamben's persuasive argument illustrates the somewhat deceptive nature of our democracies, where the veneer of freedom and legal protection may be swiftly stripped away under the threat of foreign attack or internal subversion, not to mention the threat of pandemics like the present one.

Agamben cites the military order proclaimed by the US president on 13 November 2001; it authorised indefinite detention and trial by military commissions of noncitizens suspected of terrorist involvement. He sees this as an example of law encompassing subjects through its own suspension. (One might interpret the point in the sense that the weakening of the rule of law, paradoxically strengthens it in the direction of tyranny.) Unlike the previous USA Patriot Act of 26 October 2001, which specified a time limit before charge or release, President Bush's order placed individuals in a state of limbo; they were not classified either as POWs or persons accused of a crime but simply as 'detainees' outside the judicial sphere. In Agamben's view, the state of exception defines, through suspension, the limit of the law.[109] He points out that the modern state of exception derives from revolutionary democracy, not absolutism.[110] The outcome of his argument is that democracy is a fragile flower, and easily uprooted.

In the terms of Karl Friedrich, under favourable conditions our constitutional systems can be transformed into totalitarian ones.[111] By assuming the title of 'Commander in Chief of the Army', President Bush facilitated the emergency becoming the rule, eliding the distinction between peace and war.[112]

Arising from Agamben's argument, it could be argued that what passes for peace may simply be a suspension of the normal state of war, or indeed a façade hiding a more-or-less continual state of war, as has been the case in the United States for a long time. Indeed, the United States has been engaged in war or invasion almost continually since independence.[113]

Agamben traces the state of exception in the post-war Federal Republic of Germany, as well as in Switzerland, Italy, England and the United States.[114] Interestingly, even Fascist Italy felt it necessary to introduce a sunset clause whereby emergency legislation fell out of effect within sixty days – if it wasn't transformed into law in the meantime.[115]

This raises the issue of whether contemporary forms of proto-totalitarianism, or the forms of totalitarianism that they foreshadow, deserve the name fascism. In some ways, it could be argued that they go beyond historical fascism – for example, in terms of the potential of modern surveillance to creep into every crevice of life and thought. It might be observed that responses to the recent pandemic, including mass house arrest, radical curtailment of travel and the banning of religious services, are virtually unprecedented, even in totalitarian systems. It is true that they depend to a large extent on public acquiescence, but such agreement is reinforced by extensive media control.[116]

The consequences of Agamben's argument in defence of the rights of individual citizens in the face of a potential diminution of freedom and autonomy, are fairly clear. Widespread ignorance of history on the part of the electorate, and of the value of freedom and democracy, leads either to a shoulder-shrug attitude to their disappearance, or else to impotent fury – a fury that, ironically, buttresses the ambitions of authoritarians on the far right.

Agamben cites a notion at the basis of emergency powers as 'necessity has no law'.[117] However, the process of invoking this phrase seems fraught with problems – for who is to decide that, in any given situation, the conditions are sufficient to invoke the 'natural' right of the state to self-preservation? It could be argued that national security is prior to written constitutions in terms of vital importance. A state without a constitution may be viable, but a constitution without a state is impotent – like a grin without a cat, in the terms of Lewis Carroll.

Once again, the fragility of liberal-democratic forms of government is evident. When push comes to shove, power prevails over abstract ideals of freedom and autonomy – the inevitability of a self-appointed deep state apparatus becomes apparent.

Agamben denies that historical figures like Hitler and Mussolini were dictators, in a technical sense of the word: both assumed power legally, and both allowed the existing constitutions to remain in place. Crucially, they installed a separate structure along with the legal constitution, allowed for by the state of exception.[118]

The state of exception is not the same as a dictatorship; it is an anomalous space where the distinction between public and private no longer applies.[119] We may already see hints of this abolition of privacy in airline travel (even in normal, non-pandemic times). When passing through airports, we are made to partially disrobe (in public) at security checkpoints; body scanners, and their operators, can look through our clothes.[120] The historical echoes with the processing of internees in camps may be faint, but they are there.

When the state of exception becomes the rule, as Agamben observes, then the system becomes a machine of death. He attempts to show that the state of exception has persisted from the First World War up to our own time, at which point it has extended throughout the world.[121] While Agamben's argument may be exaggerated for rhetorical effect – we do not live in a machine of death, at least not yet – the potential remains for our systems to degenerate to such a level.

Agamben refers to Michel Foucault's observation in *The History of Sexuality* that the state began to tally and take control of natural life at the dawn of modernity.[122] This is in the context of Foucault's growing emphasis on biopolitics – though Agamben points out that Foucault never focused on the totalitarian biopolitics of the twentieth century.[123] The frame of reference is the overall distinction Agamben makes between *zoê* ('bare life') and *bios* ('political existence').[124] The former refers to the basic biological condition of life, while the latter refers to life as lived, including its potentialities.[125]

For Agamben, democracy has failed to save bare life and has become complicit with its enemy, totalitarianism.[126] In our time, the state of exception begins to become the basic rule. The 'absolute space of exception' is the concentration camp.[127] For Agamben, the camp is the paradigm of the biopolitical space of the modern.[128] In the process of extermination of the Jews, the lines of demarcation break down between police and politics, eugenics and ideology, health and battle.[129] In Agamben's terms, we are now all virtually in the category of *zoê*, or bare life.[130]

Overall, Agamben's position may be seen as involving something of a rhetorical exaggeration. Inhabitants of stable Western democracies are not, at least in practice, in the same boat vis-à-vis the pandemic as their counterparts in some other parts of the world. The potential remains, however. James J. Criss, in the context of a discussion of the difference between voluntary medicine and its compulsory counterpart, describes how the state has become increasingly concerned with the regimentation of bare life in its attempts to grapple with the problem of disease.[131] Others argue that coercive measures instituted under pressure of the pandemic have sapped the struggle for increased democracy.[132]

Agamben notes Arendt's observation that the camps are laboratories in the experiment of complete control.[133] But he reverses this; he argues that it was the deep-rooted metamorphosis of politics into the sphere of bare life that gave legitimacy and necessity to domination. It was only because politics had morphed into biopolitics that it was possible for it to transform into totalitarianism.[134]

In the era of biopolitics, according to Agamben, the sovereign – who already had the ability to decide the state of exception and consequently the power of life and death – now has the power to decide the point at which life no longer has political relevance. One of the key features of biopolitics in recent times has been the fusion of medicine and politics. In the Third Reich, this process began to take on its final form. In the medical-political coalescence, sovereign and doctor appear to exchange roles.[135]

This issue of fusion of medicine and politics has increasing relevance in the context of current debates around assisted dying.[136] This provision from one perspective, increases individual choice, freedom and autonomy. From a negative perspective, it raises the possibility of future state coercion or duress – its potential overextension in regard to people whose lives might be deemed unproductive or superfluous.

On the face of it, this seems an example of the familiar confusion between rights and duties: if I assert a right to avail of assistance in ending my life, that statement is logically quite distinct from the assertion that I have a duty to do so. In practice, though, the world is less logical than that – rights do, in practice, sometimes morph into duties. To take one example, the right of women to work outside the home has, through economic adjustments, meant that it has become much more difficult than it was before to be a stay-at-home mother. Similarly, the right to die may, under certain socioeconomic pressures, change into the (perceived) duty to die.

Agamben goes on to argue that regardless of whether the first concentration camps were instituted by the Spanish in Cuba or by the British in South Africa, what happened in both cases was the result of a state of emergency and martial law. In Germany, the camps developed on the basis of the concept of *Schutzhaft*, or 'protective custody', originating in Prussian law. People weren't interned because of actual criminality; they were interned to avoid endangering the state.[137]

He points out that the first concentration camps in Germany were actually set up by social democratic governments, not the Nazis, to intern Communists and refugees.[138] The Nazis simply followed an earlier practice when they proclaimed the 'decree for the protection of the people and the state', which indefinitely suspended constitutional protections of freedom and privacy.[139] In Agamben's view, when the state of exception becomes established as the norm, the camp is the result.[140] In the camp, any atrocity becomes possible.[141]

For Agamben, the camp may be viewed, in essence, as 'the materialization of the state of exception' – refugee centres, for example, may be seen as partaking in the essence of what the camp is. The issue here is not that of ill-treatment *per se*, but pertains to the situation of the centre under the control of the police and outside of judicial authority. In contemporary society, spaces such as airport *zones d'attente* hint at the presence of the camp.[142]

In our own time, we could point to the example of Guantanamo, whose inmates live in a perpetual state of legal-political limbo.

The camp, in Agamben's terms, emerges when the political system enters into a crisis of extended duration and the state takes over the care of biological life. In the camp, the system becomes a killing machine. When bare life and the nation state split apart, the camp is the result.[143] The potency of the Führer, his word as law, derived from his oneness with German biological life.[144]

It would be a mistake to believe that we have overcome such challenges to freedom and individual autonomy; in our own time, refugees take the place of Jews in the context of the reduction to bare life, and the potential for similar forms of inhumanity arises. Today, alarm about the repressive possibilities of the state of exception seems to be largely a concern of liberals, libertarians and right-wing conspiracy theorists. The left often ignore these kinds of concerns. With some notable exceptions, such as Klein and Agamben, they tend to accept the narrative regarding the necessity of more-or-less repressive measures that governments and their scientific-medical advisors put forward. Whether such a response is wholly wise will, no doubt, be revealed in time.

It should be noted that not all commentators agree with recourse to Agamben, in regard to the state of exception, as a means of responding to the pandemic. In an otherwise enlightening review of recent pandemic literature, Joelle M. Abi-Rached dismisses the state of exception perspective as 'trite and passé' without, however, explaining why this is the case. Abi-Rached believes that what we require are 'new ways of rethinking our modes of production, socioeconomic priorities, and modes of consumption', arguing that '[i]magination and critical thinking will be more than ever vital in reimagining our post-pandemic future.'[145]

It may be a helpful response to envisage new and more positive ways of living as a response to the negative experience of the pandemic, but an understanding of the fragility of our democratic systems, and of our freedoms, is surely imperative as well. Agamben contributes to that understanding in significant ways, despite a certain tendency – which he shares with other prominent thinkers of the last century or so – to look for the worst and to dwell in the Grand Hotel Abyss.[146] Shorten argues against the tendency – which Agamben shares – to understand modernity in totalitarian terms.[147]

For the moment, though, the 'sanitary state' where the health of the citizenry has priority, has taken control of our lives. It is based on a key, unstated belief: that the presumed exigencies of public safety outweigh those of freedom. This is something that has not been thought through – or at least not publicly verbalised, if it has. Paradoxically, this mindset has been largely accepted by the left, with reinforcement by the media. This may have something to do with the marginalisation of the issue of freedom on the left in favour of (more-or-less) authoritarian forms of state control, in the interest of implementing the goal of equality.

The largely unexamined assumption that necessity trumps freedom prevails, regardless of concerns that could be raised about the long-term effects of the erosion of freedom in the presumed interest of biological safety and security. The seamless fusion of medicine and politics should raise urgent questions as to the dangers of the erosion of freedom; it should also bring into focus the fragility of our democratic systems. Unfortunately, it has tended to obscure both.[148]

THE FRAGILITY OF DEMOCRACY

Reading key thinkers such as Arendt and Agamben intensifies one's sense of the precarious state of freedom and democracy in the modern world. In the face of a pandemic, the apparent willingness, and even eagerness, of various populations to submit to draconian measures – measures unprecedented even in wartime, or under the totalitarian regimes of the twentieth century – raises concerns regarding the erosion of freedom.

This erosion may transpire under innumerable threats – for example, global warming, resource depletion, and mass migration from no-longer-liveable areas of the world. This is in no way to diminish the threat of the pandemic – or, indeed, any of the other potential threats that we may face as a result of our out-of-control depredations on nature and the prevalence of military adventurism. But finding a balance between freedom and security is a major challenge, and this has been the case ever since democracy took hold on our society.

The key is informed consent. Insofar as populations are convinced of the need for serious erosion of the freedoms they have hitherto taken for granted, they will permit the partial, temporary diminution of those liberties under certain circumstances. However, permission that is not informed by rational thought and judgement aids the slide towards the permanent erosion of freedom. The statement that freedom is easy to give up but difficult to regain is no less true for being a cliché.

Attempts to steer discussion in particular ways, or to marginalise or censor particular viewpoints, are potentially harmful. The public, as a result, may disbelieve information that they might otherwise have accepted, had it emerged in the process of free and vigorous debate. Free speech and untrammelled debate are not absolute values, but they are vital to the healthy functioning of democratic systems.

The political necessity is for an informed populace. This prospect is problematic in an era where media communication often takes the form of mind-control, and the previous exhilarating anarchy of social media seems to be giving way to new forms of regulation and restriction (under the guise of the prevention of dangerous forms of expression).

The exponential pace of technological development offers the possibility of a form of total control by the state, working hand in hand with corporations. In this scenario, they would have complete knowledge of the most minute details of the lives of the citizens – details of which the individual may indeed be unaware. This is a prospect of which Hitler and Stalin could only dream, and which greatly exceeds Orwell's worst nightmares. Media manipulation and the union between state and medical establishment are worrying signs. They signal an acceleration towards the kind of total system outlined by the thinkers referred to above.

Even in the nineteenth century, Tocqueville was aware of the negative tendencies and potentialities of the state. In his terms, the state seeks to keep us in eternal childhood. Every day it curtails free agency, covering society with a web of small regulations. 'Such a power does not destroy, but it prevents existence; it does not tyrannise, but it compresses, enervates, extinguishes, and stupefies a people, till each nation is reduced to nothing better than a flock of timid and industrious animals, of which the government is the shepherd.'[149]

INVERTED TOTALITARIANISM

At this point it is worth mentioning Sheldon Wolin's influential, and persuasive, notion of 'inverted totalitarianism' whereby the economy dominates the state, unlike the reverse situation in more traditional forms of totalitarianism. Wolin cites the influence of money on elections, lobby culture and the judicial and penal system skewed by class. Inverted totalitarianism, in the terms of Chris Hedges, is expressed in 'the faceless anonymity of the corporate state'.

While paying lip service to the trappings of democracy, the corporate state has total control of power, at the expense of the power of the citizen. This situation is reinforced by keeping the populace in a perpetual state of insecurity and passivity – an 'economy of fear', in Wolin's terms. The society of the spectacle replaces any substantive democracy. Image takes the place of substance. Cultural wars, for Wolin, are a substitute for political involvement.

The key point in Wollin's compelling argument is that unlike classical totalitarian regimes such as Nazism or Soviet Communism, where economics took second place to politics, the reverse is the case in inverted totalitarianism: politics is dominated by economics.

The system Wolin describes is that of the management of democracy. The corporate state enhances the rights of corporations at the expense of those of citizens. Intellectuals are bought off. The militarists and the corporatists have effectively extinguished American democracy, wasting resources and dismantling labour unions in the process of normalising war. The dominance of the military and the Department of Homeland Security represent a form of disguised statism, hidden in plain sight.[150]

For Wolin, in his key text *Democracy Incorporated*, inverted totalitarianism emerges from the reciprocal relationship between government and corporations. It involves what he calls 'the political coming-of-age of corporate power'. Inverted totalitarianism succeeds by fostering political lack of engagement on the part of the populace; this is in contrast to the extreme engagement characteristic of traditional totalitarianism. The leader is the product of the system rather than its author.[151] Inverted totalitarianism, according to Wolin, encourages 'predomination': control by a combination of varied powers.[152]

This situation might be contrasted with the historical phenomenon of Nazi political control, which operated largely through competition and duplication of power whereby officials were deliberately put in potentially vying positions– the US version encourages co-operation among controllers rather than competition.

Wolin notes a further difference between inverted totalitarianism on the one hand, and the Soviet and Nazi versions of totalitarianism on the other. The older forms of totalitarianism developed a substantial system of social services. Inverted totalitarianism, in contrast, tries to weaken such services, reducing individual power as a consequence. In other words, political apathy is welcomed.[153] In this sense, inverted totalitarianism is the opposite of conventional totalitarianism, which fed off the enthusiastic participation of the masses.

Inverted totalitarianism relies on the passivity of the citizenry; it flourishes on the basis of a 'politically demobilised society'.[154] Universities, science and scholarship in general have been assimilated into the system.[155] As a consequence, the status of science has been diminished; it is left vulnerable to institutional manipulation – and also to reactionary, fundamentalist attack.[156]

Religious fundamentalism, which historically marginalised the social gospel, or the practical application of Christian ethics in the organisation of society, in favour of an emphasis on the natural depravity of mankind, finds confirmation of its bleak view in the destructive excesses of neoliberal capitalism.[157]

The 'managerialisation' of the political scene, the domination of a management culture, has come about through the switching of personnel between politics, corporations, government departments, the military and the media. The system considers the operation of politics and government in managerial rather than political terms. A ruthless business-based approach flourishes, while the public ethic deteriorates. State and corporation are seamlessly intermingled in the corporate state.[158]

In Wolin's compelling terms, the United States is transformed into an imperial superpower, a combination of empire and the expansive corporation.[159] The superpower provokes political instability and exacerbates the problem of terrorism.[160] Imperial control by the United States abroad has, as a side effect, the extension of surveillance to the home population as well.[161]

Manipulation of the populace by the system of managerial capitalism and inverted totalitarianism occurs through a paralysing fear of terrorism and natural disasters; of incursions of illegal immigrants; of epidemics, such as Asian flu and avian flu, for which there will be a limit on the supply of vaccines. (Wolin was writing pre-Covid-19, but subsequent events seem to bear out his line of argument.) The citizen is forced to look for help from a government that has been presented by conservative forces in the United States as the enemy of freedom. The individual experiences a consequent insecurity and uncertainty, on the basis of which inverted totalitarianism flourishes.[162]

At the same time, the US population is controlled by the system of managerial capitalism and inverted totalitarianism through corporate manipulation,[163] distraction and obfuscation – through the foregrounding of non-crucial issues.[164] In Wolin's persuasive terms, 'the consummate union of corporate power and governmental power heralds the American version of a total system.'[165]

Wolin traces the historical origins of what he terms 'managed democracy' to the institutional constraints on the majority; these include checks and balances, separation of powers, the Electoral College and judicial review. In his terms, managed democracy has its roots in the designers of the US Constitution.[166]

The role of the Electoral College in the recent Trump triumph seems to substantiate Wolin's critique in this regard. In Wolin's terms, the US political system originated with a prejudice against democracy – majority rule was seen as a menace to the republican system. The goal was the management of democracy through an elite.[167] Executive overreach is a consequence of the success of this philosophy. This overreach has included secret wiretaps and rendition, the violation of treaties, and the ignoring of whistle-blower protections. The US Constitution, and democracy itself, are marginalised in the process.[168]

For Wolin, elitism is a basic element of inverted totalitarianism.[169] Elites have fomented catastrophic wars, including the American Civil War, Vietnam and Iraq.[170]

Wolin cites the concept of 'civic demobilisation' through fear and insecurity (though the citizenry, by allowing itself to be manipulated to such an extent, is not completely blameless).[171] Both historically and in contemporary terms, Wolin sees the chief dangers to democracy as lying in elitism and in the tendency towards imperial expansion.[172]

In the context of the United States, he cites the key tension as being between republican elitism and democratic participatory politics.[173] The US Constitution, by limiting the political role of the citizen to the exercise of periodic choice, was actually designed 'to minimize the direct expression of a popular will'.[174]

For Wolin, the essential problem is the political involvement of corporations, the corrupting effect of lobbying, the growth of executive power, and the obfuscation of political discourse (bolstered by the media).[175]

Since the publication of Wolin's book, the disintegration of Republican politics (that of the Republican Party) has brought into sharp relief the limitations of the Republican mindset, with its elitism, self-interest, appeal to narrow sectional interests and dismissal of the ability of the *demos* to make enlightened and rational choices. Wolin does tend to favour the Democratic Party over that of the Republicans, a position that may be open to question by those who regard them as two sides of the same coin. Nevertheless, his defence of people power and democracy vis-à-vis Republicanism, with its suspicion of democracy, is persuasive.[176]

The main priority of democrats, according to Wolin, is to regain popular control of politics and renew representative democracy. Means to that end, in a US context, include restoring the authority of Congress, limiting the expansion of the president's power, deactivating the lobby system, ending the Democratic–Republican duopoly and reining in the system of campaign finance.[177]

The interest of restoring democracy, for Wolin, also necessitates curtailing the evils of empire, managed democracy, globalization, military interventionism and a biased tax system. At the same time, he encourages the strengthening of environmental protection, populist politics, individual rights, an independent judiciary, separation of powers, checks and balances, oversight, public welfare, and governmental regulation of the economy.[178] Wolin endorses the development of local politics, though acknowledging that politics cannot be confined to the local. He further urges a reinvigoration of the ethos and practice of public service, along with the de-commercialisation of broadcasting.[179]

Such measures are no doubt needed; arguably, however, they ought to be supplemented by an expansion of direct democracy, as well as by the general reining-in of corporate capitalism. This should be accomplished not simply through state control – the relationship between corporations and the state is already more than cosy – but through the establishment of grass-roots alternatives, including direct democracy, to the current economic and political establishments.

Despite his indications of how things might develop in a positive direction, Wolin's overall perspective is a bleak one; it may be incorrect to speak of the fragility of democracy if the institution in question no longer exists as anything but a Matrix-like simulation.

In recent times, we have seen the power of corporations increasingly enmeshed with that of the state. We have watched the strengthening of corporate and state control over the media, and have also observed the proliferation of the state itself, with its intrusion into every facet of our lives, facilitated by the growth of technology. The important question is whether this will inevitably lead to the triumph of some form of totalitarian system – perhaps a version of Wolin's inverted totalitarianism. And the further question is how such a scenario might be resisted. These, and related, issues will be examined in succeeding chapters.

Chapter 3

TOTALITARIANISM
AND THE LEFT

An old joke from Soviet times goes something as follows. A man loses his pet parrot. He receives a call from the police to say the bird has been found, and he can come and collect it. On arrival at the police station, he turns to the officer on duty and remarks, 'I'd just like to say that my parrot's political views are very different from my own.'

The joke is no longer as funny as it might once have been. Even in the contemporary West, we recognise that our political opinions have become of increasing interest to the state, or at least that the state is more easily able to satisfy its interest than had previously been the case – the normal excuse being the war against terrorism, or other forms of criminality such as recreational drugs – whether legitimately regarded as such or not.

The contemporary problem of terrorism is in large part the result of military adventurism, deriving from the Western desire to prop up the fossil fuel industry; the concomitant, somewhat crazy belief that democracy can be exported through the use of force; and the self-perpetuating dynamic of the military–industrial complex.

Other forms of criminality that threaten society result from an inappropriate extension of criminal law to areas where it has no business. For example, the war on drugs has resulted, unintentionally, in the accumulation of wealth and power by criminal gangs, police corruption, and the growth of a self-serving prison industry.

In the context of modern technology, the methods of finding out our opinions are greatly enhanced from those of twentieth-century totalitarian regimes. It is true that citizens of Western First World countries are – for the moment, at least – unlikely to end up in a labour or concentration camp because of their views on the government. But a liberal democracy can, given favourable circumstances, morph into something that threatens the safety of citizens. Surveillance technology – and the information it provides – may outlast the relative benevolence of any current system.

Hannah Arendt made little distinction between totalitarianism of the left and the right; indeed, there are resemblances between the two in practice, despite the fact that Stalinism focused more on perceived enemies within the Communist movement than on those outside it. Internecine struggles within left politics often exceed in bitterness the supposedly more fundamental tensions between left and right.

Despite apparent similarities in practice, there is not much resemblance between the motivations of, for example, Marxist state socialists and National Socialists. This is so at least on a conscious level, though the lure of power may operate even in the case of those who are unaware of it. And there are others who consciously exploit the chance for domination opened up by the institution of dictatorship,. A political movement may include both idealists and cynics.

Overall, though, the conscious ideals of Marxists have tended to be – at least in principle, and in the long term – benevolent. Though admittedly, at their worst – for example under the Pol Pot regime in Cambodia – the atrocities perpetrated in the name of the Marxist political tradition at least equalled those of their ideological opposites on the right.

By contrast to those of most Marxists, the ideals of Nazism were exclusive and often malevolent – at least to those who were viewed as not belonging to the master race.

The programme of Marxism was primarily (though not explicitly) ethical. Marxist politics may be seen as a kind of materialised version of Christianity, with its concept of *agape* (altruism or unconditional love) and social justice. Though in the case of Marxism, the project was not that of some life beyond this one; it was the construction of a perfected system on earth. Such a project is not, perhaps, as far from the Christian ideal as is commonly supposed, though in the case of Marxism it is conceived as – initially, at least – an enforced rather than a voluntary mode of organisation.

By contrast, the programme of Nazism was primarily aesthetic – a politicised version of Plato's ideal of *eros*, the basis of romantic love, with its inherent element of desire and exclusivity. Here, however, it was applied to an ideal of racial improvement and dominance. In this romantic, neo-pagan, pre-Christian mindset, racial improvement and elitism trump freedom and justice. In Nazi ideology, the ideal of beauty was mapped on to that of a European (or at least northern European) ethnicity – a mapping that is clearly absurd, since no one ethnicity has a monopoly on beauty.

This chapter focuses on the propensity of left-wing politics to slide into totalitarianism, though with some reference to the politics of the right as well – and the latter will be examined more thoroughly in the following chapter.

There is undoubtedly a significant development around groupthink on the left – a form of mental totalitarianism, or perhaps proto-totalitarianism. This illustrates how even a liberal society, or state, can function to control our words, our actions and even our thoughts. It also stimulates a right-wing reaction: the right, in responding, can pose as defenders of freedom against wokeness, groupthink, cant culture, political correctness, and the rest of the bugbears of conservatives and libertarians.

At the same time, right-wing forms of groupthink flourish in the form of bizarre conspiracy theories, religious fundamentalism, blindness to the reality of the corporate state and fear of largely bogus enemies such as cultural Marxism.

Furthermore, the growth of a surveillance culture develops out of a process of articulation of capitalism and the state, so that it combines the negative aspects of both right and left, with their respective manifestations of commercialism and authoritarianism. The corporate state combines the worst of both worlds.

POPPER, PLATO AND TOTALITARIANISM

This chapter will focus on ideas of the philosopher Karl Popper, an exile of Jewish origin who fled from Austria following the rise of Nazism. Of particular interest are those ideas presented in his influential book *The Open Society and Its Enemies*, dating to the mid-1940s.[1]

Together with those of Hannah Arendt, Popper's ideas represent probably the most significant philosophical critique of totalitarianism in general, and of the Marxist version in particular.

Popper was in some ways an admirer of Karl Marx, though not of the outcome of certain manifestations of Marxist politics. It's also important to note that Popper's book, which played a significant role in the intellectual ferment that led to the fall of Communism, does not promote neoliberalism or hyper-capitalism as an alternative.

Popper, in fact, seems to be a kind of piecemeal reformer: he believes in incremental improvement steered by the state, rather than in a kind of root-and-branch restructuring of the economic system. Nevertheless, it's an indication of how far we have veered to the right in our own times, in the context of our prevailing systems and mindset, that Popper's ideas seem to be well to the left of centre. Indeed, the international businessman and philanthropist George Soros, whose ideas have been strongly influenced by Popper, is a major target of the ire of the far right – ironically so, given Popper's stature as the most important philosophical critic of Marx and Marxism.

Popper is not on the right, however, any more than he is on the far left. In fact, he comes across as a kind of social democrat; he promotes piecemeal change, or social engineering, and state involvement in the structuring of the economic system (as distinct from the state having overarching control of the economy). The extent of state involvement is an issue that may become increasingly relevant in a post-pandemic world – if indeed we are ever to be free from the threat of recurring pandemics, given our unsustainable socioeconomic system.

Presumably, for the foreseeable future, most people will want to continue to avail of public transport, air travel, cafes, restaurants, cinemas, theatres and other facilities. In a situation where social distancing threatens the viability of the market, it is difficult to see how such institutions can thrive without the – somewhat robust – intervention of the state, and the concomitant abatement of the role of the market. In such a situation, the neoliberal or hyper-capitalist approach – where people are crowded together to maximise profit and traditional mass travel flourishes – seems to be a non-starter: the only issue of contention is as to the extent and depth of state intervention.

This could involve massively increased state regulation of the economy, such that many of the amenities we take for granted – and that the market currently facilitates reasonably well – would be taken under public ownership/control, or at least under some combination of state and co-operative ownership and/or control. In that case, profit maximisation would no longer hold sway in large sectors of the economy; the design of goods for health could take priority, regardless of its economic downside. This would, presumably, have to be paid for with increased taxes of one kind or another, or a different emphasis on what is taxed – or both.

The alternative would be the annihilation of small-scale, human-friendly enterprises; large-scale business would thrive, inequality in society (already massive) would deepen, and electronic cocooning would become a permanent way of life for the population as a whole.

For good or ill, however, it looks as if some kind of socialism, at least in the sense of increased state involvement in the economy, may win out after all. Whether or not that would be a good thing is a separate question.[2]

For Popper, the origin of totalitarianism lies in the work of Plato. According to Popper, Plato regarded the society in which he lived as being in a state of historical degeneration; he wished to restore it to a primitive, 'tribalist' form of lost unity. Popper sees the political influence of Plato as being almost wholly malign. He traces Plato's influence, particularly through the German philosopher Georg Hegel, on left- and right-wing forms of totalitarianism in the twentieth century.

Popper sees Plato – with the latter's proposals for eugenics, communism, the community of women and children, social and ideological control, and rational ordering of the state – as the originator of the sinister forms of anti-freedom that have developed in the modern world. Popper regards Plato's position as a form of 'historicism', which he opposes.

Historicism, for Popper, is a view that there is some kind of logic in history – for example, that society is either currently in a stage of degeneration from an original, ideal situation (as Plato believed) or progressing towards a future state of social freedom and justice (as Marxism assumes).

Plato's views may be interpreted as a kind of philosophical idealism. For Popper, though, Plato's belief in underlying 'Forms' or 'Ideas' does not represent some kind of redeeming spirituality; instead, it is at the root of various forms of totalitarianism's attempts to institute, or at least facilitate, a utopian society – whether a 'social' utopia, in the left-wing version, or a 'natural' utopia, on the right.

Popper's thought, summarised briefly above and formulated at length in *The Open Society and Its Enemies*, needs to be historically contextualised when viewed from the perspective of our own time. On the one hand, there was the defeat of fascism including National Socialism in the 1940s, the later collapse of the Soviet Union in the 1980s, and the fairly recent transition to democracy of authoritarian regimes in southern Europe and South America.

On the other hand, there has been the recent resurgence of authoritarian nationalism in, for example, Brazil, Poland, Hungary, Turkey and

Russia. In the United States, there has been instability, racial violence and the associated threat of a strong-arm leader; China, with its strange blend of Communism and neoliberalism, is rising in power and influence. This is not to mention the threat posed by the Covid-19 pandemic to the EU ideal of supranationalism, open borders and international co-operation (there is a direct contradiction between the mobility of viruses and the desire to maintain globalist ideals, in terms of free trade).

Popper's views also need to be seen in the light of contemporary ecological politics. The question might be asked whether this escalation can be understood as a new form of Platonism, harking back to a pristine view of nature – uncontaminated by the challenges of pollution, species extinction and myriad other environmental issues. Nonetheless, the existential nature of the current ecological crisis calls into question any attempt to categorise ecopolitics as fundamentally aesthetic or cultural – as it is literally a question of life or death.

In Popper's view, writing in the mid-twentieth century, a return to a congenial state of nature is not possible. To turn back would mean going the whole way – back to the animal state. According to Popper, society can never return to the supposed state of lost innocence; reason and the advancement of knowledge preclude a return to what Popper calls 'tribal magic'. He argues that an attempt to return to tribalism would bring us the Inquisition, the secret police and 'romanticised gangsterism' (presumably a reference to Nazism).[3]

Understanding the historical context of Popper's writings is of central importance. Popper was writing in the 1940s, at a time when the world faced a somewhat different range of problems from those that confront us today. The latter include global warming, species extinction and the threat of future pandemics, themselves consequent on our depredations on nature. Unrestrained capitalism no longer threatens just human well-being – which is bad enough – but the totality of nature itself.

Nevertheless, a politics based on nature or natural values may itself be problematic. The slogan 'return to nature' is by no means a new one; it goes back, at least, to Rousseau. It was an important feature of the ideology of National Socialism, with its doctrine of 'blood and soil', and Social Darwinism; it was also a counter-Enlightenment foregrounding of racial instinct, the exaltation of the supposed will to self-perfection on the part of a superior ethnic group. Searching for a balance between humane values and the values of nature is by no means an easy project.

It should also be noted that Green politics, with its highlighting of 'nature', has a dubious antecedent in fascist theory and practice.[4] Some kind of Green authoritarianism, particularly under the pressure of environmental collapse, is conceivable as a future prospect – though mitigated by the fact that the people who are most concerned about the environment are seldom the people who actually rise to power. A more pressing danger would be ecological-economic collapse, followed by the takeover of the state by power-hungry people with no concern about environmental matters, but who manage to deflect public attention away from the real issues.

It is, however, crucial that the concept of nature within Green thought be clearly demarcated from that of its sinister predecessor; that the relationship between natural and humane values be articulated and contextualised. Eco-authoritarianism, or even eco-fascism, is one possible direction that a variety, or deformation, of Green politics could take, particularly under the future socioeconomic pressures of immigration, resource wars and economic dislocation.

The tension between natural and humane values is not the only one that looms in environmental politics. There is also a tension between respect for nature and deference to science. From a personal perspective – in the context of my own involvement in Green politics over a number of decades – a noticeable chasm has developed between those who harbour a suspicion of aspects of science and technology, particularly as those practices are economically-influenced, and others who take their cue from those sets of disciplines.

Heated debates among Greens around such issues as genetic engineering and the environmental effects of mobile phone technology may signal that the struggle between the 'two cultures' (in novelist C.P. Snow's terms) is as alive as ever; that the relationship between the ideals of nature and progress is no more settled now than it was in Popper's time.[5]

For Popper, Plato's totalitarian political programme is based on the idealist notion of arresting change, combined with the naturalistic 'back to nature' project. Elements of the programme include a strict class division, with the ruling class being accorded priority, including a monopoly on military involvement and education. To avoid being undermined by trade, Plato's state – in Popper's argument – should have economic autarchy or self-sufficiency as its goal.[6] For Plato, Popper argues, the state's interest is the benchmark of morality.[7]

Popper believed that Plato wished (sincerely though erroneously) to free his contemporaries from the strain of social change and dissension, consequent on the social revolution that was linked to democracy and individualism. This was to be brought about by a reversion to a static society and to tribalism.[8] For Plato, then, the ideal of a tribal or collectivist organisation was 'the closed society', as distinct from 'the open society' (endorsed by Popper) wherein the individual is called on to make personal decisions.[9]

The terms 'open society' and 'closed society', deriving from Popper's dichotomy, have been extremely influential in our contemporary world, denoting a tension between freedom and its lack. Popper draws a parallel between reactionary Platonism, with its desire to return to a static way of life, and orthodox Jewry around the time of Christ, which rejected the Christian movement together with its humanitarian ideals. Nonetheless, Popper argues that a totalitarian element, echoing that of Plato (and Aristotle), developed in the practice of the institutionalised Christian Church, resulting in medieval authoritarianism and the Inquisition.[10]

It should be noted that the tension between the values denoted as humane, natural and scientific runs deep within the Christian tradition. One influential critic, Lynn White, doesn't blame Christianity for its supposedly anti-scientific influence; instead, he blames it for the historical dominance of science and technology, with the deplorable environmental results of such dominance.[11] Christianity has consequently been blamed on the one hand for anti-scientific obscurantism, and on the other for fostering a scientific spirit that has led to the degradation of the earth.

POPPER ON HEGEL

The German philosopher Georg Hegel ranks second on Popper's hit list of malign influences on politics, both left and right. Hegelianism, for Popper, involved the rebirth of tribalism. Popper viewed the French Revolution not as an anti-Christian revolt but as a reinstatement of the positive ideals of Christianity (liberty, equality, fraternity), together with the positive aspirations of the Greece of Pericles and Socrates. Hegelianism, with its Platonic roots, was in Popper's view a philosophical reaction against the progressive ideals of the French Revolution. This reaction included the worship of the state and the corresponding denigration of the individual.[12] Hegel, for Popper, was – through the influence of Plato, and his pupil Aristotle – the direct progenitor of the historicism and totalitarianism of our time.[13]

Popper also attacks Hegel's writing style, quoting the philosopher Arthur Schopenhauer (whom he admires):

> [T]hese monstrous accumulations of words that annul and contradict one another drive the mind into tormenting itself with vain attempts to think anything whatever in connection with them, until finally it collapses from sheer exhaustion. Thus any ability to think is so thoroughly destroyed that the young man will ultimately mistake empty and hollow verbiage for real thought. A guardian fearing that his ward might become too intelligent for his schemes might prevent this misfortune by innocently suggesting the reading of Hegel.[14]

Popper's critique of Hegel is addressed in this chapter primarily to contextualise the Popperian analysis of left-wing totalitarianism, but it should be pointed out here that Popper blames Hegel, to a great extent, for right-wing totalitarianism as well. Popper notes, in particular, the combination of Hegel's 'mystical metaphysics' with the form of Darwinism espoused by Ernst Haeckel as lying at the root of fascism. In substitution for Hegel's concept of 'Spirit', racialism exalts the material, quasi-biological notion of Blood or Race. What we get is a religion of, in Popper's terms, a 'self-developing biological essence' – characterised by George Bernard Shaw as a 'meta-biology'.

Popper argues that almost all the most important concepts of twentieth-century totalitarianism derive from Hegel.[15] These concepts include nationalism; the warlike, self-assertive, amoral state; the promotion of war; the leadership principle; and the principle of the heroic life.

For Popper, these have, in political practice, fed into the ideology of race with the aim of state creation. The resultant state is a totalitarian one that pervades and dominates the life of the people. For Hegel and his followers, Popper asserts, nationalism answers people's need to situate themselves in the world and in a collectivity. The state exists only in contrast to other states; it is not subject to any standard other than that of the judgement of history: might is right. This results in the exaltation of war. Popper refers to this syndrome as the 'Platonic-Prussian morality'. Propaganda, lies and distortion of the truth prevail. Hegel, in Popper's view, promulgates the cult of glory, anti-egalitarianism and the 'Great Man', the 'tribalist ideal' of animal heroism.[16]

In contemporary terms, regarding the ideology of 'might is right', we might point to the United States' refusal to accept the jurisdiction of the International Criminal Court and, in a broader sense, its routine use of war as a means of furthering its aims. Further back – in an avowedly totalitarian context – we may recall Hitler's habitual breaking of his word when it suited him.

Unfortunately, and if one accepts Popper's critique, it would appear that Hegel's influence is alive and well in the contemporary era, with the emergence of 'great men' (in their own eyes, at least) – regardless of whether such individuals have ever read Hegel, or even heard of him. In the light of Popper's account of Hegel's exaltation of the state, its legacy seems to remain, even in the aftermath of the great totalitarian regimes of the twentieth century.

POPPER ON MARX

While Popper is generally regarded as the most influential critic of Marx and Marxism, he is in many ways sympathetic to Marx, and an admirer of his work. This, indeed, is the case for most people who have studied Marx in any detail – if one can successfully bracket the malign influence of a version of Marxism on the politics of the twentieth century.

Nonetheless, Popper's interpretation of Marx's position on some key issues is not one that Marx himself would have endorsed. It would probably have made matters clearer if Popper had clarified where his own ideas departed from those of Marx rather than attempting to find them, at least implicitly, in the previous author. There seems, indeed, to be a key incoherence in some of Marx's ideas – particularly around historical materialism and the determination of consciousness by social being – that Popper might have explicated more clearly.

Popper regards Marxism – the left-wing of Hegelianism, with its crucial appropriation of Hegelian dialectics – as the most perilous manifestation of historicism (despite conceding its humanitarian motivation). For Popper, Marx replaced Hegel's Spirit with material and economic interests – similar to the way in which Nazi racialism replaced the same notion with the material concept of Blood or Race.[17]

Popper distinguishes between what he calls Marx's historicism (his endorsement of historical prophecy or the notion that a study of the past and present can yield insight into the future), which he dismisses, and his economism (an emphasis on the study of economic conditions as an explanatory mechanism), which he endorses. Popper, though, believes that Marx carried economism too far; to him, its general importance as an explanatory mechanism is clear, but it is a mistake to overrate it in particular cases. The example Popper gives is that of mathematics: economic conditions may illuminate the history of mathematical problems, but a knowledge of the problems themselves is much more important.[18] Putting it another way, the class background of a mathematician may explain how he or she became a mathematician in the first place, but it tells us nothing of interest regarding the substantive issues of mathematics.[19]

Popper goes on to argue that certain ideas are more basic than the material means of production. Suppose, he posits, our economic system were destroyed but that scientific and technical knowledge survived. The consequences would be dramatic, but not terminal. If the reverse were to happen, however – for example, if people from an undeveloped culture occupied a developed but deserted country – the civilisation would disappear.[20]

The argument is intuitively persuasive. A slightly different version involves a thought experiment regarding a switch of populations. Imagine swapping populations with completely different mindsets between an undeveloped country and a developed one, where the two countries have roughly similar climates, natural resources, etc. In such a situation, the new population would, in each case, have to fit into a radically different social and economic structure than the one they were used to.

It seems clear, by intuition, that the systems would tend to change, in each case, to reflect the mindset of the new population – to a greater extent than the mindset would change to reflect the new structure. This kind of thought experiment, where it seems that consciousness determines social being rather than vice versa, calls into question the whole basis of Marx's analysis.

One could argue, though, that there is no clear definition of historical materialism in Marxist theory. The notion that social being determines consciousness[21] seems to cover the whole spectrum, from the minimalist (trivially true) contention that the economic basis is essential to society to the maximalist (highly reductive) viewpoint that the economy explains society in every important way. In practice, the Marxist approach seems to vacillate from one extreme to another. The issue is further complicated by the difficulty, or impossibility, of disentangling cultural and ideological elements from economic practices.[22]

Marx's goal was that of freedom for the worker from bondage to drudgery and material conditions as a result of the capitalist system. Popper describes this aim as 'idealistic' – a loaded term, which Marx himself would certainly have rejected. Nonetheless, it does fit into Popper's conception of Marx as implicitly, if not explicitly, championing the cause of spiritual liberation from bondage to material conditions.[23]

Marx's 'realm of freedom', with its liberation from subjection to toil and material pressure, and its abolition of capitalist injustice and exploitation, arguably bears more than a passing resemblance to the 'kingdom of heaven' extolled in the New Testament. It should be emphasised, however, that it is a resemblance that Marx himself would have been unlikely to acknowledge.

An implicit reliance on religious ideology runs deep in Western culture, whether commending a life free from capitalist subjugation or the (related) slavery of fascism. On the other hand, there have been notorious defences of fascism within the Christian tradition, including nationalist Spain in the 1930s and collaborationist France during the Second World War – not to mention the 'ratlines', involving Catholic aid to escaping Nazis after the war.

One of Popper's key criticisms of Marx involves the latter's (false) belief in historical prophecy: the idea that the revolution is inevitable. This, in turn, led to a failure to elaborate, either in theory or practice, a functioning system for a post-revolutionary society. For Marx, in Popper's view, all a society can do is facilitate the unstoppable development of socialism.[24]

This, it should be emphasised, is arguably one of the crucial failures of Marxism: the failure to elaborate not only what a socialist or communist society might look like but also how to get there without setting up a self-perpetuating system with the potential for tyranny. The issue here seems to be the perennial tension between democracy and freedom.

From a democratic point of view, it seems perfectly logical that democracy should be extended to the public organisation of society as a whole, including the socialisation of the economy. From the perspective of the defence of freedom, such a project highlights, once again, the potential conflict between democracy and freedom – since democratic control of the economy may serve, in important ways, to limit not only economic freedom but also personal freedom.

The problem here, though, is that if you push that argument – involving suspicion of democracy - too far, you end up with a defence of untrammelled capitalism against the encroachments of the state, with negative effects including the emergence of a class of self-regarding oligarchs or plutocrats. The result in practice has been the triumph of neoliberalism, the reality of corporate domination, the marginalisation of democracy and the restriction of individual freedom.

On the one hand, the citizen is presented with the choice between a bureaucratic and controlling state, with the loss of freedom it involves. On the other, he or she is faced with the prospect of a massively unbalanced capitalist structure, with the atomisation, insecurity and social fragmentation – in short, the loss of freedom – characteristic of such societies.

There is, consequently, no easy resolution of the relationship between democracy and freedom. Each may be regarded as desirable in itself, but they exist in a somewhat uneasy tension – a tension that has seldom been resolved, either in theoretical or practical terms.

Apart from the belief in historical prophecy, Popper's key critique of Marxism is based on his interpretation of the Marxist theory of the state – though that theory exists in a fairly rudimentary form. The state, in Marxist theory – as Popper elaborates it – is organised class oppression; all government involves dictatorship of the ruling class. Politics on its own, in Popper's interpretation of Marxism, is powerless to change the underlying economic system. However, Popper points out that politics, at least in its radical form, can have the function of stirring up class consciousness in a revolutionary direction.

Popper summarises Marx's position on progress towards a future society in the following terms: after the revolution, the dictatorship of the bourgeois, capitalist state is initially replaced by a dictatorship of the proletariat; the proletarian revolution leads to a society with only a single class, and consequently to a classless society where class dictatorship cannot exist. In effect, the state has to vanish.[25]

Popper's encapsulation of the Marxist position highlights one of its key drawbacks. The problem is that dictatorship has its own dynamic; the mindset of people who are drawn to the capturing and exercise of power within a system of dictatorship is likely to represent the mindset with the strongest resistance to the relinquishment of power. This, indeed, seems to be borne out by history.

One could argue that the flaw comes down to a radical underestimation of the role of ideational, or psychological, factors in politics – an underestimation that has the consequence of instituting and perpetuating tyranny. Furthermore, the Marxist tendency to downplay the role of psychological factors may lead to the – disastrously false – notion that if you change socioeconomic conditions, the mindset of the population will adjust in due course.

Popper views Marx's theory of the state as being limited by its own time; the revolution of machinery led to a change in the class structure, and political and legal transformations merely followed on. For Popper, the notion of the juridico-political system as merely a superstructure contains an element of truth, and Marx's cynical views on liberalism and democracy are borne out by the appalling workplace conditions of his time, as well as by the structure of the capitalist system itself.[26]

Popper suggests a positive role for the state in limiting the excesses of capitalism (i.e. a political remedy). This involves the construction of social institutions, backed up by state power, for the protection of the weak; economic interventionism, for Popper, must replace unrestrained capitalism. This, according to Popper, is what has already happened in the capitalist system of his time. The state has not withered away; it has been replaced by interventionism. In theoretical terms, historicism has been supplanted by social engineering.[27]

Popper's persuasive criticism of Marxism is that while the latter sees the revolution as inevitable, and politics as potentially making the transition as quick and benign as possible, this downgrades the potential of the political. In contrast, Popper regards political power as being crucial in its potential to control economic power, particularly in regard to protecting the weakest in society. It can limit exploitation and the length of the working day, and install a safety net for workers or the citizenry as a whole. Political power is the key; in Popper's view, it should dominate economic power if necessary.[28]

Popper criticises Marx, then, not just for underestimating the positive potential of political power but also, more crucially, for underestimating the threat of political power to human freedom. Marx, in Popper's view, fatally disregarded the importance of democracy in protecting society against the misuse of political, and economic, power.[29]

Popper's key point, and perhaps his most important insight, is that Marxists ignored the most basic problem of politics: how to control the dangerous aggregation of power in the state. Consequently, they never grasped the danger that lies in increased state power. They believed that only bourgeois control was bad; that power wielded in the name of the working class was the exception. In Popper's view, all power – including political and economic power – is dangerous. In political practice, the dangers of the 'dictatorship of the proletariat' were ignored, as was the possibility of the wrong people getting hold of the expanded powers of the state, including in the economic sphere.

For Popper, interventionism – including the kind of social engineering he endorses – can be very dangerous. Though sometimes necessary, it needs to be accompanied by the strengthening of democracy. For him, the important question is not, as the followers of Plato, Hegel and Marx believe, 'Who shall be the rulers?' The crucial question is, 'How shall we tame them?'[30]

This last question has an obvious contemporary resonance, particularly when we see public suspicion of state domination, and legitimate feelings of social and economic alienation, being channelled by entrenched economic interests for their own purposes – as in the recent phenomena of Trumpism in the United States and Brexit in the United Kingdom. One set of rulers is replaced by another that is even less sympathetic to the fundamental interests of the populace as a whole.[31] How to deal with this, and comparable developments, is a major conundrum of our time – one that Popper's analysis may serve at least to usefully contextualise, if not to resolve.

For Popper, a classless post-revolution society is not inevitable: new class divisions and a new class struggle may emerge, along with a new ruling class.[32] Popper was in a position to recall such events having actually happened in the Soviet Union – there is a certain conflation of history and speculation in his writing. His views of a likely future are informed by past developments.

From our perspective, we could point to the breakup of Yugoslavia in the 1990s – with the crucial difference that the fracture there seemed to fall along cultural or ethno-religious lines, exacerbated by nationalism, rather than mapping on to class divisions. In the case of Yugoslavia, there was a relatively neat split along the lines of societies dominated by Catholicism (Croatia), Orthodox Christianity (Serbia, Montenegro) and Islam (Bosnia–Herzogovina, Kosovo).[33] To argue that these kinds of ideational splits are somehow less fundamental than class-based fractures, or economy-based fractures, seems to fly in the face of the evidence.

Popper, while aware of the importance of cultural factors, does not follow it through to its logical conclusion – which is that in some key instances, factors of culture and civilisation outweigh economic factors (as in the case of Yugoslavia).

Popper believes that the most destructive element in Marxism is its forecast of the possibility of bloodshed in a revolutionary situation. For Popper, violence is justified only in a despotic situation where reforms are otherwise impossible. The sole aim of violence, in his view, should be to bring about a situation wherein reforms may be made without violence. The sustained use of violence, according to Popper, leads not to freedom or reason but to the rule of the strong.[34]

For Popper, the key question is in regard to the extent of power and how it is implemented, rather than who implements power.[35] Popper denigrates Marxism's 'ambiguity', in both its radical and moderate versions, towards the issue of violence and the conquest of power. This approach on the part of Marxists is rooted both in historicism and in the Marxist view of the state as a form of class oppression. Popper argues that if a minority party plans to suppress another party, it implicitly recognises the right of the other party to do the same; it forfeits any right to a moral stance and also strengthens the hand of those among its opponents who wish to use force.[36]

The Marxist doctrine of class war, in Popper's view, actually contributed to the fascist reaction. Marxists took the false – and fatal – view that fascism was the bourgeoisie's last stand; that it would be short and temporary, with no action needed to counter it.[37] This view was – as we know, and as Popper himself knew – shown to be disastrously wrong by historical events. Indeed, the logical consequence of Popper's argument against the Marxist 'last stand' analysis is that at least in one specific case, the problem was not that Marxism was too violent but that it actually lowered its guard at a catastrophically inappropriate juncture: the reactionary seizure of power by the Nazis.

Popper's analysis of Marx and Marxism may be questioned over many of its details. This includes – but is not limited to – Popper's interpretations of his subject matter in terms of historicism, economism, technological determinism and historical materialism. He sometimes conflates speculation with concrete historical experience, allowing the latter to impart an implied credence to the former. He also doesn't always clearly distinguish Marx's position from what he thinks it ought to be, or from what Marx might have thought if Popper had been around to help him clarify his ideas.

Figures from Antonio Gramsci to Louis Althusser and Jacques Derrida, and their followers and critics, have raised issues that make Popper's analysis seem rather basic. His critique of 'back to nature' politics seems overly dismissive from the perspective of our own time, with the development of Green politics in recent decades. It raises the interesting question as to what he would have thought of contemporary ecological politics (including influential, and impressive, attempts – like those of John Bellamy Foster – to redefine Marx as an ecologist[38]).

Nevertheless, Popper's (often quite friendly) appraisal of Marx remains the most thoroughgoing and important critique that we have; Popper's contribution to political theory may be seen as being on a par with his parallel contribution to the philosophy of science. In political terms, despite Popper's failure to foresee the emergence of ecological politics, his work constitutes a trenchant defence of the potentially constructive ('piecemeal') role of the state in terms of its fostering incremental change, as well as a warning about the dangers of state excesses. This is the perilous course that we have to take today – between the Scylla of unrestrained capitalism and the Charybdis of the authoritarian state, where governments of both right and left have failed.

Present-day Scandinavian social democracy, though under threat from neoliberalism, still seems to provide a beacon of hope and a functional example of left-wing capitalism. At the same time, it is part of an environmentally-unsustainable First World economy. The alternatives of ecosocialism and 'socialism from below' which rejects a top-down model of organisation, are currently undeveloped, both in theoretical terms and in terms of practical implementation.

Ecosocialism offers an integration of humane and environmental values, rather than the traditional socialist project – the domination of nature in the interest of economic growth. Socialism from below offers a possible structure whereby citizens, workers and consumers hold sway, rather than their appointed (or self-appointed) representatives.[39] A combination of the two would be 'Green' in two ways: in terms of ecological politics, and in terms of grass-roots control from the ground up.

Nonetheless, at this point we can only gesture towards the possibilities of such a development.

CONCLUSION

An articulation of ecosocialism with socialism from below may offer a constructive alternative to centralism and rule from above, whether of the social democratic or state socialist variety.

An important issue, though – at least from a public relations point of view – is the negativity traditionally attached to the term 'socialism', involving as it does a picture of statism, bureaucracy, authoritarianism and domination. Such an image, it must be admitted, is to a great extent deserved. Perhaps the ideal of an ecosocial society is more felicitous than that of an ecosocialist one.

Some questions remain unresolved, though. To what extent does, or would, the average citizen wish to participate in the minutiae of running a society, with its often-boring practical details and obstacles? How does freedom in the workplace, and in everyday life, survive under the constraints of a rationally structured society? Most crucially, how do we convince the ordinary citizen that while the democratic system they live in is highly leveraged, managed and manipulated, the alternative of full-scale authoritarianism, despotism or out-and-out totalitarianism would be even worse?

The appeal of anarchism lies in its offer of liberation from both social and economic constraints – and the anarchist ideal has its attractions, if only as a long-term goal. There are, however, formidable obstacles in its way in the short and medium term – one example being the exploitation of the relaxation of rules by asocial or antisocial individuals.

In our time, the threat of totalitarianism does not come from the same sources as those of the mid-twentieth century (fascism including Nazism on the one hand, Stalinism on the other).

Today, for the right, totalitarianism appears as a spectre (the ogre of 'socialism') to be condemned by libertarians and conservatives. The dangers of right-wing totalitarianism may be ignored by the right, or even covertly welcomed by racists and neo-fascists. All of the above groupings exist in a kind of loose, paradoxical right-wing conglomeration.

On the left, Marxism exists either as an exemplary warning (as in North Korea), as a victim of Western sanctions and undermining (as in Cuba) or as part of a strange melange with neoliberal capitalism (as in China). Overall, left politics has been in retreat for several decades, first of all under the pressure of the right-libertarian politics of Ronald Reagan and Margaret Thatcher, and more recently under the threat of a combination of populism and nationalism in countries like Brazil, Hungary, Poland, the United Kingdom and the United States. Crucial issues like global warming and the Covid-19 pandemic, however, have once again raised issues around the viability of capitalism.

Both ends of the political spectrum seem oblivious to the possibility that totalitarianism may have already arrived – in its 'soft' or 'inverted' form, as outlined by Wolin.

Simultaneously, there is the relentless push of technology, which threatens to undermine freedom, autonomy and privacy, no matter who is in control (whether they belong to the centre, the left or the right). Those who proffer the enhancement of democracy and freedom as alternatives to state control, corporatism, consumerism and authoritarianism face an uphill battle.

Chapter 4

FASCISM, RACISM, NAZISM

With the disintegration of traditional conservative (Republican) politics in the United States and the rise of mob politics, and with the growth of the authoritarian right in Europe, the main threat to human freedom seems, at first sight, to be from some new form of fascism taking hold on our society. Certainly, there are uncomfortable resonances between events in our own time, particularly in the United States, and the historical phenomenon of fascism in Europe.

Juan J. Linz, a sociologist, noted a 'confused sense of manliness' as characteristic of fascism, with its 'frankness, spontaneity, lack of manners, public use of insult and ridicule'.[1] Unfortunately, present extremist politics seems to have undergone little change since the time of historical fascism. 'Phallic panic' has prevailed on the world stage, with the bizarre excesses of President Trump seeming to represent a general crisis of masculine identity. This was balanced by the civilised humanism of his female German counterpart, Chancellor Merkel, who became – somewhat by default – the admired leader of the free world, especially through her humane attitude to the issue of immigration.

Currently, the left is divided between proponents of class politics and cultural activism. At the same time – in the United States, at least – the 'moderate' left and right converge on a centrist politics[2] characterised by aggressive war, the destabilisation of foreign countries, the domination of politics by corporations, and a subtle form of institutionalised racism whereby, under the guise of the war on drugs, the prison substitutes for the plantation and the cotton field.[3]

The cultural left, often focused on issues such as language and social amenities,[4] comes under fire from conservatives for manifesting 'cultural Marxism'. In fact, contemporary cultural politics expresses a form of postmodernism – the philosophical opposite of Marxism. The key distinction is that Marxism relies on some form of philosophical realism: the notion that there is a real world out there, beyond thought and language. Postmodernism relies on perspectivism: the belief that our perspective determines our understanding of the world.[5]

At the same time, traditional Marxists bemoan what they see as the deflection of political energy from its rightful place in support of class politics – as distinct from, for example, the politics of race and gender.[6]

The right manifests an often-incoherent mixture of conservatism, authoritarianism, libertarianism, religious fundamentalism, racism and fascism – as if libertarianism had anything in common with authoritarianism, or Christian egalitarianism with racism. Indeed, the current left–right dichotomy is somewhat misleading, since it is possible to find positive areas of common ground across the traditional divide – for example, in regard to bank bailouts, the destructive war on drugs, and foreign military interventionism.[7] Right-wing conspiracy theories may contain elements of truth, which facilitates their sale of nonsensical ideas – such as climate change denial.[8]

This is not to deny that there are real differences between the traditional categories of left and right. Among them is the trust (or lack thereof) placed in science, and the role of the state in regard to (for example) health services. Perhaps, though, the usefulness of the left–right binary is eroding in favour of alternative dualities, such as libertarianism and authoritarianism, or growth and degrowth.[9]

In the midst of this situation, modern technology opens up terrifying possibilities of surveillance and social control. In a sense, it doesn't really matter if the all-seeing-eye ends up under the control of the extreme left, the extreme right or the forms of centrist politics that disguise the will towards domination – by capitalism, the state or both. The possibilities of repression remain the same.

In the guise of protecting Western or at least US values, the established system in the United States operates a sophisticated form of oppression, from institutionalised racism at home to military adventurism and neo-colonialism abroad. Indeed, Ernst Nolte suggested that the US 'empire' is, because of its power and racial tensions, the only country of the West capable of practising fascism.[10]

A word here is needed on terminology. Capitalisation in this context can be tricky. Terms such as 'fascism' and 'national socialism' without capitals denote the general manifestations of the political phenomena in question. With initial capitals, they refer to specific instances: Fascism in Italy, and National Socialism in Germany.

Historically, the terms 'national' and 'socialist' may have moderately benign implications; taken together and capitalised in English, however, the phrase 'National Socialism' has irredeemably toxic implications.[11] At the same time, a person may define themselves as both 'nationalist' and 'socialist' wihtout any adherance to Nazi ideology.

In a somewhat parallel way, 'communism' (initial letter in lower case, as distinct from 'Communism', which is used here to refer to the institutionalised Marxist variety) may be used to refer to a primitive state of human society, to the voluntary communism of the early Christians or of monasticism within various religions, or to political aspirations that do not include a statist phase, for example those of anarchism.

This chapter will discuss aspects of fascism and national socialism, as they appeared in their most developed forms in Italy and Germany respectively, while at the same time drawing an important distinction between them – at least in terms of degree of oppression. National Socialism (or Nazism) was, like Stalinism, totalitarian[12] to an extent that other forms of fascism – including the Italian variety – were not. (Nonetheless, the Italian form of fascism certainly aspired to totalitarianism, regarding it as a good rather than an evil.)

Hitler's perverse gift for populist politics lay not in pushing some type of rightist politics, though that may have been the ultimate result. It lay rather in his success in combining, or appearing to combine, nationalism (traditionally right-wing) and socialism (traditionally left-wing) in a new synthesis of National Socialism, represented by the Nazi flag. The black swastika symbolised the Aryans, while the red background – the colour was stolen from the left – symbolised social solidarity among the German people. Similarly, scholars have found leftist elements in Italian Fascism – for example in regard to the welfare state, and its insistence on subordinating the means of production to the common good.[13]

As a consequence of its ideological looting from both ends of the political spectrum, Nazism attempted to exploit two burning issues in modern capitalist society at the same time: the lack of a sense of identity, and the lack of a sense of community. The former was to be addressed by nationalism, the latter by socialism. National Socialism was thus, at least in theory, a syncretic movement that promised to heal the psychic and material wounds of the German people.

At the outset, at least, it might have been seen as a form of radical centrism rather than a manifestation of the extreme right in alliance with business interests (as it later became under Hitler's control). Indeed, leftist tendencies were present in the Nazi Party, at least in the early stages – evidenced in certain aspects of the SA, a paramilitary organisation whose brown-shirted uniforms gave rise to the epithet applied to its members of 'beefsteaks' (brown on the outside, red on the inside), and in figures like Joseph Goebbels and the Strasser brothers.

That said, the origins of Nazism – in the 'stab in the back' theory deriving from the cessation of the First World War – have a strongly nationalist or right-wing aspect (though the feelings of grievance consequent on the Versailles Treaty, with its onerous conditions of reparation, were felt across the political spectrum).

Theorist Erich Fromm notes the appeal of Nazi ideology to the lower middle class, with its love of strength and hatred of weakness, its small-mindedness, and its thrift with both feelings and money, 'Their outlook on life was narrow, they suspected and hated the stranger, and they were curious and envious of their acquaintances, rationalizing their envy as moral indignation; their whole life was based on the principle of scarcity – economically as well as psychologically.'[14]

The German inflation involved a catastrophic loss in the value of money. Fromm points out that the inflation was a mortal blow against the principle of thrift as well as state authority.[15] The lower middle class projected its frustration and feelings of social inferiority onto the defeat in the First World War and the Treaty of Versailles.[16] This class could readily identify with Hitler, who embodied the characteristics of resentment and hatred, together with those of a servant of the industrialists and the establishment.[17]

Fromm regards the essence of the authoritarian character, embodied in Hitler, as the presence of both sadistic and masochistic drives: sadism as destructive power over another, masochism as dissolving oneself in the overwhelming power of another. Both inclinations have their root in the need for a relationship that overcomes the aloneness of the isolated individual.[18]

Left-libertarian theorist Willhelm Reich saw the authoritarian mindset characteristic of Nazi Germany as having its origin in the patriarchal family and the lower middle class, together with sexual repression in the context of patriarchy. Reich's focus on sexuality, however, led to him being at odds with the Stalinist orthodoxy of the time. Reich urged the rejection of totalitarianism in favour of organic citizen participation in the activities of life.[19]

Nazism and Italian Fascism, though they bear some similarities, are not the same thing. There are obvious resemblances: both harked back to the past at the same time as they engaged in vigorous modernisation; both fostered shirted organisations, processions, regalia and hymn-singing, sometimes recalling religious ceremonies; both made a strong appeal to youth; both persecuted their political opponents, though with differing degrees of severity; both relied on a messianic leader and mass support, and instituted forms of totalitarian state control, though to differing degrees; both manifested forms of national romanticism; and both glorified violence and engaged in a disastrous war.[20]

Both Nazism and Fascism paid lip service to some leftist, or at least anti-capitalist, ideals (socialism in the case of Germany, syndicalism in the case of Italy), though neither went very far in terms of their implementation.[21] Indeed, some leftist Nazis came to a sticky end with the culling of the SA in the Night of the Long Knives in 1934.

Both Nazism and Fascism were secular and scientific in inspiration – though Nazi ideology, with the help of Heinrich Himmler, included a dash of occultism.[22] Neither manifested the kind of clericalism that characterised other fascist or quasi-fascist movements (for example, in Spain, pre-Nazi Austria, Slovakia and Romania).

Italian Fascism and German National Socialism differed somewhat in terms of degrees of oppression. Notwithstanding Italy's destructive adventurism in North Africa, the reign of Mussolini was characterised by an initial period of relative mildness, at least compared to that of Hitler. Paul Gottfried, a philosopher, argues that there was a greater resemblance between Nazi and Stalinist tyranny than between Nazism and Italian Fascism, drawing on the distinction between 'totalitarian' and 'authoritarian' regimes.[23] On the other hand, he cites the view that by the late 1920s, there was a tendency for Italian Fascism to develop in a (leftist) totalitarian direction, with a romantic nationalist veneer.[24]

Nonetheless, Gottfried is unconvinced that Mussolini dominated the Italian people in ways similar to Hitler or Stalin. Examples of Italian Fascism's relative laxity include the concessions made to the Catholic Church, the eventual dismissal of Mussolini as head of state, and his subsequent arrest. Such events, Gottfried points out, would not have been possible in totalitarian Germany or Russia.[25]

Italian Fascism was not, initially, emphatically racist in character. Gottfried notes that before Mussolini instituted anti-Semitic measures under the influence of Hitler, there were many Jewish members of the

Italian Fascist party, and Mussolini even offered asylum to Jews fleeing Germany.[26] Gottfried downplays the connection between Nazism and Italian Fascism, emphasising the Latin character of the latter.[27]

While both National Socialism and Fascism celebrated the past, the former focused (to an extent) on the Germanic and Nordic past, and the latter (to an extent) on its Mediterranean equivalent. Whether the ancient culture of classical times – admired by Nazis and Fascists alike – was primarily Nordic or Mediterranean in nature was a matter of some dispute. Somewhat embarrassingly for Nazi ideologists, no conceivable comparison could be made between the cultural level of the ancient Mediterranean and that of its contemporary northern European counterpart, though attempts were made to assert the fundamentally Aryan or Nordic dimension of the ancient Mediterranean world.

Both Italian Fascism and Nazism embraced, and celebrated, modern technology. Despite this, in terms of the cultural output of the time, Nazi Germany severely repressed all forms of modernism – manifested most egregiously in the contemptuous Degenerate Art Exhibition organised by the Nazis in 1937. Some cultural tensions existed within Nazism, though: Goebbels, the most highly educated Nazi leader, had a personal penchant for Germanic Expressionism, as exemplified by the artist Emil Nolde. Overwhelmingly, however, in place of modernism and avant-gardism, Nazism fostered realism, classicism and kitsch. In this it was somewhat akin to its rival Stalinism, though with a dash of German Romanticism in the case of Nazism.

This cultural bent was partly due to Hitler's personal anti-modernist aesthetic tastes, but it also derived from the handy role that kitsch, or mass culture, plays in terms of propaganda. Even the classical music preferred and propagated by Nazism – particularly that of Wagner, with its repetitive leitmotifs – has a drug-like, hypnotic effect, which has the practical use of stirring up emotion that can be channelled in a political direction.

That is not to say that there was no impressive art produced in Nazi Germany. The film-maker Leni Riefenstahl is a notable counterexample to the prevailing aesthetic mediocrity. Though her work sometimes manifests an element of kitsch, it is outstanding in aesthetic if not in moral terms.

Italian Fascism, on the other hand, was much more tolerant of modernism and avant-gardism than was Nazism; members of the Futurist art movement, with their glorification of war, speed and destruction, and their hatred of institutionalised culture, were early supporters of the Fascists.

The architecture fostered by the Nazis, with a couple of exceptions, such as the Berlin Olympic Stadium and Tempelhof Airport, contributed little of cultural worth – certainly compared with the older architecture that was destroyed throughout Europe in the war. What the Nazis did envisage for a new Berlin – for example, Albert Speer's projected Germania – would probably have been an aesthetic nightmare.[28] Italian Fascism, on the other hand, fostered some notable contributions to the built environment.[29]

NAZISM AND RACISM

While racism was intrinsic to Nazism, it was less emphasised in the case of Italian Fascism, which adopted anti-Semitism only under Nazi pressure. A number of nineteenth and early twentieth century thinkers – including, most significantly, Houston Stuart Chamberlain, Arthur de Gobineau, and Madison Grant – influenced the ideological environment in which Nazi racism developed. Nazi race theorists such as Alfred Rosenberg and Hans Günther fed into the development of this ideology.[30]

It is difficult to get a grasp on Nazi race theory, as it is rather confused and incoherent. On the one hand, it elevates the 'Aryans' to the highest position in human culture and society, the term being mapped on to the speakers of Indo-European languages (Celtic, Germanic, Italic, Slavic and so on). On the other hand, Nazi and proto-Nazi race theory emphasises Nordicism (particularly in the writings of Grant and Günther), downgrading other Aryan groupings such as the Alpine and (to an extent) the Mediterranean – though Grant concedes that the superiority of the Mediterraneans in the sphere of art is unquestioned.[31] Grant indeed attributes much of the 'greatness' of the English to the fact that they comprise roughly equal numbers of Nordics and Mediterraneans;[32] he ascribes the civilizations of ancient Greece and Rome to a similarly happy admixture.[33]

Günther is at pains to distinguish racial physical characteristics from linguistic ones, seeing the Nordics (whom he exalts) as permeating numerous different linguistic groupings. He praises what he sees as the positive mental qualities of the Nordic race, such as self-mastery, creativity, steadfastness, honour, heroism, nobility and a love of nature. In his view, the French Revolution was a racial struggle between the insurgent Alpine-Mediterranean element and the dominant Nordic aristocracy.[34]

To balance their positive qualities, which he praises to the skies, Günther notes among the Nordics a lack of insight or knowledge of humanity.[35] Some of the 'threats' to the Nordics include their difficulty in bearing warmer climates than those native to them,[36] susceptibility to the associated diseases of warmer climates, and their tendency to engage in late marriages.[37]

There is also their well-known, and self-destructive, propensity to wipe each other out in battle.[38] Günther specifically references the 'Great War' (the First World War) in this context;[39] Grant refers to it as a Nordic 'civil war'.[40] The dominance of the commercial, capitalistic spirit in society further weakens the Nordics, in Günther's view.[41] To this tally of Nordic woes, Grant adds a tendency to alcoholism and consumption.[42]

In religious terms, the Nordics lean towards Protestantism, the Mediterraneans towards Catholicism.[43] Religion for Günther – for example, in the case of Buddhism – has been the enemy of the Nordics, since it promotes universality rather than racial solidarity; through sexual renunciation, he believes, it contributed to the disappearance of Nordic blood in India.[44] In the West, in his view, Christianity also had a negative role to play; the humane attempt by early Christianity to counter the Roman practice of exposing children had, he argues, a downside in weakening the race.[45]

With a Nietzschean[46] side-swipe, Grant observes that charity has had the unfortunate effect of preserving individuals of deficient mentality, who, in a state of nature, would be allowed to perish.[47] The outcome of this mindset on Hitler's policies of eugenics and euthanasia hardly needs to be laboured.[48]

In a broader sense, Günther argues that Christianity's universalism had an antiracial effect, tending to weaken racial barriers.[49] Monasticism, by effectively neutering the highest-minded individuals (who became monks), also had a negative eugenic (i.e. 'dysgenic') influence.[50] Grant blames the religious persecution of the Middle Ages, and specifically the Inquisition, for the oppression of free thinkers and intellectuals – with negative (dysgenic) results for Europe.[51] Here, we may see an interesting dismissal of one form of totalitarianism by an author whose own writings may have contributed, albeit indirectly, to the institution of another.

Günther criticises the modern welfare state as fostering the hereditarily 'inferior' at the expense of the fitter elements.[52] The overriding concern of both authors, Grant and Günther, is the supposed decline of the superior Nordic race under the pressure of other, 'lesser' races.

The issue of the relationship between race and language – in other words, anthropology and philology – becomes particularly fraught in terms of the political application of Nazi race theory. Hitler notoriously persecuted the Slavs and Roma, who are linguistically Indo-European, and made alliances with the Finns, Hungarians and Japanese, who are not. Günther's thought is suggestive of this, since he was a strong influence on Hitler. For him, anthropological measurements and visual clues (hair and eye colour, etc.) were much more important than linguistic categories; in Günther's terms, a Polish-speaking Nordic type had more of a claim to racial superiority than a German-speaking Baltic, Alpine or Mediterranean type.

Günther's ideal – one might almost say his fetish – was the tall, blond, blue-eyed, 'dolichocephalic' (long-headed as viewed from above) Nordic male. There seems more than a hint of homoeroticism in his writings on the subject. The reinstatement of the Nordic ideal to its supposedly appropriate and superior status – for which Günther praised in particular the contemporary political efforts in the United States – was his overriding aim.

While the ideas of authors such as Gobineau, Chamberlain, Grant and Günther fed into Nazi racial theory, Hitler gave them a crucial political impetus, albeit in a somewhat incoherent manner. That did not, however, limit its destructiveness.

Hitler's racist ideas are founded on a rather odd conceptual premise: that animals mate only with members of the same species (with some exceptions at the extreme).[53] Applied to humans, the example raises the question as to why, if race-mixing is unnatural, it is so easy for humans to do so. Hitler gives no answer to this, but goes on to condemn such intermingling on Social Darwinist grounds; he argues that the offspring of a mixed relationship will stand somewhere in between the two. This, according to him, is against the will of nature, which involves the domination of the stronger; blending of the strong with the weak involves the sacrifice of the greatness of the former.[54]

As noted previously, the concept of the will of nature plays a similar historicist role in Nazi thought as, in the case of Marxism, that of revolutionary progress towards a communist society. It is both fact and value – something that contains at the same time its own impetus and justification. A kind of 'applied Darwinism', it rests on the belief that the struggle for dominance and the survival of the fittest – interpreted crudely in terms of simple physical toughness – are both natural and to be endorsed.

In our own time, crude anthropological head measurements and speculative historical philology have given way, in large part, to genetics in terms of the study of ethnic origin and classification. The question remains open as to whether the dominance of genetics will serve to defuse the primitive, though historically incendiary, work of the earlier anthropologists and eugenicists. Genetics may indeed open up new, perhaps equally fraught areas of research, such as the development of designer babies, or the institution of a two-tiered society – the elite at the top and genetically stigmatised groupings at the bottom (as explored in the film *Gattaca*, for example, or earlier in Aldous Huxley's novel *Brave New World*). There is the associated prospect of genetic regimentation, opened up by the mass availability of genetic information and the erosion of privacy.

It should be added that, far from being an exploded notion, Nordicism thrives in our culture, though at an often-unconscious level. Popular culture suggests that the Aryan (or Nordic) ideal is alive and well. Blonde females (as in the novel and film *Gentlemen Prefer Blondes*) are widely preferred to brunettes (or at least believed to be so), and even dark-skinned non-European models tend to have a 'European' body shape and facial features. Günther states that until about 1600 in England, only those with blond hair and blue eyes were regarded as good-looking.[55]

The main confusion in pinning down the historical role of Nazi race theory has at least two main causes. The first pertains to the tension between philological and physical (anthropological) analysis, which was never really resolved – as exemplified by the respective exaltation of the Aryans and the Nordics. The second is the conflict between the practical exigencies of war and the purity of racial theory. In practice, the energy and resources that could have been used in an attempt to turn around a losing war were instead diverted into the project of exterminating the Jews. This raises the question as to whether Hitler used racism to gain power, or power to implement his racist goals.

The political compromises with 'non-Aryan' peoples – the Finns, Hungarians and Japanese – in the pursuit of aggressive expansion suggest the former (power as the main impetus). On the other hand, Hitler's urgent pursuit of the Final Solution towards the end of the war suggests the latter (racial purification as the overriding goal). Perhaps it is futile to try to find a rational answer in this context, since we are dealing with a fundamentally irrational phenomenon: the phenomenon of Nazism.

NAZISM AND ANTI-SEMITISM

Historically, the most egregious manifestation of anti-Semitism was the form it took in Nazi Germany,[56] where – under the influence of racist theory – the Jews were seen as the antithesis of the Aryans (or Nordics). For Günther, the Jews are not a race or a religion but a nation, and may belong to several different religions and 'races'.[57] Günther's solution to the Jewish 'problem' was in fact an overt endorsement of Zionism, with its proposal to withdraw the Jews from the Gentile nations.[58]

In Hitler's *Mein Kampf*, hatred of Jews emerges as a confused melange of antipathy – personal, political, economic, cultural, racial, religious and philosophical. Jews are regarded as culturally parasitic and racially exclusive, as tending to fight amongst themselves, as economically exploitative (from a quasi-socialist point of view) and at the same time as destructively subversive (from an anti-Marxist perspective). As a consequence, Hitler manages to have his cake and eat it: Jews, in his view, are responsible both for the ills of the capitalist system and for the destructive activities of its Marxist opponents.[59]

Anti-Semitism of the Hitler variety derives much of its ideological and political force from an appropriation of the socialist attack on capitalism, with its critique of alienation, inequity and exploitation. Nonetheless, the Nazi take on anti-capitalism focuses not so much on the system as on a particular people, the Jews, who are seen as representative of the capitalist spirit – particularly in the form it takes in the financial sphere, with its hidden power, obscurity and obfuscation.[60] Hitler and the Nazis had a simple answer to the economic travails of the German people: the problem was not finance capital or the capitalist system; in the perspective that they propelled, it was the Jews. This socioeconomic critique that gave Nazism much of its impetus has been aptly termed 'the socialism of fools'.

In Hitler's text, the racial element emerges as the most important and the most intractable. The individual Jew, in his view, can achieve nothing by changing his or her religion, politics, economic activity or personal philosophy – he or she will always be a Jew, and will always be unwelcome in the pure (one might say, inbred) Europe that Hitler aspired to create.[61]

The phenomenon of anti-Semitism remains one of the most complex problems of our time, involving a combination of racism, displaced economic resentment, and jealousy of a people who have successfully retained their ethnic identity over millennia. There are also religious roots, harking back to Catholic anti-Semitism of the Middle Ages and the anti-Semitic writings of Martin Luther, most notoriously *The Jews and Their Lies*.

In the case of Nazi anti-Semitism, there may, in addition, be a conscious or unconscious attempt to undermine the Ten Commandments – the moral foundation of Western civilisation – since Nazism explicitly repudiated most of them, whether in theory or practice, or both. In this regard, the Jews made an easier target than the better-entrenched Christians, of both major denominations. Arnold Zweig, a Jewish exile from Nazism, argued that 'it is the enforcement of this nonpagan and unnatural faith [Christianity] which the peoples of Central Europe cannot forgive the Jews.' The group-mind of the Germans, in his view, is characterised by a longing for the old native gods, which represent what people think they are or wish themselves to be.[62]

Nazism simultaneously opposed Christianity and attempted to shape it to its will; at the same time, it drew on the anti-Semitic cultural legacy of Christianity for its own calamitous purposes. It was a kind of destructive eclecticism, using for its own purposes whatever potentially incendiary elements were lying around.

Nazism made its own use of both science and the occult, drawing on a mixture of (perverted) Darwinism, philology and anthropology, and on the murky racial occultism of the time. Primarily, though, one might speculate that Nazism involved a Freudian 'return of the repressed', with the attempted resurgence of pagan and feudal values over the modern ideal of equality – the valuation of equality characterises both the Christian and secular Western mindset, regardless of other tensions that exist between the two. It is conceivable that, at an unconscious level, the real enemy of Nazism was not the Jews but the moral values and aspirations of Judeo-Christian society[63] – values that they were not, at the time, able to overthrow, despite every attempt at co-option, distortion and repression.

CONTEMPORARY SOCIETY: RACISM AND THE THREAT TO FREEDOM

Racism is a major threat to freedom, primarily because its goals cannot be instituted without draconian measures of one kind or another – whether these include restrictions on relationships, reproduction, immigration or permission to remain in a particular territory. The most notorious form that racism has taken in recent times is anti-Semitism. To this, we can add prejudice against people of recent African origin (according to the anthropologists, we are all of African origin if you go back far enough). Another prominent form is opposition to Islam, at least when the last-mentioned is a disguised form of racism.[64]

The term anti-Semitism appears – on the surface, at least – to be something of a misnomer. Not all Jews are members of groups that speak, or have historically spoken, Semitic languages – and many who belong to groups that speak such languages are not Jews. Anti-Semitism was originally a term used by anti-Semites themselves to describe their beliefs.

The definition of who is a 'Jew' is fraught and hotly contested. Since the consensus has been that 'anti-Semitism' is an appropriate term to denote opposition to Jews (rather than, for example, anti-Judaism), we shall continue to use it, having noted its complexity. (For stylistic reasons, I do not use the sometimes more politically acceptable term 'antisemitism'.) Anti-Semitism is arguably the most pernicious form of racism, not just because of the recent horror of the Holocaust but also because of the way it infuses the extreme forms of Islamism that threaten to undermine the civilised world.

Nonetheless, the problem doesn't just lie in the excesses of Islamist extremism.[65] The situation is exacerbated by Israel's mistreatment of Palestinians – which feeds into anti-Jewish racism as a reaction – and by Western meddling in the affairs of Islamic countries. The latter is under the misguided idea of exporting democracy, though the underlying impetus is the consolidation of economic and imperial power.

As a member of a historically oppressed people (the Irish), I can relate to victims of anti-Semitism. You are blamed for the results of the past oppression of your own people; they pour water on you (to put it politely) and tell you it's raining. The trauma of the Great Famine of the nineteenth century (facilitated by the British colonial power) lies deep in the Irish unconscious, allowing us to empathise – to an extent, at least – with others who have experienced their own historical trauma.

In Dublin, we mourn what has been viewed for a long time as the diminution of the city's Jewish community – a community that at one time gave life, spice and a touch of internationalism to what was in many ways a drab provincial city. James Joyce's Leopold Bloom, the main figure in his landmark novel *Ulysses*, is the prime example in Irish literature. This perception of a diminished community persists at the same time as Dublin is transforming under the positive influence of multi-national and multi-ethnic immigration.[66]

Despite the respect and warm sentiments that Irish people may express for their Jewish compatriots, criticism of the policies of Israel, specifically in regard to the situation of the Palestinians, is unusually sharp in Ireland. This is not because of anti-Semitism, whose presence is negligible in the country, but – to an extent, at least – because we expect better of the Jews, particularly given their own history as an oppressed people.

In the incisive terms of the Jewish writer Zygmunt Bauman, '*The pernicious legacy of the Holocaust is that today's persecutors may inflict new pains and create new generations of victims eagerly awaiting their chance to do the same, while acting under the conviction that they are avenging yes-terday's pain and warding off the pains of tomorrow.'*[67] In Bauman's terms, 'The macabre paradox of being a hereditary victim is to develop a vested interest in the hostility of the world.'[68]

In addition, the Irish recognise the suffering of the Palestinians with unusual clarity because it reminds us of the suffering of our own people under a historical system of penal laws instituted by the British – though Irish nationalist resistance, similar to the Palestinians' resistance today, has itself been characterised from time to time by atrocities.[69] Nevertheless, Irish people instinctively tend to side with the underdog – or at least with whomever they perceive, rightly or wrongly, to be the underdog at any particular time.

Additionally, there has been the development of secularism in Ireland over recent decades; there is also the memory of the disastrous consequences of an island divided into two components, the Free State (later the Republic) and Northern Ireland. The historical division in Ireland between a (Catholic) confessional state and a (Protestant) confessional statelet has had extremely negative results in terms of religious control, economic and political discrimination, cultural repression, and terrorism, There has even been low-level civil war over a number of decades, ending fairly recently. For their own historical reasons, Irish people are, by and large, negatively disposed towards countries where religion is seen to play an inordinate role – whether that religion be Judaism in Israel, Islam in Saudi Arabia, or indeed the dogmatic Bible Belt Christianity of the southern United States.

The separation of church and state, one of the many positive achievements of the United States, may be held up as a suggestive model for other societies as well. Enzo Traverso points out the difference between freedom *for* religion (the US version of secularism) and freedom *from* religion (the French version). The latter, in his view, is entwined with imperialism and colonialism, leading to a negative view of Islam in particular.[70]

Nonetheless, this seems a somewhat limited view of the US version of secularism, which specifically forbids the establishment of religion. In the context of engaging with Islam, it seems essential that Western countries robustly assert the distinction between state and religion, whether legally, culturally or both. For example, a recurring theme in the writings of the key thinker of political Islamism, Sayyid Qutb (there are alternative spellings of his name), is the supposed illegitimacy of the Western separation of religion and state.[71] Such ideas, with their potential to erode freedom, need to be vigorously contested.

Slavoj Žižek argues that we should accept immigrants from Islamic countries in the West; he also contends that we be cognizant of the nefarious influence of our economic system as a cause of the underlying problems of immigration. He believes, however, that we should not gloss over the cultural tensions in terms of the importance that the respective cultures place on human rights.[72]

How the ideal of separation of religion and state might be applied in the context of Israel, given that Jews define themselves in both ethnic and religious terms, is a conundrum, but one that must be solved in the interests of a lasting peace in the area – and, indeed, in terms of the spillover global effect. If Israel were to radically address the issue of secularisation, it would neutralise some of the poison of anti-Semitism, including the version that permeates radical Islamism – since the extremists often use the politics of the state of Israel, particularly in regard to treatment of the Palestinians, as a justification for their own extreme policies.

Historian Deborah Lipstadt, defending the fact that Israel has an established state religion, cites the existence of 'undemocratic Islamic theocracies' in the same geographical area. (The obvious riposte is that two wrongs don't make a right.) She also points to the fact that countries like Great Britain, Denmark, Greece and Monaco have official state religions.[73] Nevertheless, Roman Catholics, for example, are not normally accorded fewer rights than Protestants in Great Britain – though they were in the past, a situation that is now regarded as unacceptable. A situation whereby adherents of one religion are given preferential treatment over those of another is no more acceptable in Israel than (for example) in Ireland, whether north or south.

In the contemporary world, the issue of anti-Semitism doesn't just arise in regard to the far right – who have often, in recent times, concentrated their efforts on Islam as a more promising target, or scapegoat, than Judaism. The issue of anti-Semitism also rears its head in controversies around the left, and in particular around the extent to which criticism of Israel (or Zionism) may represent a form of anti-Semitism. The short answer is that it may or may not, depending on the particular case, and that Israel could help to defuse the threat of anti-Semitism by lifting its oppression of the Palestinians, which functions as an excuse for ant-Semitism.

Anti-Semitism may also be found among Muslims themselves, which brings up the weird issue around nomenclature, since Muslims may be 'Semitic' – or at least they may be members of groups that are, or were, speakers of Semitic languages,[74] while many Jews may not be. Like its mirror-opposite 'Islamophobia,' the epithet 'anti-Semitism' does not, or at least should not, apply to political criticism of states or individuals, insofar as such criticism is devoid of underlying prejudice based on race or religion. The issue may, however, be complicated by the fact that criticism (e.g. of Jews or Muslims) may appear merely political on the surface but can in fact be motivated by hatred, envy, prejudice, projection and so on. That is where things become more complicated, and often heated.

Behind much contemporary racism, including anti-Semitism, is the northern European racial ideal, whether consciously or unconsciously held. Associated with this is the belief that white dominance is under threat, and that that is a bad thing.

The fear of a threat to white dominance is based on a number of questionable assumptions around the notion of 'whiteness' itself. White people are not native to North America; their dominance there has been at the expense of the native population, who lived a life that was, by and large, in harmony with nature and did not threaten its very existence, as does Western civilisation.[75]

If, however, whites did wish to ensure their future chromatic hegemony, it would seem to have been a rather counterproductive idea to ship over large numbers of black people from Africa, the descendants of whom now threaten the dominance of their former overlords' progeny.[76]

The European racial ideal remains alive and well. The writings, already mentioned, of race theorists like Madison Grant and Hans Günther – who were extremely influential on the thought of Hitler and the Nazis – are a melange of scientific, or pseudo-scientific, studies; their research is based on observation and measurement on the one hand, and impressionistic, cultural and aesthetic preferences on the other. Again, a mixture of fact and value.

This strange relationship between fact and value remains in our society. While race 'science' has been essentially suppressed, marginalised and indeed rubbished in our societies, the Nordic ideal thrives in popular culture.

This ideal achieves explicit political articulation in claims that whiteness is being eradicated through the rise of non-white peoples, and that this is a bad thing.[77] This claim, in turn, begs a number of questions – for example, whether whiteness is something that actually exists; whether it is likely to disappear; whether that likelihood can be demonstrated; and whether its disappearance is to be deplored. Again, within these inquiries are topics (such as the likelihood of numerical diminution) that may be subject to verification or at least estimation, and others (such as the valuation of whiteness) that are not, being based on value rather than fact.

Any attempt to understand the spectre of racism in our society needs to take into account the prevalence of specific ethnic preferences in the public unconscious – for example, the preference for blondes (at least in the case of females; blond males are not so highly regarded as in the heyday of racism). There is also a prevalent preference for people with 'European' facial features and bodily structure, as distinct from skin colour. (Abundant body hair, a feature of Europeans, is seen as less attractive, particularly in females – though again, blondness may mitigate the aesthetic issue, and razors and other artificial means may do the rest.)

Such preferences may or may not be completely culturally determined. If they are, they can be changed through cultural activism. If they are not, whatever innate preferences may exist will work their way through the culture of their own accord. Heavy-handed attempts to impose one aesthetic ideal or another, whether from a racist or ostensibly anti-racist direction, should be resisted in the interest of freedom.

The crucial issue, in a political sense, is the inevitable conflation of racism and authoritarianism. Racists sometimes try to disguise this with an appeal to libertarians – an appeal that is self-defeating, since the goals of racists could not be implemented without an authoritarian, or perhaps totalitarian, society.

Contemporary racists, indeed, face a conundrum, particularly insofar as they wish to influence the non-racist right. There is no clear answer to the question as to how racist ideals could be enforced in our societies, short of drastically interfering with the freedom we currently (more or less) enjoy to breed with appropriate consensual partners and the concomitant liberty to travel across national boundaries as we wish, or to remain where we are if we that is what we want. The racist theorist Grant is explicit about this; for him, artificial devices are essential to keep races apart, and to prevent what he regards as the 'lower type' from prevailing.[78] This would involve the radical imposition of a new, or renewed, form of biopolitics – a prospect which should surely fill even right-wing libertarians with horror.

The response to the racist argument, from a freedom-loving perspective, must be that if you don't approve of 'race-mixing', you are perfectly free – and you should be – not to engage in it. You should not, however, be allowed to constrain the rights of others to reproduce across ethnic divisions. The reason is that it involves an unwarranted diminution of human freedom, which is a fundamental value in itself – or at least widely regarded as such, which is about the same thing for practical purposes.

Indeed, there is a strong connection, in practice, between racism and the impetus towards totalitarianism, since racism cannot be imposed as a national policy without greatly increasing the power of the state. And as manifest particularly in Nazi Germany and the territories it controlled, this has had disastrous historical results.

Putting it in a nutshell, you could have totalitarianism without racism, but racism probably leads to totalitarianism. Libertarians, particularly those on the right, and humane conservatives need to be made aware of this, and of what uncongenial bedfellows racists are likely to make[79]

AESTHETIC ISSUES

In contemporary society, there has been controversy around scientific attempts to assert the influence of nature as distinct from nurture – for example, in the sphere of athletic performance and IQ measurement.[80] There has even been the marginalisation of the concept of beauty in aesthetics and art theory. (It is seen as too closely allied with Nazi racism.)[81]

At the same time, people continue to fall in love and have children under the influence of aesthetic impulses of which they are largely unconscious. Which, indeed, has always been the case – at least when free from the influence of family, or political or economic pressure. Increasingly, though, in a multicultural society, race or ethnicity is becoming irrelevant in the process of mate selection. If this situation continues, it promises to render futile the attempts of racists to hem it in, in addition to exposing the totalitarian implications of any attempt to do so.

Racism, particularly in its form as the exaltation of the northern European ideal, is essentially the attempt to replace ethics with aesthetics as the basis of human striving: recent history shows us the horrific results of such attempts.

Nonetheless, ethics should not completely replace aesthetics. To take one example, the main goal of humans in the sphere of sexual relations is not to express compassion or charity towards another human being – there is an essential element of self-fulfilment in the sphere of sexuality.[82]

The distinction here is between aesthetically-based 'erotic' love, which involves an essential component of self-fulfilment, and ethically-based 'altruistic' love, which does not. (The respective Greek terms are 'eros' and 'agape'.[83])

Aesthetics has a key role to play in the successful reproduction of the species.[84] Aesthetics weighs more heavily than ethics in most people's choice of a life partner, our primary goal is to have someone pleasant with whom to live, enjoy sexual relations and (perhaps) reproduce. In the case of reproduction, felicitous results are generally, and appropriately, desired: most people, whatever their political outlook, want their children to be healthy, happy and intelligent. Erotic attraction, with its basis in aesthetics, functions, more or less, as a means to this end – albeit often unconsciously. That said, an aesthetically-based relationship without an ethical dimension (eros without agape) may be headed towards turbulence.

To take another obvious example of the importance of the aesthetic dimension, aesthetics features prominently in the desire of many people to protect the natural environment. The ideal, then, is the harmonious articulation of aesthetics and ethics, not the total attempt to replace one set of values by the other.

The Nazi ideal – indeed, the fascist ideal in general – involves the aestheticisation of politics. The potential attractiveness of such an enterprise should not be underestimated. Everyday life is boring – and it always has been for most people, even in 'ideal' societies such as that of the Renaissance or the classical world. What has come down to us in cultural terms (for example, through paintings in art galleries) is the aesthetic ideal – the memory of those societies at their cultural best. It is easy to contrast the banality of our contemporary world with an idealised image of the past; to yearn for a political shortcut to an alternative world, perhaps to the musical background of a Wagner chorus. The appeal of such a process is as illusory as it is exciting and dangerous.

The maximisation of creativity and aesthetic values in society, and the minimisation of banality, are admirable goals, but it is a catastrophic mistake to imagine that they can be achieved through the fetishism of politics or the worship of a political figure.

POLITICAL ALTERNATIVES

One proposed riposte to Nazi-style racism lies in the creation of an alternative socioeconomic system – one that would include the elements of social equality, justice and freedom, as well as the potential for creativity and an aesthetic life. Such a potential is largely denied by industrial capitalism, with its dreary labour ethic and environmental destruction.

Such an alternative system would function to neutralise the energy that Nazism historically, and deviously, embodied – that of a distorted critique of capitalism. This is a tall order. The only thing we can say with confidence is that traditional socialist blueprints – based on notions of top-down direction, the ideal of economic growth, a know-it-all vanguard party and ideological regimentation – are unlikely to work any better than the practice of their capitalist opponents has done.

Combined with the creation of an alternative to the current socioeconomic system, we also need a vigorous defence of the secular state and refusal of any attempts to temper it. There is no essential contradiction between a secular political structure and the defence of the rights of religion. The separation of church and state (or mosque and state, or synagogue and state) is as urgent a priority now as it has ever been. This is doubly the case, since racism often takes the form of a pseudo-defence of religious freedom – or of sectarian opposition to another religion, as in the case of some manifestations of Islamophobia.

Racism is one of the main possible sources of a future totalitarianism, though not the only one. A non-racist totalitarianism is perfectly possible – as manifest, for example, in the novel *Nineteen Eighty-Four*, or historically in Spanish fascism or pre-racist Italian Fascism; or, indeed, in Stalinism, before Stalin launched his own attack on the Jews after the Second World War. Nevertheless, one way to weaken the structure of a future totalitarianism is to undermine one of its potential pillars – the pillar of racism.

Nazism, or neo-Nazism, has one central proposition: the denial of the equality of human beings. In its current or future manifestations, it is unlikely to mirror the form it took in the 1920s or 1930s. For one thing, communications have changed so much, with the replacement of radio with television and the internet as our prime media, as to make that difficult to imagine. The overt manifestations of racist politics are easy to spot. The subtle ones, though, are more difficult to discern.

Whether or not one can prove the proposition of human equality, the point is, surely, that we should behave as if it were true. The fact that it is the foundation of our civilisation may be reason enough for that. Some values are essential to our continuation as a civilisation; we need to live as if they have an underlying justification, whether or not we think, in a philosophical sense, that they do. The continuance of civilisation is probably a good enough reason to act in such a way.

Fascism, at least in the form it took in the early part of the twentieth century, is unlikely to be replicated. One reason is that its key enemy, Communism, is – in a political if not a theoretical sense – either dead or discredited, or both. (The important exception is China, which strangely seems to embody both a desire for a neoliberal and a socialist society, though perhaps in the belief that the former is a necessary stage on the way to the latter.)

The most flourishing example of a new Chinese direction is the imaginative installation of an alarming form of technological totalitarianism – the so-called 'social credit system'. This is in the process of development; it is an articulation of public and private structures whereby citizens are rewarded or penalised for their behaviour, and which already interfaces with systems of facial recognition.[85] The possible outcome is a system of total state surveillance and control (of which Hitler and Stalin could only dream), whose potential imitation by the West is perhaps more dangerous than any socialist Chinese example might be.

The socialist elements to which Nazism and Italian Fascism aspired, at least in theory, are unlikely to attract many rightists, either. Particularly as the latter often tend to pay at least lip service to an anti-statist, quasi-libertarian ideal. From a political point of view, in order to loosen whatever distorted links may exist between right-wing libertarians and fascists of one kind or another, the incompatibility between socialism and libertarianism is something that needs to be emphasised.

That leaves the question of how to tackle nationalism (in its negative, exclusionary form). Nationalism is indeed a serious danger. Beyond the form of ignorant buffoonery that it takes in the United States and the United Kingdom, there is the perhaps more problematical manifestation found in Europe, in countries such as Poland and Hungary – particularly as it may threaten the breakup of the EU.[86] Nevertheless, nationalists often have problems in co-operating across national borders. This is shown by the difficulties involved in creating a fascist international (cooperation between fascists in different countries) in the early years of the movement, and by Hitler's preference for collaborationist governments within the Nazi sphere of influence (as distinct from foreign parties structured on the Nazi model).

Paxton cites the danger of a homegrown US-style politics that uses American themes in fascist-resembling ways – perhaps taking hostile aim at church–state separation, controls on gun ownership and unassimilated minorities.[87] Through some of the extreme manifestations of Trumpism, this danger may have increased in the recent past.

Nevertheless, the incoherence between the different strands of libertarianism, authoritarianism, racism and religion on the US far right may act as a brake on such an impetus. This incoherence is something that those who love freedom, and equality of opportunity, could make it their business to point out whenever possible – including, specifically, the incongruity of Christian egalitarian and neo-pagan worldviews, and the further incongruity of racism and libertarianism.

The irrationality of any putative fascist alternative to the Western corporate-capitalist-statist model should not, however, blind us to the overriding danger of a form of totalitarianism arising within the system already in place – as distinct from any monstrous threat that seems to loom from outside it, or from the political extremes at either end of the left-right spectrum.

In some cases, this danger may indeed by recognised more clearly by some on the right than by the left – however ideologically vitiated their analysis, and however distorted and ultimately self-defeating their attempted forms of resistance may be. Opposition to bureaucratisation, universal surveillance, ideological groupthink, political censoriousness, military adventurism and the negative aspects of globalisation should not be consigned to the right. To do so is to hand a powerful weapon to the enemies of freedom.

Chapter 5

POPULISM OR FASCISM?

The – almost unbelievable – invasion of the Capitol in Washington by Trump supporters raised the spectre of a fascist takeover in the heart of Western democracy,[1] calling in question the very foundations of our political systems.

As one internet meme put it, 'Due to travel restrictions, this year the United States had to organise the coup at home.' At a facile level, it seemed that the chicken of US interference in the affairs of other nations was coming home to roost.[2]

This chapter asks the question of whether the recent rise of populist politics, in the United States and elsewhere, is likely to lead to the resurgence of fascism in one form or another.

Trying to define key terms such as 'populism' and 'fascism', not to mention 'state', 'nation' and 'totalitarianism', is an unrewarding, and perhaps impossible, task. We know what the words mean when we see them – or we think we do, anyway – but the more we try to pin them down, the more they slip away.

The Oxford English Dictionary (OED) defines fascism as 'An authoritarian and nationalistic system of government and social organization'. Fascist parties, according to this definition, were typically ethnocentric and militarily aggressive. They were opposed to socialism, liberalism and communism; fascist governments tended to form totalitarian dictatorships with a charismatic leader.[3]

Nonetheless, even such a bare-bones definition is open to many questions, as we have already seen. These include issues of capitalisation, the relationship between German National Socialism (or Nazism) and Italian Fascism (and of both to fascism more widely). There was also the incorporation of left-wing as well as right-wing elements in fascist theory – and, to a lesser extent, in practice. The Nazi Party included the term 'socialist' in its official title, though the leftist tendency was neutralised in 1934 with the Night of the Long Knives, when the unruly 'socialist' elements of the National Socialist German Workers Party were culled.

Roger Griffin, a historian and political theorist, argues that an objective definition of fascism is impossible, since it is basically an 'ideal type'. It is the result of an artificial abstraction from phenomena that are believed to have certain things in common.[4]

The relationship between fascism and totalitarianism is similarly complex. The OED defines 'totalitarian' rather succinctly: a one-party system of government, with all other systems in subordination to the party, usually requiring individual subservience to the state.[5]

Such a clear-cut definition, however, raises multiple issues in regard to the actual practice of fascism.[6]

In practice, the relationship between state and party in fascism was quite complex, and fascist parties negotiated relationships with the churches. The actual implementation of totalitarianism ranged from a somewhat laissez-faire attitude in Italy to a rigid dogmatism in Germany. In the cultural sphere, this is exemplified by the positive attitude to Futurism in the case of Italian Fascism and the negative approach to modernism, including Expressionism, in the case of Nazism.

Both systems fostered an up-to-the-minute attitude in the areas of science and technology, particularly as these were channelled into war and conquest. At the same time, both looked to the classical ideal as the epitome of cultural striving.[7] Fascism had a complicated and contradictory relationship with modernity. The implicit goal, whether conscious or unconscious, may have been to reverse the historical displacement, by Judeo-Christian values, of the classical and pagan world.

If that is the case, it would seem that right-wing Christians would do well to rethink their alliance with their current neo-pagan allies. In a worst-case scenario, if fascists of one kind or another actually took power, such a cosy pagan–Christian arrangement could turn out to be a temporary one.

Nevertheless, some forms of fascism, historically, took on a Christian (or 'Christian') dimension, such as the race-based 'German Christianity' under Nazism or the forms of clerico-fascism that arose in, for example, Spain and Slovakia. We should not underestimate the energy that current forms of fascism, or neo-fascism, may derive from conservative religious attitudes, even if their ideological thrust is essentially at odds with the religious values that they ostensibly endorse.

POPULISM AND FASCISM

The key question we have to ask at this point is a speculative one: is the current manifestation of authoritarian populism in various parts of the world likely to lead to some new form of fascism, however we may define the term?

Populism is a key concept here, and again we may look to the OED for a definition: populist political parties are those that aspire 'to represent the interests of ordinary people'.[8] There are left-wing populists (the Occupy movement, for example), but populism is usually seen as having a right-wing tendency (the Gilets Jaunes in France, Trump supporters in the United States, or the Brexit phenomenon in the United Kingdom). Populism may plug into economic concerns (for example, the argument that immigration tends to undercut pay and working conditions), and in that sense it may have both left-wing and right-wing elements.

Consequently, right-wing opponents of immigration may find themselves in conflict with the neoliberalism of the centre-right; the neoliberal publication *The Economist*, for example, has traditionally supported immigration.

In cultural terms, the situation is equally complicated, as right-wing populists find themselves on the same side as some feminists, Jews, free-speech advocates and gays in opposing the growth of Islam in the West – which some fear would threaten the Western liberties we take for granted.

How to differentiate right- and left-wing populism may be problematic. In a general sense, however, the difference may be found in attitudes to immigration and the environment: positive or neutral in the case of the left, negative or cynical in the case of the right. A striking phenomenon has been the tendency for right-wing populists to take over the anti-globalisation movement over the last twenty years or so – previously, it was largely the domain of the left.

Populism is at times the outcome of genuine grievances, particularly in the economic sphere – for example, as a response to out-of-touch elites, bank and corporate bailouts that leave the ordinary individual stranded, and military adventurism that benefits no one except the military–industrial complex. The fact that populists may be asking the right questions is, unfortunately, coupled with the fact that they often give the wrong answers, since they are as much in thrall to media and other vested interests as they believe their opponents to be, albeit in different ways.

The current split within the capitalist system, between advocates of globalism and protectionism, means that most people are prisoners of one ideology or the other – and of their associated manipulators – rather than having some kind of privileged access to political enlightenment.

Populist discourse is often conspiratorial in nature. It is dependent on dubious sources and on (obvious) misinterpretations of facts and sources; it also manifests its own form of groupthink, in parallel with leftist versions of the same phenomenon. The wild speculations of the QAnon conspiracy theory, with its recycling of anti-Semitic clichés and a disparate range of followers (from the gullible to the malevolent), represent an extreme example.[9]

The political difference between populists and (for example) Marxists is that populists believe that ordinary people have, more or less, got it right – or from a more cynical viewpoint, that their instincts may be used as a useful stepping stone to power. On the other hand, Marxists tend to believe that the people must be enlightened as to where their true interests lie (as revealed in Marxist literature); otherwise they will fall prey to capitalist ideology and work against their own interests. An easily-cited example of this is the caricature of the normal Trump voter, deluded as to the cause of his or her economic misfortune and looking in the wrong place for salvation (to protectionism and isolationism, instead of socialism and internationalism).

In the populist mindset, the will of the people takes quite a different form from the role it plays in socialist (or Communist) theory. In the case of the former, the people's viewpoint is regarded as self-evidently true; 'elitist' viewpoints are routinely rubbished, but the forms of (equally elitist) manipulation that encourage the populist viewpoint are ignored. From a critical perspective, populists fall out of the frying pan of the elitist millionaires and into the fire of the elitist billionaires.

In the case of the left, populism is often suspect: it is believed the people must be educated as to the nature of their true interests. The will of the people is correct, but the people need to be instructed as to what their true will actually is – or rather what it would be, or should be, if they got it right. This raises the difficult, and perhaps unanswerable, question as to how one can claim the privilege of knowing what is good for everyone. Marxism, for instance, has no inherent mechanism whereby its truth-claims – for example, about the nature of the capitalist system – can be tested or falsified. (If the revolution fails, it means that it was not applied properly – universally, as Trotsky believed, or in one country, according to the politics of Stalin.)

Marxism's sole claim to truth is its success in the field of discourse (which, indeed, is not entirely to be dismissed as a factor in the struggle of ideas).

A related issue arises in respect to values – which, when we examine Marxist theory, are difficult to disentangle from facts. To take a key example of how facts and values are entangled, Marxism has no watertight answer to the question of whether socialism, though it may be inevitable in some way, is necessarily a good idea. Historical examples of the implementation of Marxist socialism have been, with a few marginal exceptions, unimpressive. Where it has succeeded (as in China, to an extent), there is a question as to whether the success is due to socialism or capitalism, or a combination of the two.

This historical pattern of failure should be distinguished from the achievements of social democracy – a form of mixed economy that, while not perfect, has had some success in combining the benefits of both socialism and capitalism while minimising the downside of each. One example is manifest in the countries of northern Europe, where a kind of welfare capitalism has prevailed.

In the United States, populism is rooted economically in a reaction to neoliberal capitalism, globalism and Rust Belt unemployment; culturally, it is concerned about the rise of groups such as Hispanics, Muslims and African Americans, and what is believed to be the corresponding threat to white Christian hegemony – or more recently, Judeo-Christian hegemony. It is also a reaction to what is seen as the politically correct culture of the left, and the imposition of party line thought, with its knee-jerk, stereotypical responses.

THE ROOTS OF POPULISM

Roger Eatwell and Matthew Goodwin see the roots of populism as lying in what they call the 'Four Ds': Distrust, Destruction, Deprivation and De-alignment. *Distrust* arises from the elitism of liberal democracy, and alienation from political discourse. *Destruction* of identity and customary ways refers to a fear arising from immigration and ethnic change, whether actual or imaginary. *Deprivation*, at least in a relative sense, has its roots in growing inequality and shrinking future prospects. *De-alignment* refers to the weakened links between mainstream parties and the people. The Four Ds, in the view of these authors, have made space for the rise of national populism.[10]

Eatwell and Goodwin argue that in the United States, cultural factors appeared more decisive than economic ones in determining support for Trump;[11] in a European context, however, the financial crisis made more room for national populists.[12] The authors dismiss the idea that support for Brexit (as an example) is confined to older voters who will die off at some stage, observing that as people age they become more conservative.[13] Support for Brexit seems to rise with the rate of ethnic change.[14]

The projected growth of the population of Africa vis-à-vis Europe, the shrinking size of native populations relative to that of immigrants, and the increasingly Islamic composition of national populations – with corresponding desecularisation – are in Eatwell and Goodwin's view likely to intensify national populism.[15]

Eatwell and Goodwin argue that Trump succeeded by appealing to a combination of white people without college degrees and traditional Republican-voting conservatives.[16] A basic element of populism in Europe is the support of the 'middle-educated' – people who have not graduated from college. It is often education that plays the key role in populism.[17]

Populists tend to favour direct democracy as distinct from representative democracy; they aim for a new type of democracy where ordinary people have a much stronger voice.[18] This runs counter, to some extent, to the image of populists as necessarily being authoritarian. Indeed, in some ways they may be more 'democratic' than mainstream supporters of representative democracy.

Historically, populists supported the involvement of experts in government.[19] Again, this counters the stereotype of populists distrusting 'experts'.

Marco Respinti points out how France's National Front (now styled the National Rally) aims to achieve electoral success by 'breaching into the left' – aiming for a crossover politics that would combine increased statism with opposition to neoliberal capitalism, immigration and the EU.[20] The point seems to highlight the fact that not all forms of crossover politics are necessarily desirable.

Resentment against immigrants does not become morally better by mixing it with anti-capitalism, though the right may enjoy benefits – a growing acceptability for its politics – by absorbing the positions of the left. There may, indeed, be a helpful dichotomy to be drawn between progressive and reactionary forms of crossover politics.

Eatwell and Goodwin point out that contemporary populists in the West urge a Swiss-style model of democracy, rather than dictatorial power.[21] Trump's appeal, in their view, is not fascist in nature but lies in a combination of American exceptionalism, individualism, the attraction of celebrity culture, anti-globalisation and protectionism.[22] Given Trump's appeal to the far right, both in the United States and abroad, this may be seen as a somewhat anodyne analysis.[23]

The authors draw a distinction between what they call the 'radical right' and the 'extreme right'. The extreme right is divisive, anti-freedom and shades into terrorism – for example, in the case of the Norwegian terrorist Anders Behring Breivik. The radical right, on the other hand, criticise certain facets of liberal democracy but do not seek to end democracy, and are open to alternative forms of popular rule.[24] However, radical right parties in Hungary and Poland are culturally nationalist, and opposed to liberalism and multiculturalism.[25]

Eatwell and Goodwin note the recent growth of a disconnection between technocratic elites and ordinary people, between the rulers and the ruled – a gap that populists are ready to fill. Elitism, combined with political correctness and the dominance of identity politics, leads to a rise of public discontent with the current system. This results in receptivity to an alternative, more direct form of democracy.[26] The authors argue that issues of community, belonging, group identity and the nation are often more important to populists than purely economic concerns, and that responses to populism need to address the former issues.[27]

It is true that there is no widespread rejection of democracy in the West;[28] what's more, national populist voters are, in the case of some countries, actually more supportive of representative democracy than are the population as a whole.[29] The issue here, though, is not really between direct and representative democracy. Either, or a combination of the two, might work with a clued-in population – and the enhancement of the sphere of direct democracy is not a bad idea in itself. The main issue is the lack of a developed political consciousness on the part of the electorate, which is necessary for any kind of democracy to function successfully.

With the decline of general educational standards in the very countries (the United States and the United Kingdom) where elite education has been so successful for an economically privileged minority, the outlook for politics based on public choice through the electoral system seems problematic.[30] An educated and politically aware public is needed for democracy to function properly; in addition, the media needs to be freed from the control of economic elites, whether those elites are conservative or progressive in nature. A population that can think for itself is an essential element of a free democratic society.

The alternative is that democratic politics may descend into tyranny of one kind or another. The fact that such tyranny may not be signalled by the swastika, the fasces or the hammer-and-sickle will be small comfort for those who have, step by step, lost their freedom, their privacy and their rights in general.

The English novelist E.M. Forster, speaking at an event in 1935, observed that the danger from Fascism in England was minimal. A much more serious danger was what he called 'Fabio-Fascism': a dictatorial mindset operating incrementally through legislation, secrecy and media control, beneath a constitutional veneer.[31]

In terms of iconography, Bibles and crosses may supplant *Mein Kampf* and swastikas, but in substantive terms the recent, authoritarian version of nationalism is somewhat reminiscent of the fascism of almost a century ago. Nonetheless, in today's culture it is somehow difficult to imagine the rise of shirted masses, torchlight processions, political hymn-singing, book burnings and the rest of the fascist paraphernalia – except, perhaps, on a small, derivative and theatrical scale.

For all its horrors, historical fascism undoubtedly had style: the bumbling, semi-literate buffoonery of US-style ultra-rightism has little or none. We may even give ironic thanks that reactionary politics is in such culturally incompetent hands. From a proto-fascist point of view, the problem with the red hat–wearing, overweight, predominantly white Trump supporters is not that they are politically dangerous – after all, danger may have its attractions for a bored and frustrated populace – it is that the far right in the United States are seriously uncool.

Social media (unlike the radio and film of the fascist era) at least provides the opportunity for investigation and debate around ideology, including that of the extreme right – however much entrenched interests may control the media, both mainstream and internet-based. The possibilities for political pushback are greater in some ways than in the 1930s, which is all the more reason why digital media need robust defence against political control and censorship, from whichever direction it comes.

While sections of the population in, for example, the United States and eastern Europe may have it bad, they have not undergone the kind of economic wipeout that beset the middle classes in Germany after the First World War – or at least not yet. It is not unthinkable that current economic policies based on obscurantism, environmental depredation, massive inequality and unsustainable national debt may, at some stage, lead to runaway inflation and the ruin of the middle classes.

A combination of such an eventuality with mass automation and unemployment – particularly youth unemployment – would mean that all bets were off. Environmental collapse and the regular recurrence of pandemics, with institutionalised social regimentation as a consequence, would be the icing on the cake of social chaos and totalitarian reaction.

The countries of southern and eastern Europe may be particularly susceptible to anti-democratic forms of government, since liberal democracy in those countries is a recent development.[32] The rise of populist politicians such as Matteo Salvini in Italy and Viktor Orbán in Hungary has been characterised by the pursuit of conservative culture wars, and hostility to environmentalism.[33] Right-wing religious values play a prominent role, together with opposition to immigration and to liberal values in the sphere of sexuality.[34] The phenomenon of illiberal democracy, as represented in particular by Hungary and Poland, is characterised by politics that have tended to weaken the rule of law and the principles of democracy in favour of populist nationalism.

This is achieved by the legal capture of the constitution and by paralyzing the constitutional court. This process is rooted in a specific psychological mindset, featuring a lack of respect and self-confidence, a sense of victimisation and inferiority, a subservience to authority, a need for hierarchy, and a suspicion of the values of an open society. It is problematic to reverse, and may be seen as a phase in the development towards authoritarianism.[35]

National populist leaders have emerged, in recent times, in such countries as Brazil, Egypt, the Philippines, Russia and Turkey; such countries appear to be in various stages of the road towards authoritarianism. In Brazil, big capital slavers at the prospect of denuding the Amazon and displacing its indigenous people[36] – a process hastened by the pressure of 'beef, bibles, bullets': the meat industry, fundamentalist religion and the military. In Russia, the rule of authoritarian nationalist leader Vladimir Putin is influenced by the writings of Aleksandr Dugin, which defend traditional, conservative values against liberalism and individualism, positing a version of left–right crossover politics along such lines.[37]

Authoritarianism, though – however negative it may be in environmental and human terms – is not synonymous with fascism. The key question is whether authoritarian nationalism is a step towards eventual, full-blown fascism. The jury is out on that, though in a possible future of social, economic and environmental collapse, we cannot foresee what, if any, limits would exist to the emergence of new forms of fascism, or other forms of totalitarianism.

There is, it should be said, one resource available in our society that was not accessible to potential fascist supporters in the 1920s and 1930s. That is the memory of the horrors of fascism, and the visual availability of that memory through mass media; these represent perhaps the strongest deterrent to its resurgence. The growth of mass education, for all its glaring flaws, may function to mitigate some of the excesses of would-be fascist dictators. The emergence of the feminist movement may, furthermore, act as something of a brake on the development of ultra-masculine political manifestations, with the 'phallic panic' that such manifestations involve.[38] Science has largely marginalised racism, though eugenics may arise again in new forms, with the possibilities opened up by genetics and the desire for 'designer babies'.

While a new iteration of fascism may be unlikely – at least as we know it from history – we may yet face other threats to our well-being. Threats that are at least equal to those faced by people in the early twentieth century. These include global warming, future pandemics consequent on our mistreatment of nature, and what might be termed the 'soft tyranny' of the all-seeing corporate state. The most pressing danger to democracy may in fact lie in the elitist 'extreme centre',[39] epitomised by the politics of Tony Blair and Hillary Clinton. This is not to mention the populist reactions to such elitism (such as Trumpism), which may manifest their own forms of tyranny as a response.

Enzo Traverso argues that both the radical right and its enemy Islamism are reactionary substitutes for disappeared utopias – particularly that of Communism, with its totalitarian dimension. In contrast, he cites more positive political developments, including the Arab revolutions, the Occupy movement, and Podemos in Spain. Unfortunately, though, as he notes, these new movements have been unable to offer a new vision of utopia. Nevertheless, Traverso mentions the possibility of a social Europe on a federal basis.[40] Whether such a Europe could emerge from the current EU, with its institutionalised neoliberalism, north–south tensions and immigration pressures, remains to be seen.

FEARS OF THE WHITE MAJORITY

There is a key cultural element in the rise of populism and the consequent danger of some kind of fascist outcome: the fear on the part of the white majority that it is under attack and may disappear. The mini attempted coup in Washington was characterised by a sea of white faces.

On the face of it, such fears seem open to question. Indeed, what exactly is a white person? Someone whose skin was completely white would cause alarm in the street – unless, perchance, around the time of Halloween. In contrast to the situation of a completely black person, there might indeed be an indication of the need for medical intervention.

In Ireland, we have some of the palest people in the world. Virtually the first impulse of an Irish person at the approach of the (usually brief) Irish summer is to run outdoors and expose as much of their body to the sun as may be legally permissible. The ostensible aesthetic purpose is to get a suntan and thereby darken one's skin – though there may be a related need to replenish one's stock of vitamin D, depleted over the long winter.

People, not just in Ireland but all over the 'white' world, will – at least in non-pandemic times – spend a large fraction of their income per year on a foreign holiday with the prime intention of darkening their skin colour. This may be, to a certain extent, for health reasons – the necessity to top up on vitamin D competes with the fear of skin-damage from the sun – but aesthetics predominates, at least at a conscious level.

There may be an element of class distinction involved in the Western cult of suntans. At one time, light skin was preferred to suntanned skin, as the latter was associated with outdoor manual work – which, by and large, the upper classes did not indulge in. More recently though, a suntan has been associated with the economic ability of the richer inhabitants of northern countries to take a foreign vacation in a warmer country, with a corresponding adjustment in the related aesthetic.[41] Suntans, then, have a class base.[42]

That said, the even more recent advent of mass travel has, perhaps, made some inroads into that association. Goth culture offers a pale-faced, death-infused alternative to the prevailing 'healthy' suntanned look.[43] And the collapse of tourism since the advent of Covid-19 may have had its own effects on the aesthetic unconscious, though it is probably too early to say what they are.

In contrast to the supposed preference for light skin, people of all races spend much time, effort and money trying to disguise the increasingly white colour of their hair as they grow older. The vast majority, if forced to choose between dark hair and white hair, would choose the former, since it is associated with youth – the preference for which is reinforced by cultural pressures (through advertising, for example). There seems to be no inherent aesthetic preference in the human psyche for light over dark: the stereotypical desirable male in Western culture is tall, dark and handsome. While blonde hair may be highly desired in females, white hair (apart from a few recurrent counternarrative fashion fads for grey or silver hair) is not.

There is much discourse about people's desire to lighten their skin colour or straighten their hair, and about the social advantageousness of lighter skin in countries such as India.[44] However, the corresponding desire for darker skin on the part of whites in white-majority countries is seldom mentioned. The optimistic (anti-racist) view might be that, in terms of the collective aesthetic, we are all unconsciously trying to meet in the middle, and aiming towards an eventual ethnic convergence where a permanent brown colour is the norm. But we must confine that to the realm of speculation.

Nevertheless, the issue of white concern about the pressure of growing minority populations is a politically pressing one – particularly as it feeds into extremist politics. How to deal with the issue of white alarm at the prospect of ethnic evanescence is the topic of Eric Kaufmann's book *Whiteshift: Populism, Immigration and the Future of White Majorities*. Kaufmann's basic argument, rooted in his liberal perspective, is that the cultural, political and economic concerns of white majorities should be taken seriously, and not dismissed with knee-jerk politically correct recriminations about racism.

To engage in such a negative response, he believes, is actually to play into the hands of racists, thereby strengthening their position rather than weakening it. The views of liberals or leftists can, as a consequence, be characterised by their political opponents as knee-jerk groupthink, thus reinforcing the notion of the opposite perspective as the repository of truth. Kaufmann's view is that demography and culture, rather than economics and politics, are fundamental to understanding populism.[45] Crucially, for Kaufmann, politicians should set immigration levels that take into account the feelings of the median voter.[46]

Kaufmann defines 'Whiteshift' as a likely change in Western physical appearance, though not so much in terms of language or religion.[47] The mixed population may, in the long term, gather around white ethnic nuclei to form a new white majority, albeit with a major non-white component.[48] He sums up the likely responses to this in four categories: resistance, repression, flight and incorporation (or as he puts it, Fight, Repress, Flee, Join).

The increase in ethnic diversity, Kaufmann believes, is a key factor in the present malaise of racial discord. According to him, this may be diminished by intermarriage and the production of mixed majorities – a situation that he regards as both likely and desirable. Kaufmann cites the argument that the difference between East Asia and Africa from 1960 to 1990 in terms of economic growth is down to the ethnic homogeneity of East Asia and the diversity of Africa.[49] The eventual situation he envisages, and endorses, is that of a melting pot and the emergence of a new 'hybrid' majority.[50]

Kaufmann, though, is not forecasting the disappearance of whites as we know them.[51] He believes that they may survive, particularly in the context of religious sects.[52]

One issue with Kaufmann's position, however, is that he does not interrogate the notion of whiteness as rigorously as he might have done – perhaps along the lines indicated above, taking into account the fairly obvious fact that white people are seldom (if ever) actually white, but more usually a pale pinkish-brown colour. Completely white people would more closely resemble ghosts.

Kaufmann urges the formation, in the United States, of a transracial majority – nominally 'white' but incorporating minority elements, on a parallel with the (fairly recent) fusion of Catholics and Jews to form a new white US majority.[53] In consonance with the change in the median racial type, the limits of what is regarded as whiteness may widen.[54]

Kaufmann asks the question, 'Solidarity or Diversity?'[55] In this, he tends to favour the former. In his view, it is a political mistake to dismiss what he terms 'ethno-traditional nationalism', an ideology based on a concern about cultural loss.[56] Such dismissal, in his view, potentially strengthens the hand of that kind of nationalism.

His solution to the refugee problem, which currently places pressure on majority populations and increases the power of populism, is to house claimants in secure facilities in Europe, though without offering the possibility of long-term settlement. This would, he believes, ensure refuge, the minimisation of feared cultural change, safety of transit, and diminution of the economic and cultural burden on countries; it would also, according to Kaufmann, eliminate the pressure of economic (as distinct from life-threatened) migrants on the system. Kaufmann further argues that, in the system he advocates, there would be pressure to resolve the problems in trouble spots, and to bring refugee camps near conflict areas more in line with Western standards; this, in turn, would encourage refugees to return to, or remain in, those camps.[57]

Kaufmann argues that high levels of immigration, justified on the basis of anti-racism, may in fact make it more difficult to build an anti-inequality progressive coalition.[58]

Kaufmann's perspective, while largely persuasive, highlights a conundrum facing countries that may, on the basis of humanitarian concerns, wish to increase their immigrant intake. This kind of dilemma has faced countries both in the past and present – whether it involved the prospect of Jews immigrating into Ireland during the Nazi era,[59] or Muslims immigrating into Germany in more recent times. Arguably, the more you open up immigration possibilities for endangered minorities, the more potential ammunition you give to native racists, anti-Semites and Islamophobes, with the potential social destabilisation that may result.

There is no easy or obvious answer to this question – any more than there is to the potential problems involved in relaxing restrictions on immigrants already present. If you make things too attractive for potential immigrants, including opening up the opportunity to work, how do you stop this functioning as a magnet for increasing numbers of people who want to immigrate on the basis of financial pressures, rather than on the grounds of fear for their lives? The usual answer to this, and similar problems, is to ignore such issues in the hope that they may go away.

Kaufmann raises some important and trenchant issues about immigration. Between the opposite extremes – far-right proposals to ship people of foreign origin 'home', and the desire to totally dismantle border controls (a radical solution mentioned, for example, by Rutger Bregman[60]) – there is wide scope for debate. Such discourse, in practice, is often characterised by fudge and avoidance of the key issues, rather than by an open-minded resolve to identify and tackle the problems.

Questions seldom asked include, 'What percentage of immigrants from a radically different culture could be absorbed without far-reaching, and undesirable, reactionary change to the cultural and political status quo?' One could imagine, for example, a situation where the rising sea level threatened to swamp the low-lying south-eastern states of the United States – a possibility that is unfortunately quite thinkable in the era of global warming. What number of climate refugees from these areas – conservative and fundamentalist Christian in outlook – could newly-liberal Ireland absorb without the danger of significant political regression, particularly in the area of women's rights or the rights of sexual minorities? These kinds of questions do not have easy answers,.

This issue is relevant in the context of debates about Muslim immigration to Europe, though Kaufmann dismisses the notion of a majority-Muslim Europe within the next century or so.[61] The issue is particularly to the fore in German and French discourse.[62] In Britain, Kaufmann points out that the tendency is towards disaffiliation from Islam rather than towards it;[63] however, the Muslim population of Europe is projected to rise to between 10 and 20 per cent by the middle of this century, and even perhaps to 30 per cent in the case of Sweden.[64]

It should also be noted that, historically, some Muslim cultures have been havens of tolerance, artistic culture and intellectual enquiry, in contrast to their Christian contemporaries.[65] The historical reasons for the reversal of this situation are beyond the scope of this book, but if we are to look forward to a positive future, it is surely a question that needs to be addressed urgently. In the sphere of education, an important priority would be to expand cultural perspectives for all sections of the population, specifically focussing on the requirement that children of all religious backgrounds become familiar with the ideas that influence their compatriots of other religions, and of none. Such a policy could result in a cultural broadening that would be beneficial to society – and would be harmful only to extremism of one kind or another.

How to deal with the issue of immigration, particularly Muslim immigration – which results not just from former British colonialism but from more recent Western destabilisation of Muslim countries in the interest of spreading 'democracy' (i.e. economic imperialism) – is a crucial issue of our time, and is of particular importance in Europe. Key to resolving the issue would seem to be a rational approach to immigration, the cessation of Western meddling in Muslim countries, and a vigorous assertion of the values of a secular state and of the separation of religion and state.

It should be made clear, however, that a secular state is not necessarily the same as a secular society. As the United States has shown, religion may in fact thrive better in a society where church and state are formally separated than in societies like the United Kingdom, where religion is established.[66]

Controversially, the liberal Kaufmann (himself of mixed-race background) raises the issue of the danger of majority whites – unlike minority ethnic groups – being discouraged from taking pride in their identity.[67] Such a situation he regards as politically perilous. One possibility he outlines is that whites accept people of mixed-race origin as part of their group, with a cultural adjustment to assimilation on the part of the group of mixed-race origin.[68]

Something like this does indeed seem to be happening in the United Kingdom, particularly with the rise to prominence of politicians of Indian background. There has also been the election of Irish prime minister Leo Varadkar, who is not only half-Indian but also gay.

The majority–minority fusion that Kaufmann outlines, and indeed hopes for, would offer conservative whites the possibility of continuing as an ethnic majority with a corresponding 'group consciousness', thus diffusing and undermining right-wing populism.[69]

Kaufmann's analysis is broadly persuasive, though it may come under criticism for its promulgation of assimilation and integration, in place of the current slogan of diversity.

From a cultural as distinct from a socioeconomic point of view, a diversified society would probably be more interesting to live in than a culturally homogeneous one. Nonetheless, interesting times are not necessarily safe times; as a drive towards assimilation progresses, the trade-off in terms of political stability and solidarity may compensate for an eventual decline in the variety of languages and ethnic restaurants.

Perhaps we may look forward to a linguistic future that is more creole than the present situation. This is notwithstanding the fact that English has been, in one sense of the word, a creole language for the best part of a millennium; it is basically a mixture of Anglo-Saxon and Latin (through Norman French).

CONCLUSION

Populist arguments are not to be totally dismissed. On the one hand, it seems illogical to condemn a majority's right to pride in its ethnic or religious heritage while defending that of a minority. On the other hand, it seems disingenuous to ignore the hankering for a past of racial superiority and domination that the phrase 'white pride' evokes – in a way that, for example, the phrase 'black pride' does not. In contemporary jargon, the assertion of white pride 'punches down', while that of black pride 'punches up'.

Concerns about the negative economic consequences of immigration may be substantiated in some cases – for example, if immigration can be shown to drive down wages or lower working conditions. This, however, is a complicated issue, and a matter of contention within the relevant literature.[70] Populist criticism of stereotypical thinking – political correctness, cancel culture and the like – may be, in some cases, justified. And there may be little to argue about when populists, conservatives and libertarians condemn bank bailouts by the state, burgeoning bureaucracy, foreign military adventurism that indulges the financial appetite of the military–industrial complex, and the counterproductive war on drugs.[71]

Liberals and leftists could make common cause with populists, where the views of the last-mentioned are justified – for example, in their demand for participatory democracy rather than the veneer that is offered at present, with the periodic exercise of the ballot and little more.

Populists could also point out that liberal values – for example, of free speech and the separation of state and religion – need robust defence, even against the leftist establishment – perhaps particularly so. Otherwise, the left risk losing the ideational battle against the right by default; the right could then claim to be the repository of the values of freedom that the left have cast aside.

On the other hand, where populists demonstrate against the supposed erosion of freedom consequent on anti-pandemic measures, and are joined by neo-Nazis and neo-fascists posing as defenders of freedom, the obvious contradiction needs to be highlighted. In a broader sense, if a slide to authoritarianism is to be resisted in favour of freedom, the tension within the mish-mash of populist thinking – between libertarianism and authoritarianism – should be clearly identified.

'Divide and conquer' may be the key to the intellectual neutralisation of the threats posed by right-wing populism, authoritarianism and – at the extreme – new forms of fascism. The basic incoherence of the ingredients – conservative Christianity, neo-paganism, libertarianism and corporate capitalism – in the proto-fascist far-right witches' brew needs to be highlighted. At the same time, whatever positive energy the far right draws on through its appropriation of legitimate issues – such as opposition to groupthink and to the policing of language – should be denied it, through the political appropriation of such opposition by liberals and the left.

Chapter 6

GROUPTHINK,
OR TOTALITARIANISM
OF THE MIND

Ideological intolerance, or what might be termed totalitarianism of the mind, whereby dissenting views are systematically banished and repressed in favour of an approved mindset, takes a number of different forms. These are often summed up in the phrases 'political correctness' (a bit passé at this stage), the (even older) 'tyranny of the Good', and more recently 'cant culture', or 'cancel culture'. The last-mentioned is an updated version of the more traditional 'no platform' – the practice of denying a voice to those whose opinions are deemed unacceptable. Practitioners of ideological intolerance are sometimes dismissed as snowflakes, who live in echo chambers and practice virtue signalling.

Present-day intolerance raises its head in unexpected forms. People with an intense commitment to veganism are sometimes termed 'vegangelicals', in a reference to their zealous counterparts in the religious sphere. The internet, as a platform for the exchange of ideas, is rife with such intolerance.

Regarding online debate, part of the problem is, no doubt, due to the well-known lack of non-verbal clues, such as facial expression – a problem that the recent phase of mask-wearing replicates, with its potential for social misunderstanding. Gestures and tone of voice can only go so far as a replacement for visual cues, such as a smile. In both cases, an important element of non-verbal human communication is no longer available, enhancing the potential of misunderstanding in social interactions. Emojis, or emoticons, are a meagre substitute.

Intolerance on the left is nothing new. Even anarchists, or a particular type of anarchist at least – ostensible defenders of freedom – sometimes mirror the activities and appearance of the police they oppose. A liking for dressing in black often characterises power-trippers of one kind or another, whether the black bloc on the far left, the SS on the historical right, or authoritarian clergy of traditional religions.[1]

Discussing the issue of extreme political correctness and the related phenomenon of cancel culture, Mark Fisher mentions what he calls the Vampires' Castle. In his words, 'The Vampires' Castle specialises in propagating guilt. It is driven by a *priest's desire* to excommunicate and condemn, an *academic-pedant's desire* to be the first to be seen to spot a mistake, and a *hipster's desire* to be one of the in-crowd.' Fisher describes the Vampires' Castle as 'a bourgeois-liberal perversion' involving an attempt to steal the energy of the struggle against the various forms of racism and sexism. The Vampires' Castle propagates a mindset which marginalises social class, insists that empathy is impossible for those outside a particular identity group, and transforms human suffering into academic capital. Politically, Fisher compellingly urges the rejection of identitarianism in favour of class politics.[2]

In recent times, questions around intolerance have arisen in the context of phenomena such as safe spaces and trigger warnings. There have been issues around affirmative action (otherwise known as positive discrimination or 'equity'). Objects of censure are denoted in terms such as 'hate speech', 'microaggressions', 'transphobia', 'Islamophobia' and 'white privilege'. Sometimes such accusations have merit, and sometimes not.

These issues usually arise on the traditional left, but there have been right-wing versions as well – for example, in regard to some uses of the term 'anti-Semitism' that seek to equate criticism of the Israeli government's politics with opposition to Jews themselves. The common theme is control of the narrative so that oppositional issues are not addressed through argument. Rather, argument is itself suppressed.

There are alarming manifestations at an institutional level. Anthony Lester points to the situation in Guizhou province in China, where it was planned to subject university lecturers to continual CCTV monitoring to ensure they avoided problematic issues.[3] In Saudi Arabia, a blogger was sentenced to ten years in prison and 1,000 lashes for running a website promoting freedom of speech.[4] The Organisation of Islamic Cooperation agitates at the UN to criminalise insults to religion. The potential, Lester notes, is the impairment of human rights and the suppression of religious nonconformism.[5]

In the United Kingdom, the Labour Party instituted the Racial and Religious Hatred Bill.[6] On the positive side, Ireland recently repealed anti-blasphemy legislation,[7] thereby removing a model that has been used for justification of similar laws in other countries.[8] The Charlie Hebdo massacre in Paris graphically highlighted issues of the clash between the right to free speech – however offensive such speech may be to some – and the feelings of minorities.

The phenomenon of censorship does not necessarily involve physical or state repression; it often displays a more subtle resistance to mental challenge, and the tendency to block out anything that conflicts with one's world view – or that of the group with which one identifies. This may result in echo chambers, where the individual's opinions are reinforced rather than challenged. One example of the process is the virtual disregard of the widespread persecution of Christians in Islamic countries, presumably because Christians do not easily fit into the category of victimhood,[9] at least in the eyes of Western activists.

The space of acceptable speech in a given society is sometimes referred to as the 'Overton Window'. The Overton Window functions by making previously unthinkable or marginal views politically thinkable, and thus capable of practical implementation.[10] Roughly speaking, and applied to contemporary politics, the right try to shift, or expand, the window in terms of what is permissible to express – for example, with regard to minorities – while the left try to alter it in the other direction. Conversely, the left attempt to adjust the window in regard, for example, to the rights of gay or trans people, while the right (with the exception of its libertarian component) tend to resist this process.

Issues may arise, though, when the rights of different protected minorities clash; there are interesting areas of silence that highlight the weakness of the relevant mindset involved. For example, Western social justice adherents sometimes ignore issues of gay rights and women's rights in Islamic countries and cultures, and downplay what would otherwise be regarded as flagrant abuses of human rights – a process described by one writer as 'benevolent bigotry'.[11] (The term 'selective outrage' has also been applied.) At the same time, the forms of anti-Semitism that are sometimes rampant within Islamic countries[12] and communities[13] are often understated as a problem.

There are imbalances even within the accepted categories of opposition to discrimination. To take one example, in terms of the anti-racism discourse there are crucial blind spots, such as the dominance of Asians over whites in the tech industry.[14] This has never become a political issue in the way that white-over-black dominance has.

In defence of the principle of free speech, Lester quotes a famous judgement by Justice Holmes:

> If you have no doubt of your premises or your power and want a certain result with all your heart you naturally express your wishes in law and sweep away all opposition … But when men have realised that time has upset many fighting faiths, they may come to believe […] that the ultimate good desired is better reached by free trade in ideas … The best test of truth is the power of the thought to get itself accepted in the competition of the market.[15]

The principle of the free trade in ideas[16] seems as relevant today as it was a century ago. We do not need the state to police our minds, and the tendency to slide into this situation by default, through the strict control of language, is concerning.[17]

To sum up the preceding discussion, the dominance of political correctness or cant culture is dangerous in two major ways. The first is that it has the potential to slide into a form of totalitarianism of the mind, fomented in the womb of liberal-democratic society – in effect, adding to the ongoing erosion of freedom, privacy, and individual autonomy. The second is that it operates as a handy target for the right, and particularly the far right, who gain energy by attacking what they perceive – sometimes accurately – as the infantilism of their opponents.

At the same time, their own forms of infantilism – particularly that of bizarre right-wing conspiracy theories – remain unseen, at least by them.

GENERATIONAL ISSUES

A new generation of students has made its voice heard in recent years. This is in the context of mass access to third-level education and an increase in the quantity of students, if not necessarily in the quality of education.

Students from families that have enjoyed access to higher education for generations may be used to a situation where amicable dinner-table argument – without enmity or the desire to crush the opposition – is taken as the norm. With the growth of mass education at third level, however, many students come from family backgrounds where such intellectually relaxed attitudes may not prevail. This may militate against the acceptance, on the part of the student, of easy-going disagreement as a run-of-the-mill part of rational debate. The taboo on *ad hominem* argumentation – attacking persons rather than ideas – is not necessarily a universal phenomenon, and not always seen as desirable. Consequently, the norms of debate – hitherto taken for granted – may be undermined.

In addition, particularly in the United States, students from less well-off families may have incurred large amounts of debt – a factor that does not sit well with the discomfort of having one's worldview challenged, either by lecturers or fellow students. One might add to this the increasing managerialism and commercialisation of universities, and the displacement, under neoliberalism, of the traditional values of free speech and academic freedom by economic values.[18] The student is a customer who can shop around in search of compatible ideas. Economic freedom thus becomes a road to intellectual conformity.

Not all the pressure towards intellectual conformity comes from students, it should be emphasised. Somewhat alarmingly, an Irish university recently proposed to modify its policy on academic freedom to take account of developing relationships with other countries, including China. Fortunately, the proposed change faced strong resistance by academic staff and was dropped.[19]

It is true that a new generation of students may have insights that their elders lack – on issues of, for example, race, colonialism and gender. Nonetheless, the traditional, and appropriate, way to convey such insights is through rational debate and the presentation of evidence, not the denial of an opponent's right to speak. Debate may have the positive effect of highlighting flaws in mutually-opposing viewpoints – a progressive development that takes place best in the context of reasoned argument, not suppression.

The increasing weakness of academics' career position in a neoliberal society feeds into the tendency of political correctness to predominate: if you have to choose between your livelihood and defending free speech, free speech may come a poor second.

Intolerance of opposing views is nothing new – as anyone, of any age, with memories of student politics can readily attest. Some decades ago, it was routine for left-wing students to attempt to 'no platform' people suspected, rightly or wrongly, of extreme right-wing views – for example, supporting apartheid in South Africa.[20]

That is to say nothing of the much more extreme cases of youthful intolerance: vicious forms of oppression by the Khmer Rouge, or in the context of Chairman Mao's mobilisation of youth in the Chinese Cultural Revolution. Going further back – though not too far back – there were the horrors of Nazi and Stalinist tyranny, both mental and physical; this involved the mass mobilisation of youth for ideological purposes, inculcating intolerance of those perceived as enemies.

When regarded in this historical context, contemporary forms of snowflake dogmatism by social justice activists can seem relatively minor and insignificant.

To draw the analogy further, former student generations in Western countries, around the time of the Cold War, tended to ignore the monstrous forms of leftist repression taking place abroad. At home, they focused on the minutiae of what was, or was not, acceptable in abstruse theoretical terms, often revolving around the relative merits, or demerits, of the ideas of Stalin and Trotsky.

In a similar way, the current younger generation tends to ignore the excesses of some Muslim regimes in regard, for example, to the repression of gays and women, while expending much energy on minute analyses of hitherto-invisible flaws in Western culture. The biblical reference to 'straining out gnats and swallowing camels' seems apposite in this context.

One can excuse the excesses of youthful intolerance on the basis that the heart of young people is in the right place. Opposition to various forms of sexual, racial and religious discrimination is surely a good thing in itself, though occasionally taken to unwarranted extremes – as, indeed, political energy almost always is.

Nevertheless, the sometimes-bizarre excesses of cultural politics represent an important political issue, insofar as they are a major factor in the growth of right-wing populism as an oppositional force. A survey of Trump voters in 2017 revealed political correctness on racial matters as a top three issue among 18 per cent of respondents.[21]

Furthermore, the marginalisation of the forms of class-based social inequality still endemic in our society isn't just bad in itself; it risks skewing, in a right-wing direction, the worldview of the victims of class oppression, as manifest most recently in the groundswell of support for Donald Trump. It seems that the contemporary left have abandoned the working classes in favour of identity groups.

The phenomenon of intolerance is not a recent one. Young people, at whatever point in time their youth occurs, tend to see things in terms of black and white, as distinct from the more nuanced view that develops (ideally, at least) as people mature. The tendency to view things in shades of grey may, indeed, appear to the younger generation as the result of moral exhaustion, unacceptable compromise and a process of selling out.

And in fairness, that is sometimes an accurate assessment. For an elected politician, when the necessity of making mortgage payments and feeding one's children conflicts with political principles, the resulting moral-political dilemma may be difficult to resolve.

With the growth of social media, young people have much greater access to an audience, and to debate, than they would have had some decades ago. The liberal dialectical process of argument is often foreign to youth, and is perhaps not as natural a phenomenon as their elders may assume. This method, with its roots in ancient Greece, of teasing out weaknesses in an interlocutor's argument in order to achieve a greater approximation to truth – whatever truth may be – is foundational to western civilisation. It should not, however, be taken for granted. The desire to not be 'triggered', to avail of 'safe spaces', and the phenomenon of online echo chambers – it all has roots in a failure to appreciate how learning develops. Intellectual complacency, silos, safe spaces and echo chambers replace dialogue.

IDEOLOGICAL CONFORMITY

There is also a growing tendency to attempt to use the law, and the monopoly on force of the state, to ensure linguistic and ideological conformity. This issue has been critically highlighted by the well-known public intellectual Jordan Peterson, who argues for the importance of individualism versus collectivism. Peterson argues for the central importance of free speech, and disagrees with the goal of equality of outcome (as distinct from equality of opportunity)[22]

This dichotomy is, indeed, at the heart of a liberal society. Equality of opportunity is one of the basic principles of that society, but that is quite distinct from equality of outcome. Unequal outcomes are the norm in life. If they were not, we would experience a nightmare of dreary cultural sameness.

There is a crucial difference between using gender-neutral language because you've realised that it makes sense and is respectful, and being forced by the state, or your employers, to do so. The former is part of the continual development of thought and language. The latter is a form of ideological dictatorship, outlined in extreme fictional form in Orwell's *Nineteen Eighty-Four*.

Eric Kaufmann notes the phenomenon of expanding the definition of hate speech to include whatever offends 'the subjective sensibilities of the most affronted individual' – or whatever the affronted's defenders believe to be a cause for offense.[23]

The phenomenon of ideological conformity isn't solely of interest because it describes something that is usually negative. Such required docility is also of political concern because it provides potential ammunition to the right in its attack on the left – and on liberal, progressive political positions.

One example of the reign of ideological conformity was manifest when philosopher Rebecca Tuvel took the position in the feminist journal *Hypatia* that we should defend an individual's decision to change their race, just as we would the rights of a transgender person to assert their chosen identity. A huge oppositional backlash followed, which Kaufmann attributes to the relative disadvantage of transracials vis-à-vis trans individuals in the hierarchy of victimhood. Trans individuals are viewed as more disadvantaged than women, whereas transracials are not seen as more disadvantaged than people of colour; consequently, transgenderism tends to win out in the victimhood stakes, while trans-racials lose.[24]

On the face of it, this negative reaction to transracial possibilities seems illogical, since there is no reason to believe that one form of iden-tity (for example, racial) is more natural than another (for example, gender). Furthermore, we are all of African origin if you go back far enough.[25] Consequently, it's arguable that I – normally presenting as a white Irish male – should be able to define myself as Irish, European or African as I wish.

To take the argument a step further still, why should these possibilities be confined to such areas as sex, gender and race? Suppose, for example, an individual became tired of the psychological and social limitations culturally associated with ageing, and decided to redefine themselves as being of a different age – whether younger or older.[26]

Ageism is the last of the 'isms' to be theorised, for reasons that prob-ably include issues around limitations of biology and reproduction – limitations that may or may not be overcome by science in due course. It is not impossible that longevity, and reproductive capability, of biblical proportions may be achievable in the future.[27]

To take a somewhat science-fictional flight of fancy, imagine a situation – which may indeed be possible at some future stage – of a 25-year-old who travels at great speed into space for (say) five years from their point of view, and arrives back on earth at the chronological age of 70. From the point of view of the person in question, only five years would have passed in psychological and physiological terms, so on arrival back home, they would present – and be perceived – as being 30 years of age. However, from the point of view of those who had been left behind, forty-five years would have passed: the individual would be seventy years old, in chronological terms at least.

To consider the issues that such an individual might face (for example, in terms of identity documents, the job market, family, social relation-ships, dating, health systems, travel, insurance, bank loans, mortgages and government welfare services) is to become aware of the relativity of the forms of limitation and constraint that we routinely accept as a part of ageing, not all of which may be natural, inevitable or potentially incurable.

In such a sci-fi thought-experiment, barriers of bureaucracy, prejudice and disbelief would tend to offset, at every step, the advantages of still being young, in psychological as well as physical terms. That is, until institutional systems and attitudes changed to accommodate the new possibilities.

Nonetheless, it is difficult to imagine an individual in such a time travel situation succumbing to the (socially reinforced) ritual self-denigration and psychological self-limitation in which older people routinely indulge. Age in such a case would be – psychologically speaking, at least – just a number. The example perhaps illustrates the extent to which the negativity attached to age is cultural in essence, as distinct from being rooted in nature. The nature–culture distinction, already familiar from other forms of identity politics, once more raises its head.

Another way of looking at the issue is to consider the various forms of negativity and positivity that are attached to numbers in different contexts. If a teacher or lecturer were to assign a mark of 70 per cent to a student, the student would normally be pleased to receive such a reassuring grade – unless, perchance, she or he were expecting an even higher one. Less gratification would result from a mark of 50 per cent, while 30 per cent would normally be a cause for alarm. If I earned €70,000 a year, I would be happier than if I earned less – and I'd be even happier if my salary were to increase to €90,000 per annum.

Yet the opposite is the case when it comes to human ageing: the larger the figure, the more psychological negativity ensues – at least after a specific, usually quite early point in life. The issue seems to be connected to life expectancy, though it is not a completely logical connection. Some people die young, while others live to an advanced age. Why should averages constrain us? At the height of the Cold War, when you went to bed you never knew whether or not you would wake up to the sound of sirens, or indeed the flash of an atomic bomb. People who lived around the time of the Cuban Missile Crisis had a (subjective) life expectancy of close to zero.[28]

Apart from whatever physical and mental limitations ageing may involve, there is also an expectation that, as one ages, one should adopt a tendency to a kind of rueful self-putdown, observing various forms of social and physical limitation, regardless of one's actual physical or mental condition. Individuals who would be horrified to be accused of racism or sexism often feel OK with casually ageist remarks, whether directed against themselves or others.

The phenomenon of intergenerational hostility recurs in every generation; it is perhaps, however, exacerbated by the current massive economic inequality between the generations, and is consequently understandable to some extent.

Orson Welles, in his mid-twenties, gave a very creditable performance as the much older Charles Foster Kane in the film *Citizen Kane*. One seldom, if ever, comes across the reverse – of an actor of an advanced age playing the part of someone in their twenties (though digital technology has made some halting steps in the direction of cinematic age-reversal – for example, in the recent film *The Irishman*).

One can only expect the relevant technology to improve, so that a future older actor may find it as easy to play a younger part as the reverse.[29] This is still in the realm of spectacle, but no one knows the extent to which comparable possibilities may develop in the sphere of real life, perhaps with the aid of drug therapy, plastic surgery or whatever other measures – in genetics, biotechnology or some other area of science – may contribute to transforming our human experience.

All that said, there is a certain blindness among social justice advocates to issues of ageism (like other marginalised issues, such as the suppression of women and Christians in some Muslim countries, or of Muslims by Chinese Communists). This lack of emphasis – as distinct, for example, from opposition to racism or (non-Muslim) sexism – may be due to the fact that, almost by definition, age discrimination is a less 'sexy' or sexually inflected topic than other forms of discrimination may be. That said, younger people are also sometimes the victims of specific forms of ageism – for example, with regard to premium payments for car insurance, or being taken less seriously at work than their older colleagues.

Relatively few artists deal with ageing as their subject matter, though there are some exceptions. Ageing forms a key part of the writings of Irish author Samuel Beckett, while the Irish-based Manx artist Kevin Atherton engages in thought-provoking video dialogues with his much younger self – an intriguing concept that raises philosophical issues about the nature of time, identity and intergenerational discourse.[30] Films such as *Midsommar* and *Amour* deal shockingly, though in different ways, with issues around age and mortality.

Racial inequality, as Kaufmann points out, is only one aspect of the problem of equality; there are other important aspects, such as those of income and age.[31] Nonetheless, such relative emphases are subject to the vagaries of fashion. If I attempt to defend gender-change, I can expect vocal support from the trans community. An attempt to defend a change of race would be much less successful, and could generate efforts to silence me.

Such opposition may arise from a combination of unstated reasons – for example, that the issue of race-change potentially holds the trans community up to ridicule, or that it denigrates the suffering experienced by racial minorities.

Nonetheless, to attempt to defend the possibility of age-change would, it seems, put one completely beyond the pale. This is not because a change of age is necessarily less logical than a change of gender or race, but because ageism has been much less subject to theorisation – for reasons that are cultural rather than logical – than have racism or various forms of gender discrimination.[32]

Totalitarianism of the mind appears across the political spectrum, though it is sometimes difficult to pin it down politically. Is verbal opposition to the expression of extreme forms of Islamism a left or right position, or simply a justifiable resistance to what is itself a form of intolerance? Allegations of anti-Semitism may be aimed either by the left, at neo-Nazis, or by the right, at left-wing opponents of the policies of Israel. The most recent example of the latter was the sustained media attack on the UK Labour Party, which – while it may have had some justification – was carried to unwarranted extremes.

INTOLERANCE

Various forms of mental totalitarianism have one thing in common: an intolerance of the opinions of others, often coupled with a desire to silence them. This is linked to an often-irrational devotion to one's own position, or to the position of the group with which one identifies – an orientation that might be summed up in the term 'groupthink'. The syndrome may involve a corresponding adherence to the practice of 'cancel culture': the desire to deny someone a hearing because they disagree with a viewpoint to which one subscribes. This may even take the form of a concerted attempt to wreck someone's career, or otherwise to disadvantage them in a major way.

The phrase 'political correctness' originally derived from the kind of party-line totalitarian thinking characteristic of Stalinist countries and political parties, and the means used to enforce ideological conformity. The latter included purges, show trials and ritualised forms of self-condemnation. The terms 'political correctness' and 'political incorrectness' are normally used parodically nowadays, and with a libertarian slant. Counterintuitively, the first normally has a negative sense, denoting a stifling orthodoxy, while the second usually has a positive sense, having the meaning of a liberating, if challenging, heterodoxy.

The term 'political correctness' has been used by the political right and conservatives to denote the perceived excesses of the left and progressives, particularly in regard to issues of race and gender – but seldom vice versa. Internal struggles over political correctness are also manifest among the left and progressives, with conservatives and libertarians watching from the sidelines in gleeful fascination. One example is the struggle between proponents of trans rights and radical feminists as to whether trans women rightly belong to the category 'women' or not.

It should be noted that conservative thought manifests its own forms of mental totalitarianism, including the knee-jerk use of blanket phrases of dismissal like 'cultural Marxism'. This phrase is often used incorrectly to denote postmodernism, which in philosophical terms – the denial of epistemological realism – is actually the opposite of Marxism.[33] Individuals proposing to speak against conservative norms – around abortion, the policies of Israel vis-à-vis the Palestinians, or militarism – have been censored by the right. Nonetheless, as Kaufmann points out, the problem is mainly to be found on the Left.[34]

While many rightists are not racists, racism is found almost exclusively on the right, and it is explicitly or implicitly totalitarian, as we have seen. Conspiracy theories, rife on the far right, are often the result of a skewed interpretation of reality, whereby particular groupings (like the Jews) are seen as being the root of all evil. On the other hand, accusations of anti-Semitism, sometimes exaggerated, have been used to undermine the position of the British Labour Party, or at least of the left within it.

CYNICAL THEORY

Cynical Theories, a recent book by Helen Pluckrose and James Lindsay, is, on the face of it, a breath of fresh air.[35] It offers a comprehensive summation and critique of the phenomenon of ideological intolerance. The authors' argument is that the recent rise of the politics of identity (particularly in the realm of racial and sexual politics) involves a large-scale use, or rather misuse, of the theoretical position of postmodernism. Postmodernism is rooted in the writings of such authors as Michel Foucault, Jacques Derrida and Jean-François Lyotard; it involves the rejection of traditional framing accounts or metanarratives (such as Marxism and Christianity) in favour of a radical deconstruction that calls in question what we can know, or say, about the world.

In the view of the authors, Cynical Theory misuses postmodernism, mainly by 'reifying' it so that – in opposition to postmodernism's original impetus – it turns into a kind of dogma or metanarrative itself, focused on issues of identity. Cynical Theory consequently involves the conflation of 'is' and 'ought' – description and prescription – so that scholarship and activism become indistinguishable. This, the authors argue, has enormous, and largely negative, political and social consequences.

It may be noted here that this position – the conflation of 'is' and 'ought' – was famously embodied by Karl Marx in one of his 'Theses on Feuerbach', where he argued that 'philosophers have only attempted to interpret the world in various ways; the point, however, is to change it.' Interpretation is ostensibly value-neutral,[36] while the desire to change something is based on the value judgement that the given situation is bad and should be replaced with a better one. The failure to distinguish 'is' and 'ought' goes back a long way in radical thought.

Pluckrose and Lindsay argue that the advocacy of a particular 'ought', as distinct from a detached assessment of 'is', is normally associated with churches, not universities[37] – a point that, however, ignores the fact that universities originally developed under the aegis of the church. The authors also argue that what they call 'applied postmodernism' weakens the academy by making it more like a church, substituting the focus on 'ought' for the focus on 'is'.[38]

This signals what may be an urgent need – that of secularising the university by moving away from 'applied postmodernism', detaching the search for truth from that of the search for spiritual comfort. The latter is, arguably, the appropriate province of the church, synagogue or mosque, not of the academy. Once again, the political importance of secularisation raises its head.

In contrast to what they describe, and denigrate, as Cynical Theory, Pluckrose and Lindsay laud liberalism[39] and the value of science; they cite the positive aspects of the contemporary world that are often overlooked by Cynical Theory. Nevertheless, the authors make no attempt to elaborate or defend the theoretical opposites of postmodernism – for example, realism, conventional scientific method (Popper seems to hover in the background of the book but is nowhere cited) and the correspondence theory of truth. These are taken for granted, on the basis that they work and have given us the benefits of modern society.

Curiously, there is not – that I noticed, at any rate – a single mention of global warming or indeed of any other environmental issue in the book. A neglect that apparently characterises both Cynical Theory (insofar as it focuses on issues of human identity rather than the natural environment) and its most trenchant critics.

Environmental politics, and the science that underlies it, doesn't just raise issues for the Cynical Theory that has tended to overlook this crucial area. It also raises questions for its critics, such as the authors of *Cynical Theories*, who tend to ignore the downside of science and technology, and of a society based on them.

To take the Covid-19 pandemic as a case in point, either it arose from a combination of deforestation, animal exploitation and globalisation, or it came about as the result of a lab escape (which is apparently less likely, according to the current consensus). In either case, the pandemic exposes the limitations of our society in alarming ways – ways that are inadequately addressed either by identity politics or by its science-based opposition.

Pluckrose and Lindsay criticise the concept of 'research justice', which holds that science, reason and objectivity have been overvalued as means of obtaining knowledge. At the same time, according to the mindset they critique, emotion, experience, tradition and spirituality have been undervalued.[40]

Nonetheless, a blanket dismissal of such concerns – such as characterises the stance of the two authors – ignores the negative environmental outcomes of science and technology, the prioritisation of practical results over 'pure' science, and the relationship between scientific method and 'masculine' modes of thought, with their tendency towards domination and control.[41] There is also the influence of economics, power, status and psychological conservatism on the practice of science, each of which often militates against the triumph of truth (if, indeed, there is such a thing as truth).[42]

Putting such issues aside for the moment, *Cynical Theories* is an alarming, though often entertaining, critical account of how one particular mindset, which sometimes began with the best motives, resulted in over-extending itself. Such an over-extension had potentially totalitarian implications, somewhat ironically becoming a dominant metanarrative itself.

The suspicion of Western values means that it becomes difficult to criticise the violation of human rights in strict Islamic countries without opening up the issue of the implied superiority of occidental norms, or the discussion ending with an ascription of the ultimate blame to the West. According to the authors, the focus on colonialism as the root of all the problems means, in practice, the neglect of the rights of women and of minorities in strict Islamic countries.[43]

Their position on this is surely to be endorsed. In a recent case in Iran, a female human rights lawyer was sentenced to thirty-eight years in prison and 148 lashes, illustrating the cruelty and barbarity of the legal system in that (Shia) theocratic state.[44] In a well-known historical example from (Sunni) Saudi Arabia, the bizarrely named 'Committee for the Promotion of Virtue and the Prevention of Vice' – a so-called morality police – forced teenage girls to stay inside a burning building because they were inappropriately dressed to appear in public. Fifteen died.[45]

It might be argued that few contemporary examples of the excesses of Islamic theocracy can outweigh the historical brutality of the Christian Inquisition. Nevertheless, Christian societies have undergone, under much protest, a process of secular enlightenment over the centuries. That process has tended to mitigate the negative influence of religion on society – though it has had its own downside, as mentioned later in this chapter. Islam awaits its own Enlightenment.

Nor, it should be added, does the solution lie merely in enhanced secularism: the secular regimes of Hitler, Stalin and Pol Pot far outdid any historical religious forms of repression – though availing, in each case, of technological aids to extermination that were unavailable to the likes of Torquemada or Louis XIV. The contemporary persecution of the Muslim Uighurs in China, largely a blind spot for the left in the West, is a further example of the excesses of a secular society.[46]

It appears that neither religious values nor a secular society are sufficient for a healthily functioning socio-political system. The nearest approximation we have to the latter – for example, the Scandinavian countries – are those which appear to be secular on the surface, but in which religious values (specifically the widely agreed value of equality) play a major role, though largely at an unconscious level.

In terms of postmodernism's influence on the analysis of racism, Pluckrose and Lindsay cite the way in which a focus on discourse and power leads to a displacement of issues such as material lack. They admit, however, that the analysis in terms of race tends to be less obscure than, for example, the analyses involved in postcolonial and queer theories.[47] The perspective of intersectionality, whereby multiple forms of victimisation may need to be analysed in any particular case, can lead to problematic situations when such priorities clash with one another.[48]

Feminism, the authors argue, has been a victim of its own success. Progress towards sexual equality had left feminists with little to do – top-down models in terms of patriarchy and oppression had begun to seem less convincing. This problem was solved by intersectional thought, which opened up new possibilities of enquiry – in particular, within feminism itself.[49] One notable, and important, casualty of intersectionality is the marginalisation of economic class in terms of the problems faced by women, and by racial and sexual minorities.[50]

With an echo of Mark Fisher's point cited earlier in this chapter, Pluckrose and Lindsay note the fear that left politics has been hijacked by middle-class academics, and that this could impel working class voters towards the right.[51] They point out that economic class tends not to be mentioned unless it is intersectionally linked to some other kind of identity. As a consequence, many economically disadvantaged people tend

166

to feel estranged from the left. The authors note the irony of a privilege-questioning movement led by people who are themselves privileged in educational, social and economic terms.[52]

The litany of complaints that Pluckrose and Lindsay cite against Cynical Theory includes the criticism that it utilises the double bind (you should try to understand marginalised people on their own terms, but not try to get them to explain their knowledge).[53] By assigning evidence and reason to the West, they argue, Cynical Theory implicitly denigrates non-occidental cultures.[54] It is intolerant of disagreement,[55] and conflates education with a quasi-religious activism.[56] The last-mentioned (confusion of the search for justice with the search for truth) is an important point, since we cannot outline in advance the political implications of the aspiration towards truth.

In the terms of the authors, Social Justice theory has become a new religion, inimical to science and criticism. Ironically, postmodernism itself has facilitated the institution of a new religion – one that hallows victimhood.[57] The authors cite the fallout of 'Social Justice in action', referring to people losing jobs for transgressing the norms of the new metanarrative. They cite deplatforming and restrictions on freedom of speech, attempts to enforce conformity in the sphere of publishing,[58] and attacks on showbusiness figures who have departed from the straight and narrow path of political orthodoxy.[59] Even mathematics is not exempt from the attacks of Cynical Theory, due to 'its focus on objectivity and proof and because of disparate outcomes in mathematics education across racial groups'.[60]

Indeed, excesses of zeal in the area of political correctness are legion. One local example occurred recently when a prominent Dublin hotel ordered the removal of a group of statues of African women; they had stood outside the building for over a century, and were removed on the (erroneous, as it turned out) grounds that the statues in question depicted slaves. The statues were reinstated.[61]

Pluckrose and Lindsay explain the failure of many university administrations to defend freedom of debate by citing the increasing bureaucratisation and commercialisation of universities, with the concomitant sidelining of academic freedom. They point out that online platforms are subject to criticism for restricting the freedom of those who transgress Social Justice norms – though such platforms also come under fire for allowing the spread of fake news and far-right extremism.[62]

The issue of the transformation of the university – from its origins in religion to a bastion of the Enlightenment to its current morphing into an outpost of neoliberal capitalism – is a matter of huge concern, signalling the marginalisation of traditional intellectual values such as freedom of speech. In a sense, the university seems to be returning to its religious roots, and not in any positive way. The search for truth becomes overshadowed by the desire to adhere to the dictates of political orthodoxy under the quasi-religious reign of profit maximisation.

Universities are, to a great extent, the intellectual backbone of our society. Their status in that regard is currently under threat, from a combination of managerialism and neoliberalism at an institutional level, and a wish for the reinforcement of accepted values (as distinct from welcoming challenging ideas). Recently, as an example of the last-mentioned, the world-famous author Richard Dawkins was disinvited from the oldest debating society in the world (the College Historical Society at Trinity College Dublin) because of disagreement with some of his views on social issues.[63]

Pluckrose and Lindsay argue that the focus on minute examples of deviation from political correctness is indicative of a society devoid of 'directly life-threatening' issues.[64] This seems a rather odd remark, however, in the era of global warming, the collapse of biodiversity, the threat of nuclear and biological terrorism, and the rise of new forms of right-wing extremism. Indeed, one of the features of the book is a somewhat unquestioning adherence to the notion of progress.

Nonetheless, the authors' conclusions in regard to Cynical Theory are hard to argue with: that its dogmatism risks provoking a right-wing, authoritarian backlash, and that secularism is an important component of a free society that denies the right to impose opinions on others.

'Declarations of *ought* have replaced the search for what *is*.'[65] The authors believe – correctly – that the process should be reversed. The problem, though, is that it's not that easy to disentangle 'ought' from 'is' (as, indeed, the preceding sentence illustrates). The question of why truth should be valued over falsity, fiction or illusion is seldom explored; it is taken as a given, though it may have something to do with the fact that human societies are built on trust.

Science is seldom pure, and is often vitiated by issues of power, status, commerce, and intellectual conservatism ('misoneism', or dislike of the new). While scientists may believe at a conscious level that they are motivated by the search for truth, the reality may be more complex.

Furthermore, the apparently dispassionate search for truth may involve the marginalisation of qualities such as compassion – resulting, for example, in the suffering of laboratory animals. There is an argument that the scientific method, as it is generally accepted, involves an element of domination, summed up in the term 'sado-dispassionate', coined by the feminist theorist Val Plumwood.[66] Scientists often deploy phallic imagery in descriptions of the scientific method and its application, so that it is not that far-fetched to regard scientific practice as involving masculine role-playing.[67]

The pure search for scientific truth is typically channelled into the search for practical applications, often with a military or commercial dimension. Indeed, the notion of an abstract truth involves an 'ought', or valuation, since there is no clear reason, on the face of it, why truth should be preferred to falsity. In fact, it might be argued that the search for truth is itself a kind of religious quest.

Indeed, one influential historian, Lynn White, assigns to Christianity the credit – or rather the blame – for our modern society dominated by science and technology, with its catastrophic environmental consequences.[68] Nonetheless, this might be seen as an overly cynical view, if not itself an example of Cynical Theory that ignores the positive contributions of science and technology to human well-being.

ENLIGHTENMENT

Dialectic of Enlightenment, a scathing critique of modernity (first published in 1944), is a book often attacked as the apex of cultural Marxism by people who, one suspects, have read it only cursorily, if at all. The authors, Theodor Adorno and Max Horkheimer, point out the Enlightenment suspicion of whatever cannot be calculated or utilised. Enlightenment, in their analysis, is totalitarian.[69] Humanity is alienated from nature, which turns into an object.[70] Enlightenment involves the domination and subjection of nature.[71] The process is decided from the beginning;[72] the means is elevated to the status of an end in itself.[73]

The viewpoint of Adorno and Horkheimer may be seen as somewhat extreme – the positive contributions of Enlightenment-based science are ignored. To take one contemporary example, global warming theory – which in its political application challenges the whole basis of industrial society – grew out of scientific research, though it took decades to infiltrate the mainstream of political thinking. Indeed, the process is still in train.

The negative side of contemporary scientific progress, however, is represented by such prospects as that of human-animal hybrids, which raise deep ethical, cultural and perhaps even existential issues.[74]

It should be said that Adorno and Horkheimer, writing in the middle of the twentieth century, did not possess a crystal ball. Their analysis is suggestive of a negative side to Enlightenment thought, but is not an all-encompassing revelation of the basic negativity of modernity.

Nonetheless, the authors offer an incisive critique of the Enlightenment mindset, and one that has been extremely influential. They write, 'Thinking objectifies itself to become an automatic, self-activating process; an impersonation of the machine that it produces itself so that ultimately the machine can replace it.'[75] This seems an uncanny anticipation of issues in our own time around artificial intelligence.

For Horkheimer and Adorno, fascism was a much more recent phenomenon than it is for us. Fascism, from their perspective, involves the triumph of (totalitarian) Enlightenment calculability, treating humans as things.[76] In their view, the dirty secret of Enlightenment rationality is that it is impossible to find, in reason, a cogent argument against murder – a lack exploited by writers like the Marquis de Sade and Nietzsche.[77]

The argument seems defensible as far as it goes, insofar as reason is morally neutral: it is at best a useful tool, like a knife. You can use a knife to make a sandwich, or to kill your grandmother. Reason doesn't have a moral or ethical dimension, nor can it justifiably claim to have one. The problem arises when reason becomes the be-all and end-all of thought and action.

Sade and Nietzsche may be considered as belonging to the dark side of Western philosophy – writers who made domination central to their philosophy, and indeed celebrated it. Enlightenment rationality was in their thought taken to its destructive extreme. In contrast, the tendency of modern (post-fascist) attitudes is to exalt the values of, for example, equality and compassion. Such values, absorbed from religion, form the (largely untheorised) basis of the contemporary liberal, secular mindset.

In the terms of Adorno and Horkheimer, moral nihilism lurks within Enlightenment: our popular culture echoes the political culture of fascism. For example, advertising, with its continuous repetition, recalls totalitarian watchwords such as 'Blitzkrieg'.[78] This raises the issue of mind-control by the contemporary advertising industry, and of widely disseminated catchphrases (such as 'the new normal') within what passes for media-disseminated news. These seem to recall the propagandistic methods of historical fascism.

One element of the totalitarian nature of fascism, in the view of Adorno and Horkheimer, is that 'it seeks to make the rebellion of suppressed nature against domination directly useful to domination.'[79] Such insights have a vital resonance in the context of the recent Trumpian misdirection; here, the oppressed strata of society, rather than supporting their potential liberators, flocked to the far right – including those who could institute or facilitate new forms of oppression.

To sum up, the supposedly value-free search for truth has its own downside in an Enlightenment mindset, whose negative aspect is often ignored. Cynical Theory has an unsettling totalitarian potential, but so does the 'scientific' Enlightenment-based mindset that its opponents rely on – despite the fact that most defenders of Enlightenment, which includes most scientists, are unaware of that potential.

CONCLUSION

A phenomenon that has recently arisen has been a kind of unconscious adaptation of Cynical Theory – but this time with an apparently right-wing rather than left-wing dimension. (In both forms, however, there are anti-establishment leanings.)

Conspiracy theories in regard to the rollout of 5G, vaccination, Covid regulations, the deep state, the Great Reset, chemtrails, geoengineering, weather modification, and so on, involve a new morphing, or perhaps deformation, of Cynical Theory. This innovation focuses specifically on the role of science and technology in society, the influence of commercial priorities on both, and science and technology's overreaching effect on government.

Conspiracy theories are very much a pale imitation of the more established Cynical Theory, and are for the most part ideologically at odds with any right-on mindset. Indeed, they tend to operate in the outer suburbs of intellectual respectability,[80] if not in the actual boondocks – though the reasons for such relegation may vary in terms of their justifiability. To take one example, the sovereign citizen movement[81] whereby citizens claim rights in defiance of the law as conventionally understood and implemented, may be viewed as surreal nonsense. Nonetheless, its bizarre claims to legal validity may function to call in question – whether consciously or not – the somewhat fragile, unspoken and taken-for-granted claims to authority of the state itself. This authority is, to a considerable extent, based on force, manipulation, and various forms of censorship, whether overt or covert, under the guise of pious fictions, such as that of the social contract.[82]

Adherents of such conspiracy theories may indeed regard themselves as conservatives rather than progressives, though their complaints about, for example, media control and the role of the pharmaceutical industry may echo more traditional left-wing criticisms. Such criticisms have been largely muted on the left in recent times, under media influence and the normal pressures of intellectual consensus and conformity. Besides conservatives, conspiracy theorists often include people who would normally be regarded as apolitical; their sentiments may be exploited – as in the case of Covid-19 politics – by right-wing elements for the latter's own purposes.[83]

At the same time, in the pandemic era, the left – even in its libertarian forms – manifests a widespread faithfulness to the official 'tackling Covid-19' regime, which combines the power of government and media, the medical and scientific establishment, and the pharmaceutical industry. Such a combination is one towards which, under normal circumstances, one might expect a greater degree of scepticism from the left.

This fracturing of cultural politics promises to further problematise an already complex oppositional situation – one arising from the role of science in society, and the control it exerts over our lives. Such control is less visible; it appears, on the surface, more benign than the apparent desire of Cynical Theory, the cultural politics of identity, to impose an ideological strait-jacket on our thoughts and actions.

Nevertheless, the intellectual conformity and media control of Covid orthodoxy is as open to criticism as is the ideological conformity that the scientific perspective – as manifest in the book *Cynical Theories* – rightly opposes. And as long as the left allow the right to control the emerging movement that questions the all-encompassing role of science and technology in shaping our lives, the left hands a further gift to its opponents on the extreme right – whose overriding political aim is to stifle freedom in the name of defending it.

The focus of the cultural left on postmodernist-influenced identity politics risks not only strengthening reactionary forces on the right but also alienating a new generation whose main concern is, and should be, to save the world from burning up under the pressures of industrial capitalism. This issue, together with that of economic inequality, is considerably more pressing, and more deserving of the expenditure of political energy, than the enforcement of correct pronouns. There is a strong case to be made for the use of kind, polite and respectful language – but as something to be encouraged, not imposed in a process of domination disguised as liberation.

Chapter 7

THE THREAT OF UNIVERSAL SURVEILLANCE

I n an era dominated by technology, the all-seeing eye of the state
combines, and interacts, with the private, profit-maximising sphere.
This combination may serve to completely undermine the crucial
values of privacy and freedom.[1]

Both political and economic security are under threat, and major
powers are struggling to update their systems to deal with the rapidly
developing erosion of privacy.[2] At the same time, the spread of information technology threatens to influence the democratic system in
unprecedented ways, through the microtargeting of voters.[3]

Increasingly, algorithms (procedures for accomplishing specific pro-
jects) seem to be in control, with the prospect of unlimited power over
our lives. This potential sphere of influence includes the market system
itself, and encompasses the manipulation of demand.

Technological developments once again make thinkable the democratisation of planning (i.e. socialism) – a utopian or dystopian scenario,
depending on how you look at it. A definitely dystopian prospect is the
creation of a kind of science-fictional 'Borg' or hive mind.[4]

As well as the danger to privacy, there is a threat to the concept
of truth. This occurs through fake news on the one hand, and growing censorship on the other. We have seen the development of online
echo chambers whereby anything that runs counter to the consensus

is screened out. There is also widespread commercial manipulation via search engines and social networks.

Simultaneously, the prospect of a cashless society[5] threatens to destabilise individual economic security. If your assets can be confiscated with the click of a computer mouse – by the bank, the state or both – this may render you powerless against the control of government, or government in tandem with powerful financial interests. A sudden unexpected bank holiday, and a bank bail-in, are all it would take to strip savers of their assets, or at least those not informed enough to scent the danger in advance, shifting their money somewhere safer. This threat has, in recent years, fed into the rise in the price of gold and the growth of cryptocurrencies – particularly the meteoric ascent and subsequent descent of bitcoin.

This is not to mention the threat of online criminal activity to financial security, and of political hackers from enemy states. If you can't stash actual cash, your freedom and status are diminished to that extent.

In our brave new technological world, genetic data becomes a commodity to be bought and sold. Such a situation raises forebodings about whatever technological security may remain for individual citizens.

Current dangers include issues involved in facial recognition software,[6] data mining, digital and video surveillance, cyberstalking, online shaming, revenge porn, doxing (online divulging of private information), identity theft and the threat to digital security through developments in quantum computing.

One might add to this the cloning of human voices, the deep fake phenomenon of false hyper-realistic depictions,[7] digital prediction of the future behaviour of citizens or employees, Byzantine online contracts, and terms of condition and privacy agreements that no one has time to read.

Who, in the worst dystopian nightmares of the early twentieth century, would have imagined that the 'right to be forgotten' would raise its head as one of the most urgent priorities of the coming century?

Cloud computing, embedded chips, machine learning, smart homes, driverless cars, all loom on the horizon. The 'internet of things' involving objects in constant communication with one another, raises the possibilities of mass surveillance. Artificial intelligence and a myriad of other benefits, real or imagined, are dangled in front of us to entice us into a technological society for which, to say the least, we are ill-prepared.

The spectre of artificial intelligence calls in question the very survival of the human species, except as pets or slaves – which may be worse than annihilation itself.[8]

The Chinese social credit system, which rewards good (or socially acceptable) behaviour and punishes bad (or socially unacceptable) behaviour, looms as an example of the actions of a paternalistic state that knows best, or thinks it knows best, or at least pays lip service to the idea that it knows best.

In the West, prominent figures such as Edward Snowden have tried to stem the tide of impending techno-totalitarianism, though with limited success and at a heavy price. Writing about Snowden's revelation of data collection by GCHQ (Government Communications Headquarters) in the United Kingdom, Anthony Lester points out that 'instead of identifying specific people who pose a threat and then putting them under surveillance, the idea is to put everyone under surveillance and decide later who poses a threat.'[9]

The uncontrolled use of metadata (information about data excluding its content) by government surveillance systems, often in tandem with capitalist corporations, threatens to undermine not only privacy but also public confidence in corporations themselves. In the United States, this has led to some cross-party opposition to an out-of-control system of surveillance.[10]

Snowden's revelations had included evidence of the NSA (National Security Agency) infiltrating links to major internet companies' data centres.[11]

According to journalist Glenn Greenwald, an analytical tool called XKeyscore can function as a means of widespread internet surveillance, allowing analysts to search through huge online databases, accessing content and search history, as well as metadata. Both current and historical activity can apparently be accessed. The target of attention can include social media, including Facebook chats and private messages. While data can be stored only for a limited amount of time due to storage limitations, 'interesting' data can be kept for much longer. The existence of such a surveillance tool illustrated Snowden's assertion, quoted by Greenwald, that he 'could wiretap anyone, from you or your accountant, to a federal judge or even the president, if I had a personal email'.[12]

Snowden himself describes the symbiotic relationship between the intelligence community and the private companies:

> IC [intelligence community] directors ask Congress for money to rent contract workers from private companies, congresspeople approve that money, and then those IC directors and congresspeople are rewarded, after they retire from office, by being given high-paying positions and consultancies with the very companies they've just enriched.[13]

American computer companies, subject to US law, are governed by classified US policies that permit the US government to spy on everyone.[14] In Snowden's terms, the ultimate goal of the NSA is to store all collected files forever,[15] redefining the personal communications of citizens as potential intelligence.[16]

As Snowden expresses it, the metadata collected can tell your surveillant virtually everything they would want to know about you, with the exception of your personal thoughts:[17] 'Once the ubiquity of collection was combined with the permanency of storage, all any government had to do was select a person or a group to scapegoat and go searching [...] for evidence of a suitable crime.'[18] From a constitutional perspective, Snowden points out, the basic laws of the United States are actually there to make the job of law enforcement more difficult rather than less.[19] In Snowden's terms, the major clash of our time is that between authoritarianism on the one hand, and liberal democracy and privacy on the other.[20]

On the positive side, the US Court of Appeals for the Ninth Circuit found, in 2020, that the mass surveillance of US individuals' phone records – which Snowden had exposed – was in violation of law, and possibly of the US Constitution.[21] Snowden approvingly cites pushback by major corporations – for example, Apple's development of strong default encryption for its iPhones and iPads.[22] Journalist Yasha Levine, however, believes that resistance to government surveillance by corporations is largely an illusion. Crypto apps, he believes, offer an illusory promise of technological security and are a poor substitute for political and democratic resistance to surveillance.[23]

Issues of privacy, freedom, dignity, individual rights and civil liberties tend to be a long way down the list of governmental priorities, if indeed they feature at all. Since computer-facilitated access to social media is virtually an extension of the human brain, the demand of private and governmental systems to inspect our social media accounts – for example, in the case of potential incoming travellers from abroad – verges on being an insistence on reading our minds.[24]

The vexing goal that lay beyond the reach of Orwell's thought police – that of mind-reading – seems on the verge of being reached.

Developments in the sphere of what might be termed 'techno-telepathy' (machine–brain interfaces) bring the scenario closer.[25] As the Bible remarks, though in a different context, 'all things *are* naked and opened unto the eyes of him with whom we have to do.'[26] The corporate state threatens to replace divinity as the omniscient power in our lives.

On the positive side, while there are some serious threats to individual privacy, there are welcome political developments, such as the General Data Protection Regulation (GDPR) in Europe. The obstacles such initiatives seek to overcome, however, are formidable.

In 2017, a former Irish chief justice claimed that current data retention law amounts to 'mass surveillance'.[27] Journalist Karlin Lillington notes that the EU, with its Common Identity Repository, has 'a database that brings together a variety of biometric data held in systems used by law enforcement, border control and immigration agencies'.[28] Lillington's columns in *The Irish Times* have, over the years, offered a relentless exposure of the threat of a surveillance society – including the specific, and ongoing, issue of the Irish Public Services Card.[29] In the context of the pandemic, she has flagged the possibility of vaccine passports as a threat to privacy.[30]

The Covid-19 pandemic opened up a further issue on the surveillance front, with the development of track and trace technology that utilises our personal data. Citing examples from China, Hong Kong and Israel, Jennifer O'Connell writes, 'All over the world, another red line is being washed away. Covid-19 is helping to normalise […] mass government surveillance of citizens.' She points out that supposedly temporary measures often become permanent – we may have difficulty getting back our rights.[31]

Klaus Schwab and Thierry Malleret note the 'coercive and intrusive' digital tracing methods employed in Hong Kong and South Korea. Individuals were tracked non-consensually via mobile phones, credit cards, video surveillance (in South Korea) and electronic bracelets (in Hong Kong).[32] The authors surmise that the surrender of individual rights to the power of the state may result in a situation where countries have been transformed in such a way that people no longer want to live in them.[33]

They speculate that, as the health crisis recedes, there will be a move towards enhanced corporate surveillance of workforces. Health and safety will be cited to justify increased surveillance. The authors argue that such surveillance methods are likely to stay in place, even after the health issue has receded: in terms of monitoring employee productivity, employers have much to gain and nothing to lose.[34] They cite writer Evgeny Morozov's foreboding of a techno-totalitarian surveillance state following the pandemic – one based on a philosophy of punitive solutionism and focused on technological repression.[35]

Yuval Noah Harari, a historian, argues that the choice we face is that between 'totalitarian surveillance and citizen empowerment'. Sensors and algorithms have replaced the traditional methods of the secret police. In China, mass surveillance is effected through the monitoring of smartphones and facial recognition. In Israel, anti-terrorism technology, through an emergency decree, was directed towards tracking corona-virus patients. The direction is towards health-oriented under-the-skin surveillance. Surveillance technology wheeled in to counter pandemics could be utilised to monitor the political reactions of the population. Harari notes that 'temporary measures have a nasty habit of outlasting emergencies, especially as there is always a new emergency lurking on the horizon.' In his view, People will tend to choose health over privacy. Harari urges citizen empowerment as an alternative to totalitarian sur-veillance – surveillance technology works both ways, and can be used on governments as well as by them.[36]

The overall problem, even apart from the pandemic and associated countermeasures, is that with the unprecedented growth of technology, the impetus towards power on the part of the state apparatus tends to marginalise values such as freedom, privacy and autonomy. In addition, the profit-maximising drive of the capitalist system tends to sweep away whatever freedoms may still remain. The paradox is that an excess of freedom in the economic realm may lead to the diminution of liberty in other, no less important, spheres of life.

In this context, one might note that individual freedom and corporate freedom do not necessarily coincide. There is no contradiction between arguing for the enhancement of freedom of the individual and for the simultaneous limitation, where necessary, of the freedom of corporations.

An increasingly close relationship between capitalism and the state is manifest in a recent form of feudal corporatism – what might be termed 'plutosocialism', or socialism for the wealthy, in the form of handouts to the rich in the spheres of business and finance. In this system, the inter-ests of the large majority of the populace are marginalised (socialism for the rich, capitalism for everyone else.) Since the left is sometimes seen as complicit in the oppressive system – through bank bailouts, corporate welfare, globalised trade, support for militarist adventurism and bur-geoning bureaucracy – bewildered working people may turn to the right for aid and comfort, as has happened notoriously in the US.

Added to this, the traditional and somewhat stereotypical left–right conceptual divide means that whatever libertarian desires may be common to both sides – potentially, at least – are sidelined through the handy device of divide and rule. If you question state control, you risk being condemned as right-wing; if you raise issues concerning the domination of billionaires, you are consigned to the left. It is possible to be suspicious of the excesses of both state and corporate power, but that doesn't fit well into the current left vs right political dichotomy as an all-explanatory mechanism.

Politically, a key priority is the development of a movement that defends the rights of consumers, as well as the traditional emphasis on the rights of workers (i.e. producers). This is particularly crucial given the eroding distinction between producers and consumers, consequent on the ubiquitous use of digital media – an issue to be examined in the following section of this chapter.

In this connection might be mentioned the uncertain philosophical status of such (supposedly) fundamental values as freedom, dignity and privacy, and the vexed issue of rights connected to them. There may or may not be such things as natural rights, but no one has ever seen them. Consequently, an appeal to such invisible entities has unstable foundations.

Once rights are enshrined in law, however, they have a tangible, and enforceable, reality. If enough people believe that freedom, dignity and privacy are desirable values, then those values will tend to prevail; they will be established and consolidated in law, in the form of legal rights, regardless of whatever philosophical foundations they may or may not have.

On the other hand, if enough people don't know, or don't care, about such values, they will tend to evaporate. To some extent, it doesn't matter whether or not our laws are founded on myths and fictions: if a sufficient number of people believe in the desirability of the values that such laws enshrine, the laws will accomplish their goals.

It should be added that not everything about technology – digital technology in particular – is negative. It is relatively easy to check in to the Grand Hotel Abyss, and declare freedom to be a lost cause.

To take one positive example, the ubiquity of mobile phones and video recording makes it easy to stream and document political demonstrations – including cases where such activities are ignored, or downplayed, by the mainstream media. Such ubiquity also makes it easier to document racist or antisocial behaviour, including inappropriate behaviour on the part of the police, whether in the context of political demonstrations or everyday life. This is part of the wider phenomenon of 'sousveillance', or counter-surveillance of those in authority by those under their control – a political practice that extends to the areas of art, fashion, and associated cultural intervention.[37]

That said, the deep fake phenomenon[38] may soon call in question the authenticity of video imagery, tending to erode the persuasiveness of video evidence. This has both positive and negative implications. The positive implications lie in the fact that the existence of convincing fake videos potentially undermines attempts at, for example, blackmail and revenge porn. If no one can tell if the figure depicted in the video with a Ruritanian sex worker is really you, attempts by the government of Ruritania, or its agents, to blackmail you may fall through. It could, after all, just as easily be a deep fake as a depiction of the real thing.

The negative implications of deep fake developments lie in the danger that they may destabilise genuinely needed evidence of misbehaviour, rendering it invalid. If even video evidence is not to be trusted, who is to say there is an accurate record of wrongdoing, be it that of law-breakers or law-enforcers.

To counter-balance the negativity of the deep fake phenomenon social media – like Facebook and Twitter – makes it easier, in principle, for ordinary people to have a political voice, however much that voice may be limited by the constraints of the system in question, and however much it may be subject to censorship of one kind or another.

Social media in the form of messaging services like WhatsApp can facilitate communication with family, friends, and social and political contacts. Digital technology and genetic tracing make it easy to find long-lost distant relatives – though the downside may be the unwanted capture of our genetic information, in ways that may have negative consequences in the future, if not in the present.

The issue of anonymity – or lack of it – around DNA tracing is a matter of global concern.[39] Stories abound of family breakups consequent on children realising that the people they called their parents were not, actually, their biological parents.[40]

Insurance companies could tailor premiums around genetic predispositions to disease, in the event that they acquired such data.[41] The money to be made – or saved – in the process constitutes a potentially enormous motivation beside which any economic impetus towards individual privacy pales into insignificance. Consequently, action at the political level seems essential in order to halt, or at least slow down, a business-aligned encroachment on freedom.

It is hardly a new observation that technology has both positive and negative aspects,[42] but the problem with contemporary digital technology is that it's progressing so quickly that most of us cannot hope to keep up with the dangers that lurk within it, either immediately or in terms of understanding future perils. There is an ongoing tension between the profit motive (with its veneer of free speech) and the less economically weighty matter of individual privacy.

The rise of a surveillance culture, and the associated phenomenon of social, political and economic manipulation in the context of contemporary technology, is by far the most ominous development in the scenario of techno-dystopia. Nonetheless, it is a somewhat depressing fact that the issue of surveillance has been to the fore of our collective political nightmares for over seventy years, with apparently little effect.

While Orwell and others may have helped to inform the debate, and to stave off some of the worst threats, the growth of technology has opened up the possibilities of surveillance in ways that could not have been imagined in the middle of the twentieth century. Indeed, it sometimes seems as if Orwell's literary nightmare is functioning as a guide to action on the part of the authorities, rather than as a dreadful warning to the populace.

Technological surveillance is a vast subject that I can't hope to cover in any depth. Instead, I will cite some of the most egregious examples, referring – to a large extent – to the recent ground-breaking and essential volume by Shoshana Zuboff, entitled *The Age of Surveillance Capitalism*.[43]

SURVEILLANCE CAPITALISM

Zuboff's book is an investigation of what she calls surveillance capitalism. This involves the transformation of human experience into behavioural data, and the corresponding change of the capitalist system into a system dominated by surveillance. Some of this data becomes what she describes (with an echo of Karl Marx's concepts of surplus labour and surplus value) as a 'behavioural surplus'. In this analysis, the user of technology takes the place of the traditional exploited labourer, who was the focus of Marx's analysis.[44]

According to Zuboff, this behavioural surplus, in turn, is made into 'prediction products' that anticipate human behaviour. These are traded in what she describes (drawing on more recent economic theory and practice) as 'behavioural futures markets'. Human communication, personalities and feelings become sources of behavioural surplus, and the manipulation of behaviour feeds into profit maximisation.

As noted, Zuboff's exposition seems to echo Marx's concepts of surplus labour and surplus value in *Capital*[45] – concepts that Marx applied to the unequal relationship between capitalist and worker, and that are fundamental to his whole investigation and critique of the capitalist system. Far from endorsing the conventional dismissive mantra of 'Marxism = totalitarianism', Zuboff's position reminds us of the libertarian possibilities in applying Marx's thought to the realm of human behaviour. We are all objects of exploitation, insofar as we all participate in the digital realm, and we all need to be freed from that form of subjection.

Marx's traditional analysis of capitalism is that of a vampire that feeds on labour. In contrast, however, surveillance capitalism – in Zuboff's discussion – feeds on human experience itself.[46] She transposes the concept of the exploited individual from proletarian status as in Marx, to the status of someone who is exploited by virtue of his or her activity as (supposed) consumer. The transposition is both persuasive and unsettling.

Insofar as we have been induced into participating in the digital economy, virtually all of us have become, to some extent, objects of exploitation. That said, there is a marked difference between the crippling forms of exploitation endured by the nineteenth-century worker and the exploitation of information in the digital sphere.[47]

Nevertheless, from a political point of view, a key consequence of Zuboff's analysis would seem to be the need for a movement to foreground the interests of digital consumers, insofar as the line between producers and consumers in this area is becoming increasingly blurred.

A political response to the situation Zuboff describes might involve an argument for compensation – perhaps a digital tax repayable to the population through a universal dividend. That would solve only one part of the problem, though, the problem of unfair use of resources. The other part involves infringement on freedom: it is that a large, and increasing, part of our individuality is circulating, out of control, in the public space of the internet.

Zuboff argues that ownership of the means of behavioural modification has supplanted ownership of the means of production as the wellspring of the capitalist system.[48] 'Primitive accumulation' involving the original appropriation of capital is not a once-off phenomenon of the early stages of capitalism, as it was according to Marx's original analysis; it is an ongoing process.[49] From smart-home devices to augmented reality, the overriding goal is 'behavioural surplus capture'.[50]

The 'internet of things' opens up vast surveillance possibilities, in addition to the already-established state monitoring of our activities. It may, with lack of sufficient security, permit hackers to gain access to personal data. These possibilities have been flagged for some considerable time, but have yet to feature significantly in the public mind.[51]

In a society increasingly dominated by technology, 'smart cities' involving the collection of data and its use in management, contribute to the undermining of our freedoms. The concept of medical privacy becomes increasingly meaningless. Our phones become devices for listening to us. Drones will be able to listen to our phone calls, monitor the insides of our homes, track our actions and potentially overpower us.[52]

In theoretical terms, Zuboff argues that users should not be regarded either as workers or customers, or even as the product – rather, they are the sources of the supply of raw material. The products of surveillance capitalism are about predicting our behaviour rather than analysing its current status.[53] Previous resistance to techniques of mass behaviour modification has been largely overcome.[54]

This situation, Zuboff suggests, is in the context of a commercial 'state of exception' whereby high-minded digital ideals become suspended under financial and social pressure. The 'extraction imperative' comes to the fore: users become means to the ends of others rather than ends in themselves.[55]

The political 'state of exception', consequent on the 9/11 attacks, tended to favour the growth of the surveillance phenomenon in the private sphere, producing what Zuboff describes as *surveillance exceptionalism* whereby surveillance was given free reign under the pressure of a threat to national security.[56] This, it might be noted, is an intriguing illustration of the issue already highlighted in the thought of the theorist Giorgio Agamben, whereby normal liberties are suspended under pressure of political circumstances.

Zuboff writes that the defence of free speech in the United States tends to consolidate the defence of property rights, due to a conservative interpretation of the First Amendment which closely links the two kinds of rights.[57] It might be observed here that there is a potential clash between two manifestations of freedom: my freedom to say what I like may clash with your freedom from intrusion into your private affairs. In the context of the capitalist system, it is not difficult to foresee which freedom will tend to triumph; the right to freedom of speech, particularly on the part of media corporations, has greater money-making potential than the individual's right to privacy.[58] In an observation that may be (sadly) outdated, Slavoj Žižek argued around the turn of the millennium for the socialisation of cyberspace rather than a 'retreat into islands of privacy'; the totalitarian potential of cyberspace was in his view a misperception.[59]

This tendency for freedom of speech to triumph over privacy is not necessarily because the former outweighs the latter in a moral sense; however, in the case of a clash, the prevalence of the former is more likely, because it feeds into the exigency of profit more than the latter does. To the extent that the public increasingly values privacy, however, there may be an economic pushback in the form of heightened demand for counter-surveillance software and other means of resistance.

For Zuboff, surveillance capitalism, by ignoring the rights of individuals, claims human experience as raw material to be appropriated for translation into behavioural data. The system of surveillance capitalism then owns and analyses this data – deciding on its use, and asserting rights to the conditions that structure that process.[60]

While the law has not kept pace with the threat to privacy that Zuboff outlines,[61] negative developments have met with some opposition and protest. She cites resistance to practices including digitalisation of literature, bypassing of privacy settings and holding on to search data. Zuboff also anticipates future defiance against drones and neurotransmitters.[62]

For Zuboff, the roots of surveillance capitalism's anti-democratic tendencies don't lie in technology or the state, but in the economic system. The effects of surveillance capitalism are the results of the logic of accumulation.[63] At the core of this new capitalism is 'the original sin of simple robbery'.[64]

Here, there is a restatement of the implicit moral judgement at the heart of Marx's analysis, which seems to be that capitalism is evaluated and condemned on some kind of moral basis. What that basis might be, Marx seldom elaborates. Zuboff, however, makes a valiant attempt throughout her book to defend the values of freedom, privacy and autonomy. In some ways, these values may be seen as being as conservative as they are liberal. This situation of 'crossover' values represents a potentially significant political issue, offering the possibility of transcending the traditional left–right divide.

Nonetheless, the key distinction between leftist and conservative conceptions of freedom is that the former is predicated on the necessity of radical socioeconomic change to deliver the 'realm of freedom' (specifically the socialisation of the means of production to deliver the minimisation, rationalisation and humanisation of work) while the latter is not. Indeed, conservative thought denies claims of the need for social reconstruction as a means towards a freer society. While that basic divergence is unlikely to be overcome, there are other areas – specifically, the defence of freedom – where a crossover politics between libertarians of left, right and centre is conceivable.[65]

Zuboff refers to what she calls the 'apparatus' of inescapable computing that is, or will be, everywhere around us, citing the ubiquitous 'datafication' of all things and processes, whether natural or artificial. Activity in the real world is constantly rendered back to the digital realm, where it becomes data for morphing into predictions.[66] The goal is the domination of reality itself.[67]

One example she cites is that of behavioural monitoring. Among its possibilities, it offers the enticing prospect of the minute control of drivers' behaviour by insurance companies.[68] (That is, as long as drivers haven't been rendered superfluous by driverless cars.[69]) A further example of the process of moving towards a monitoring culture is the growth of surveillance of third level students as a consequence of the increase in online learning, with its worrying implications for privacy.[70]

All of this is under the aegis of what Zuboff describes as 'inevitabilism' – a concept of which she is critical.[71] The idea behind the concept seems to be that a specific event is going to happen anyway; those in power urge you to get used to it. Whatever the case, you will have no choice. The concept of the inevitable recalls Popper's critique of the Marxist utopia. It is regarded as both desirable and destined to arrive – a unity of value and fact.

Nonetheless, from Zuboff's perspective the result of the inevitable is posited as undesirable – a kind of 'negative inevitabilism', perhaps. There is, it should further be pointed out, little obvious consumer enthusiasm for the internet of things – the demand seems almost entirely producer-driven.

As one commentator ironically observes, 'we all know our dishwashers have long harbored a pent up desire for scintillating conversation with our doorknobs'.[72] By and large, the internet of things may be described as a capitalist solution to problems that don't really exist – the traditional formula of the creation of false needs in order to make a profit by fulfilling them.

Zuboff describes the rhetoric of inevitability as being formulated to make us supposedly defenceless against powers that are both irresistible and indifferent.[73] An oppressive bureaucratic tangle, from terms of service to privacy policies, imposes an additional burden that few have time to engage with Cconsequently, most people tend not to do so.[74] For Zuboff, in these circumstances,, the internet of things is transforming into a network of coercion in which everyday activities are in the service of behaviour surplus.[75]

Our mobile phones function as tracking devices, enabling not only the pursuit of those wanted by the law but also the targeting of users by advertisers.[76] Sensors incorporated into clothing offer the means to decipher human body language, as well as to monitor health.[77]

Information on health, it should be noted, is of particular interest to insurance companies; access to it may open up the prospect of premium levels being affected, or even the diminished likelihood of future coverage.

The information power grab and its technological facilitation also tends to undermine traditional patient–physician confidentiality. Like its spiritual counterpart – in the context of the religious confessional – it seems to be going out the window, almost unnoticed.

Facial recognition opens up the possibility of enhanced machine learning of human attributes and behaviour, which in turn greatly increases marketing opportunities.[78] Individuals who are at risk of shifting their brand preference can be aggressively targeted.[79] The prospect Zuboff critically highlights is that we will give up much of our privacy for the convenience consequent on permanent monitoring.[80]

Arising from Zuboff's analysis, it may be observed that few of us remember how comparatively convenient life was before digital technology intervened, with its enticing offer to solve our problems. Technology steps in with an offer to make life smoother for us. Eventually, its seductive alternatives become inescapable, and we become imprisoned in a maze of passwords that can never be safe enough; we become shackled by solutions that open up a myriad of further technical problems, both time-consuming and expensive to resolve.

Most of us are by now familiar with the eternal regress in regard to computer problems: you can't fix problem A because there is a problem B; you can' t fix problem B because there is a problem C. The bottom line is that you need to upgrade to (or purchase) X, Y or Z. For that, however, you may need a new computer. And then arises the issue of transferring files and deleting old files. Without access to an open volcano, the latter may be a feat that is difficult or impossible.

In earlier forms of communication, such issues, including the disposal of no-longer-needed but sensitive information, were largely absent. If you broke your quill pen or ran out of ink, the solution was relatively quick, simple and straightforward. And because writing was somewhat labour-intensive, you had to pause and think before committing pen to writing surface – a situation that had its advantages as well as its challenges.

Technological progress inserts problems, as well as solutions, at every stage. If you need a new car, good luck in finding one that is an automobile rather than a sophisticated computer, requiring a steep learning curve – and probably opening up its own privacy issues as well.

Computer technology starts with an apparently liberating promise. Credit and debit cards, for example, begin as an offer of alternative methods of everyday payment. Eventually, as seems to be happening under the pressure of the pandemic, they become the only means of payment possible. The initial promise of freedom turns into a form of universal constraint: freedom gives way to necessity, and to the prospect of increased control by the state – potentially in tandem with financial institutions – over our financial security.

If banknotes are no longer in use, our vulnerability to state control (specifically, in times of financial crisis, the prospect of bail-ins) increases. For all except the very rich, there is no escape from the machine – with the possible exception of buying land and burying a pot of gold in it (assuming that the possession of gold is not eventually prohibited).

Zuboff describes how the incursions of capitalism in the digital realm were unprecedented. They involved 'invasion by declaration', dispossession, the historical disfavour of government regulation of business, and the parallel favouring of surveillance post-9/11. There has been an increasingly cosy relationship between business and government, and a growing dependency on technology both by businesses and individuals. Revenues are increasingly tied to the prediction imperative. Surveillance capitalists become admired role models, and hype predominates. Alternatives are dismissed in the march towards the 'inevitable' future; mere human thought is marginalised in the march of the all-powerful machine. Obfuscation and obscurantism predominate. In a shock and awe process, velocity negates awareness and overtakes democracy.[81]

To counter the situation outlined above, Zuboff calls for laws that repudiate the legitimacy of surveillance capitalism and impede its fundamental activities – specifically, the transformation of human experience into behavioural data and associated forms of exploitation and manipulation.[82] Zuboff writes (italics in original), '*if industrial civilization flourished at the expense of nature and now threatens to cost us the Earth, an information civilization shaped by surveillance capitalism will thrive at the expense of human nature and threatens to cost us our humanity.*'[83]

The fact that such key terms as 'nature', 'human nature' and 'humanity' are problematic in terms of contemporary thought, should not blind us to the urgency of the problem that Zuboff outlines.

INSTRUMENTARIAN OR TOTALITARIAN?

Somewhat surprisingly, Zuboff rejects the description of the new digital regime as 'totalitarian', suggesting instead the notion of 'instrumentarian power', or control through behaviour modification as distinct from naked domination.

Totalitarianism, she points out, employed genocide and soul-engineering. Zuboff cites the Italian philosopher Giovanni Gentile, with his concept of the 'total': the state as an organic entity to which individual lives are subordinate.[84] In the words of Mussolini:

> Fascism is totalitarian and the Fascist State – a synthesis and a unit inclusive of all values – interprets, develops, and potentates the whole life of a people .... [It] is an inwardly accepted standard and rule of conduct, a discipline of the whole person; it permeates the will no less than the intellect ....sinking deep down into his personality; it dwells in the heart of the man of action and of the thinker, of the artist, and of the man of science: soul of the soul. ... It aims at refashioning not only the forms of life but their content – man, his character and his faith ... entering into the soul and ruling with undisputed sway.[85]

Zuboff notes that the concept of soul-engineering also characterised the thought of Stalin, though in the case of Nazi Germany the movement rather than the state was emphasised.[86]

By contrast, the origins of instrumentarianism are, she argues, in the project of a 'technology of behaviour'. In contradistinction to totalitarianism, which operates through violence, instrumentarianism works through behaviour modification.

The key origin of instrumentarianism's perspective is 'radical behaviourism'.[87] This mindset, Zuboff contends, is rooted in the sinister approach of the behaviourist psychologist B.F. Skinner, which viewed humans as 'others' – the object of scientific experiment and manipulation.[88] This worldview annihilates the concepts of freedom and privacy. In this view, the environment plays a deterministic role on behaviour, and there is an associated desire to control such behaviour.[89]

Zuboff argues that Skinner's instrumentarianism – as elaborated, for example, in his book *Walden II* – is the exact opposite of Orwell's nightmare as set out in *Nineteen Eighty-Four*.[90] This is because the scientific social order that Skinner's utopia embodied replaces force and domination with manipulation. In this nightmare scientocracy, control is focused on behaviour rather than on the human spirit. Totalitarianism and instrumentarianism, for Zuboff, are both nightmares, but they are at opposite ends of the spectrum of horror.

Nonetheless, Zuboff's totalitarianism–instrumentarianism dichotomy seems somewhat overstated. To take one obvious example, Nazism relied heavily, through the perverse genius of Joseph Goebbels, on behavioural manipulation via propaganda in the cultural sphere. While the iron fist was certainly a central feature of Nazism, it was combined with political persuasion – and would have been much less effective without it.

Hitler, for example, made use of his perceived status as an object of attraction for German women by remaining unmarried, until shortly before his death. His mistress Eva Braun was shunted to the sidelines right up to the time of their grotesque, funereal wedding in the Berlin bunker. In some ways, the carrot of ideological attraction was as important for the Nazis as the stick of brute force – the sugar as powerful as the whip. Hitler's power lay in the extent to which he could shape himself to the ideological desires of the German people – desires which the Nazi system and establishment simultaneously, and reciprocally, moulded to their will.

Leaving that example aside, Zuboff's totalitarianism–instrumentarianism dichotomy seems, to some extent, a restatement of the traditional literary polarity between Orwell's dystopia in *Nineteen Eighty-Four* and Huxley's *Brave New World*: the tyranny of despotism versus that of subtle control and manipulation.

The difference is that between the world as a gigantic concentration camp and an enormous sheep pen. Perhaps both analogies are appropriate. In our present experience, rather than the kind of total control attempted – with all its lacunae – by Stalin or Hitler, society is under the aegis of a sophisticated neo-feudal corporate capitalism.

Indeed, the forms of surveillance and control available to our political and economic masters could hardly have been dreamt of by the two most prominent dictators of the twentieth century. Given contemporary technological developments and the possibilities they open up, the dusty files in the offices of the Gestapo and NKVD seem amateurish compared to the kind of total knowledge, and associated power to control society, to which we are moving at present.

The forms of democracy that exist in our time seem to ameliorate, to an extent, the sinister spectre of technological domination. Nevertheless, the prospect of the corporate-dominated surveillance system falling under the control of the total state as a consequence of economic and societal breakdown – not to mention the consequent rise of tyranny – is alarming to say the least.

Zuboff gives the title 'Big Other' to the digital apparatus that confronts us everywhere, with its monopoly on power, and that alienates us from our own behaviour.[91] The goal of universal power is achieved through the offer of convenience.[92] In particular, the internet of things opens up immense opportunities for state surveillance.[93] One specific aspect of the digital apparatus is the possibility of 'predictive policing';[94]

this is reminiscent of the film *Minority Report*, in which future crimes are identified before they happen (the notion of 'pre-crime').

An oft-cited example of a burgeoning technological dystopia is China's social credit system, with its assignment of privilege or penalty in response to behaviour. Admittedly, Zuboff sees this as more of an example of instrumentarianism than of totalitarianism. Nonetheless, in China's case the focus is social rather than (as in the West) economic – an attempt to heal, through technology, the widespread public distrust deriving in part from existing totalitarianism.[95] Social credit makes total-itarianism bearable, or appears to do so at least.

The cornerstone of the social credit system is the judgement defaulter's list, which can impact travel, accommodation, education, career choices and business.[96] The Chinese state is in the process of developing a system where the control of knowledge, in the service of the state's self-perpet-uation, trumps freedom;[97] to that end, it is currently developing a smart city run by artificial intelligence.[98] There are alarming implications for the monitoring and control of people's lives.

The 'Nosedive' episode of the television series *Black Mirror* offers a familiar though chilling outline of the social credit system, if it were to develop in the West. The crucial difference between the dystopian tele-vision episode and the Chinese real-life version, however, is that in the latter, your score does not reflect the judgement of your fellow citizens but manifests the power of the state or corporations.[99]

A similar development in the West might result in an individual's credit score being affected by his or her web browsing. This could have positive as well as negative implications, giving people access to credit who might otherwise be denied it, but the implications for privacy are of major concern.[100]

In the Chinese example, we are back to the old problem endemic in state socialism: that of the self-perpetuating tendencies of the state itself. The recent Chinese hesitancy – to put it charitably – to facilitate the search for the origin of the coronavirus is a case in point. When the search for truth inconveniences the priorities of politics, it is easy to see which is likely to win out – particularly given the top-down centralised power of state social-ism (or perhaps state capitalism, in the case of China). Truth is no more likely to prevail against state power than it is against capitalist power in the West, and perhaps less so. Means are enthroned as ends: freedom of thought is subordinate to political control in the service of the goal of socialism. When ideas are subordinated to social being in a conceptual sense, there is a practical outcome as well: power overrides the search for truth.

The goal of surveillance capitalists, in Zuboff's terms, is the develop-ment of a new society modelled on machine learning.[101] Such a society would replace a supposedly obsolete and inefficient system. She outlines the opposing alternatives: the use of the digital revolution to strengthen democracy, or a future without freedom.[102]

Zuboff's analysis involves a devastating exposure of a technology out of control, dominated by a rampant corporate system that is itself out of control. In combination with an ongoing power grab by the state in the guise of combating crime and terrorism, and public ignorance of an exponentially developing technology's downside, this corporate domina-tion has undoubtedly sinister implications for human freedom.

Danger, it should be observed, lurks even in the ranks of opposition to the technologisation of society. Carl Schmitt and Martin Heidegger, two of the most influential thinkers of the twentieth century – both German – were deeply critical of technology, and the dominant modes of thought associated with it.[103] It may be that their notorious association with Nazism was not as strange as it sounds. Nazism didn't just pervert technology in unprecedented ways: it offered a back-to-nature cultural recipe – one fitting of their slogan 'blood and soil' – to counteract the various alienations of modern life.

These forms of alienation included the ubiquity of technical or tech-nological thinking, and domination by technology. It may be that a future form of fascism, perhaps eco-fascism of some description, may offer a similarly beguiling alternative to the current attempts of technol-ogy to colonise the human soul.[104]

Nonetheless, such a project would be self-contradictory, because no species of fascism could triumph in the modern world without itself employing the very technology that threatens to alienate us from personal and social fulfilment. The cure would be worse than the disease, which is not to say that it may not be tried.

WHERE ARE WE GOING?

All is not lost in the struggle against the form of technological domination manifest in the burgeoning of surveillance capitalism. Zuboff notes and endorses efforts by individuals to assert the right to privacy, specifically under the GDPR.[105] However, the GDPR statements of many companies often use language that is formulated to 'encourage you through the path of least resistance'.[106] This may compromise the effects of the regulations.

On the positive side, Zuboff also cites collaboration between artists and scientists to counteract the all-seeing eye. Examples include devices to defeat facial-recognition software.[107] The overall impression she gives – probably correctly – is that resistance is, and will be, an uphill battle. Nevertheless, there are indications of defiance against the power of the giant technology companies.[108]

However, the possibilities opened up by surveillance developments are daunting.[109] The problem is that resistance to surveillance capitalism, like resistance to previous manifestations of capitalism, is not a straightforward matter.

In the twentieth century, opposition to the depredations of finance capital was notoriously deflected towards support of anti-Semitism ('the socialism of fools') and its political manifestation in Nazism.

In the twenty-first century, instinctive opposition to surveillance capitalism, and the overall power of the state that it represents, often feeds into mass paranoia rather than reasoned analysis; it is displaced onto bizarre conspiracy theories such as QAnon. Weird associated beliefs include the strange notion that Trump and his billionaire backers could, or would wish to, lead the electorate into the promised land of freedom and economic opportunity, liberated from the control of the deep state. Instead of a new freedom, novel forms of potential tyranny loom – the spectre of right-wing authoritarianism.

It should be added that not all paranoia is unfounded – in terms of the old cliché, the fact that you're paranoid doesn't necessarily mean they're not out to get you. And conservative political reactions, though often characterised by bizarre nightmare fantasies, should not necessarily be completely dismissed. The sacrifice of babies on the part of the elite is doubtless a fantasy; however, it is not so far from the truth of contemporary war and military adventurism, with its catastrophic effects on the populations of countries like Iraq and Yemen.

The left are often obsessed with the minutiae of cultural politics, while class issues remain unaddressed – globalism has contributed to the growth of the Rust Belt. To add to the problem, the phenomenon of ideological displacement, intensified by the control of the media, means that political resistance in our time often takes a reactionary rather than a progressive form, focussing on false targets (such as immigration) instead of real ones – those of corporate-capitalist domination.

It should be emphasised that reaction is not always bad, and progress is not always good. Some things are worth reacting against, and the 'conserve' part of 'conservative' is not to be dismissed as a matter of course. It depends on what is proposed to be conserved – the natural environment yes, obscurantism no. Similarly, not all forms of progress are commendable – as we have seen with the various environmental menaces manifest in contemporary society, from threats to the rain forest and biodiversity to the associated peril of global warming.

Insofar as right-wing conservatives and libertarians have a point, they should be listened to – even if the solutions they propose are misconceived. The problem is that capitalism channels forms of opposition to damaging effect, either neutralising such opposition or transforming it into active support. Consequently, for example, resistance to declining living standards in the United Kingdom among large sections of society has been directed against immigrants and the EU; in the United States, the reaction is against immigrants and in favour of protectionist (Trumpian) capitalism.

Opposition to surveillance capitalism – from activists in the legal, political, artistic and technological spheres – will go some way to counteract the total system of instrumentarianism that Zuboff describes in such devastating detail. Without a major shift of public consciousness, however, and the advance of practical solutions – including the reining in of dominant players in the digital world and the development of more socially appropriate alternatives – the future seems bleak.

As noted already, the problem of surveillance culture was already to the fore more than seventy years ago. Far from being headed off by the literary efforts of Orwell and others, it has, in many ways, intensified in the interim. The problem is not just the familiar one of deflected opposition from appropriate targets onto inappropriate ones. It also involves the exponential growth of technology – technology that exceeds the understanding not only of the general public but also of those with expertise in specific technological fields. Even experts in different areas of technology may have difficulty understanding one another, and even greater difficulty in grasping the big picture.

This may be seen as part and parcel of the overall problem of the academic division of labour, whereby it is increasingly difficult to see the overall situation, even when one is a part of it. In other words, to distinguish the wood from the trees.

The problem of overspecialisation lies, in part, in the inherent difficulties involved in individual knowledge domains. But another part of it is systemic, and perhaps psychological, whereby a specialised, analytical approach is favoured at the expense of a wider contextualising perspective. The fact that such a narrow approach intensifies the problem of alienation experienced by non-specialists – never mind the general public – is overlooked, with potentially disastrous political consequences.

One could add to this the paternalistic, self-perpetuating growth of the state. This goes hand in glove with a rapacious capitalist system (neo-liberalism in the West, capitalist socialism in China), together with the out-of-control development of technology.

There is also the divide-and-conquer mentality, which neutralises the desire for liberty through the insistence that freedom be parked in one political corner or another. From the point of view of the prevailing system, the wish for freedom cannot be allowed, even in limited circumstances, to transcend the prevailing left–right dichotomy. Such a replacement would be truly dangerous for the system and its beneficiaries, since it opens up the possibility of bringing freedom forward as an agreed priority. Instead, freedom is marginalised in favour of more accepted values, such as equality (on the left) and prosperity (on the right).

In a review of Zuboff's book, John Gray argues that the surveillance capitalism described by Zuboff derives from an 'illiberal tradition of Enlightenment thinking' that focuses on remaking humanity. Gray points out, correctly, that surveillance societies are possible wherever the necessary technology exists; that they are not confined to the capitalist world. Socialist societies have devastated their natural environments, and have the potential to do the same to our freedoms through surveillance.

Gray is dismissive of what he sees as Zuboff's optimism regarding the democratic potential to rein in surveillance, pointing to our more-or-less universal dependence on technology – specifically, the smartphone. It is, he points out, hard to imagine the effective countering of criminality, terrorism and tyranny without intrusive technology. Gray's optimistic view is that internal conflict will destroy the 'ugly utopia' of the surveillance society.[110]

One can only hope that he is correct; however, probably a lot more is needed. Zuboff's book is long on naming and short on taming, but it goes a long way to diagnosing the disease. In terms of the main culprit, Zuboff's analysis places the emphasis on business rather than the state. Nonetheless, in the era of an increasingly cosy relationship between the state and capitalist corporations, the line between the threat of corporate and state domination becomes more and more blurred. Business corporations' access to every detail of our lives becomes, potentially, the state's access as well. This is particularly the case given the spectre of inverted totalitarianism, outlined by Sheldon Wolin, whereby business increasingly dictates to the state.

Naming the problem is, as Zuboff admits, only the first step. Fixing it is a matter for another day. At the individual level, it will involve a considerable amount of time-consuming, and ongoing, personal defence.[111] At the political level, it will involve a lot of struggle – aimed, crucially, at foregrounding the interests and rights of digital consumers, however difficult this may be given the opposing powers of capitalism, technocracy and the state. As Snowden remarks, it may involve 'removing the greed from the process' of technological development.[112] Given the current state–corporate relationship, this may be seen as something of a tall order, though no less imperative for that.

CONCLUSION

At this point, I will try to sum up some of the main issues arising from the foregoing account. The following discussion involves both description and prescription. In other words, it is not just a summary of major threats to freedom but also a series of broad-brush suggestions as to how we might counter them in practical terms.

Issues regarding the role of the state, particularly in the era of pandemics, are not clearly to the fore in the public mind. Key questions around apparently abstract issues, such as the nation state, biopolitics, freedom, democracy, authoritarianism, globalism, nationalism, supranationalism, postcolonialism and the spectre of totalitarianism, are not generally matters of public concern. On the contrary, such concern usually has to do with immediate practical challenges facing groups or individuals.

The extent to which present and future pandemics, resulting from our depredations on nature, are compatible with current forms of neoliberalism and globalism – not to mention the system of corporatism, or indeed capitalism itself – is not widely debated by the public.

Part of the reason for this lack in public consciousness is the gulf between academic and popular thought. This is the result of a specific kind of dichotomy between two cultures. In this context, 'two cultures' does not refer to the traditional split, famously identified by C.P. Snow, between the sciences and the humanities. Rather, it references the gulf between an obscure academic culture of extreme analysis and specialisation, and a popular culture where facile and simplistic – even crazy – ideas abound.

The decline of the public intellectual, mediating between academic specialisation and public knowledge, has helped to enhance the problem of widespread political incomprehension on the part of the public. This, in turn, feeds into the political system itself – since in a democracy, rather than those possessing specialist knowledge, the public as a whole ultimately determines the kind of government we have.

The disastrous political consequences of the split between academic thinking and popular sentiment hardly need to be laboured. On the one hand – for example, in the United States and the United Kingdom – we have world-beating excellence at the top educational level; on the other, we have voters, or potential voters, who don't know who won the Second World War, or where Australia is on the map.

Everyone, regardless of their knowledge or ignorance, has the same vote under our system. How people who are ignorant of contemporary politics, basic history and basic geography can be expected to make responsible choices in an election or referendum is something of a mystery.

THE ISSUE OF FREEDOM

The political sidelining of freedom's importance is a major part of the overall problem. The issues of freedom and civil liberties tend to be pushed to the margin in the dominant discourse; in their stead, inequality and the distribution of wealth are favoured as the main political question.

Liberty and equality are foundational values of our civilisation. In important ways, they support each other – and indeed overlap to a great extent. Achieving a balance between these complementary, but sometimes conflicting, values is crucial to our social well-being.

In times of pandemic, a dominant, if largely untheorised, viewpoint is that public health should necessarily trump freedom. Such a position is at least questionable, for reasons outlined earlier – basically, people have valued freedom so highly that they have been prepared to sacrifice their lives, not to mention the lives of others, to preserve it.

While issues of wealth distribution are undoubtedly vital, the relative marginalisation of the question of freedom confines debate to the traditional left–right socioeconomic split and pushes aside, for example, crucial issues around the erosion of civil liberties.

This marginalisation is, currently and counterintuitively, particularly marked on what is called the left, where questions regarding civil liberties tend to take a poor second to issues around wealth distribution. (And in turn, the latter are marginalised by the focus on identity politics.)

The result is a gift for the right, including the far right. The far right can, somewhat bizarrely, pose as defenders of civil liberties in the face of state repression – even though some of the worst forms of such repression have historically come from the far right itself.

Traditional political boundaries of left and right are based on a somewhat limited conceptual split – that between the philosophy of high tax, high spend and low tax, low spend. Such a dichotomy has its validity as far as it goes, but it should not diminish the important struggle between libertarianism and authoritarianism, which may go beyond traditional left–right divisions.

In other words, there are both authoritarians and libertarians on the left, and their counterparts on the right. The political priority, for those who cherish liberty, is to maximise freedom and minimise authoritarianism.

In political terms, for lovers of freedom there may be scope for some (limited) co-operation across the traditional left–right divide, particularly in regard to the erosion of civil liberties. At the same time, crucial left–right differences – social, economic and cultural – will undoubtedly remain. There are limits to the possibilities of crossover politics.

The fragility of accepted norms of freedom within the democratic state is a matter of urgent concern. The most pressing issue relates to public political consciousness – particularly the need for the development of a critical mindset that interrogates imposed norms, party line thinking and propaganda.

State repression feeds on aggressive militarism abroad; it is also bolstered by the consequences of the latter at home. Foreign military intervention fosters terrorism, both international and domestic, and political instability. Both, in turn, provide the rationale for increased spending on military goals. The extension of the state into areas of personal morality where it has no legitimate place (such as in the prohibition of recreational drugs) also leads to the burgeoning of the repressive elements of state power.

This adds to the problem, as the power and wealth of gangsters and drug cartels becomes entrenched; they profit from distortions in the market that state repression engenders. There are related issues of police corruption, and class and racial oppression through the prison system – and the further inevitable spread of the drug problem itself.

Foreign military intervention and adventurism serve to prop up a self-serving military elite; this, in turn, operates to destabilise the world through the growth of terrorism. Military intervention encourages this growth. Political destabilisation abroad leads to the pressure of mass immigration on the West – which may function as a rationale for the further erosion of civil liberties. Framing all this is the phenomenon described by Wolin of inverted totalitarianism, whereby the tail of corporate capitalism increasingly wags the dog of the state.

WOKE CULTURE

The mental totalitarianism of political correctness or extreme forms of woke culture is a danger not so much in itself, but in the reaction it tends to engender. Radical politics has historically had a tendency towards intolerance, giving rise to the saying, 'Inside every revolutionary there is a policeman trying to get out.' The major danger in our time is the extent to which party line thinking or groupthink gives ammunition to the enemies of freedom on the right, who – bizarrely – often masquerade as defenders of freedom.

Nonetheless, insofar as it involves merely social pressure, woke culture is part of the way customs and values inevitably change over time. The current pronoun wars will no doubt be resolved one way or another. At its best, woke culture is simply politeness taken to extremes. At its worst, as when people's lives and livelihoods are destroyed by online bullying, woke or cancel culture shows its deplorable side – but this is nothing essentially new.

Intolerance has been a feature of youth-dominated politics going back at least as far as the 1960s. The main difference in our own time is the unprecedented public access to technology – surely a good thing in itself, despite its occasional, and inevitable, misuse in terms of enforcing ideological conformity.

POLITICAL URGENCIES

Both capitalism and traditional top-down forms of socialism are inherently flawed.

The current dominant form of government, particularly in the United States, may be viewed as a kind of disguised or, in Wolin's terms, 'inverted' version of totalitarianism. The accumulation of citizens' personal data by corporations is doubly threatening – not only in itself but in terms of its potential for contributing to the virtual omniscience of a future corporate-dominated repressive regime. Such a system could conceivably arise as a consequence of economic collapse.

Such a regime, or regimes, with immeasurable technological power, could have nightmarish consequences for the values of privacy, autonomy and freedom – which are rapidly being eroded by technological, economic and political developments.

Democracy and freedom are fragile entities. They usually reinforce each other, though occasionally they may be at odds – most notoriously in terms of the tyranny of the majority. The threat of totalitarianism to both democracy and freedom arises from numerous sources. One key threat is the possibility of authoritarian nationalism consolidating and developing in a totalitarian direction, with corporate backing and all the power of media manipulation that goes with it – perhaps as a consequence of global economic collapse.

Such a development might, or might not, be accurately definable as fascism, but that may be somewhat of an academic issue. There is indeed a definitive threat from the far right. Its racist ideology, aimed at 'defending the white race', calls for a clampdown on freedom – specifically the freedom to reproduce as we wish. This is a considerable threat, particularly given the various forms of conscious and unconscious racism that already exist in the public mind.

Such a threat is clearly at odds with any form of libertarianism, including libertarianism of the right – a fact that needs to be made plain in order to shove a wedge between the contradictory forces, both actual and potential, of the right. In these kinds of cultural wars, the priority for freedom-lovers is to divide and conquer.

Totalitarianism of the left is a less obvious threat to our civilisation than totalitarianism of the right – at least insofar as we may think of specific instances, such as Stalinist Russia or North Korea. Pyongyang is unlikely to feature as a socioeconomic-political model to be emulated, even in the most extreme circumstances of Western destabilisation or disintegration.

Nevertheless, the example set by the social credit system in China should be considered a serious threat to the freedoms we have hitherto taken for granted in the West. The desire to keep on good terms with China – its potential influence – should also be mistrusted.

At the moment, though, it is difficult to establish how far China will itself develop in a neoliberal-capitalist direction – in economic terms, at least – as distinct from aiming towards the goal of socialism. It is possible that the Chinese Communists – or a section of them – see the development of a dynamic neoliberal-capitalist economy as a necessary step on the road to socialism.

In a similar way, it is crucial that the welcome (rightly) accorded to refugees and immigrants from non-Western countries should not be at the expense of the liberties that the West enjoys. Freedom from clerical control was hard-won in the West; it should not be given up either to Christian or non-Christian manifestations of such control.

The pandemic may result in the state being more involved in the economy and in our lives, for good or ill. Biopolitics' encroachment on civil liberties is an increasing danger, and something to be aware of. The prosperity of the few, consequent on the triumph of large-scale capitalism at the expense of small-scale economic enterprise activity – in the context of the pandemic and the restrictive measures taken to deal with it – may add to the social and economic inequity already characteristic of Western society, unless radical measures are taken in the area of wealth redistribution.

The redistributive priorities of the left are vital, albeit they should not be allowed to overshadow the importance of freedom. To this end, it is important that they take a universal and unconditional form – specifically, that of universal basic income – so as not to be swamped by the bureaucracy and obstructionism that are an ever-present danger whenever the state steps in to try to rectify society's problems.

THE SURVEILLANCE SOCIETY

The main threat of totalitarianism arises from universal surveillance – the creeping incursions on privacy by the state, and the hijacking of our freedom and private lives by corporations – as so devastatingly outlined by Shoshana Zuboff. This unprecedented development isn't just malign in itself; it also opens up the prospect of making our everyday lives totally visible to the state, or to a future corporate-dominated state that may be less benign than its present manifestation. Such an all-seeing corporate state would be a good deal more threatening than the worst revelations of Edward Snowden and other whistle-blowers.

Resisting the surveillance society will involve considerable effort. At a personal level, insofar as participation in the digital world is more or less inescapable, it involves taking time-consuming, and apparently never-ending, precautions online – maintaining whatever remnants of privacy we have left, and doing our best to regain what we have lost. Nonetheless, the exponential growth of digital technology makes this an uphill task.

Specifically needed is opposition to the philosophy of technological inevitabilism, or 'technology for its own sake', whereby developments like the internet of things are assumed to be obviously good in themselves. And indeed they are, from the point of view of the producers – though not necessarily from that of potential consumers. No one is gagging for the internet of things, except those who stand to profit from it, and their propagandists.

Questions need to be persistently raised about the dominance of means over ends. Technology's encroachment on the values humans hold basic, such as those of freedom, privacy, dignity and autonomy, also needs dissection. There is no essential contradiction in limiting corporate liberties while maximising individual freedoms.

RESISTING THE SPECTRE OF OPPRESSION

There are possible forms of resistance, mentioned already, through art, design and cultural action. Sousveillance, or the technological subversion of surveillance, may operate as an oppositional antidote to universal oversight. Political and legal resistance is fundamental to the defence and preservation of whatever freedoms we have left, and the possibility of regaining those we have already lost. In particular, given the increased corporate exploitation of consumers and the blurring distinction between consumers and producers in the digital realm, there is an urgent need for the foregrounding of the rights and interests of consumers, and the public in general. This emphasis is in parallel with the more traditional emphasis on workers' rights per se – for example, through the revitalisation of the trade union movement and its reorientation to the digital world.

Fascism involves a kind of parody of masculine identity. Domination, aggression and violence are exerted to the extreme. The domineering, assertive leader exerts control over the submissive masses. For those who wish to resist the possibility of a new kind of fascism – however technically inaccurate such a term may be when applied to the spectres that currently threaten us – there are several fronts to fight on.

The first is anti-fascism itself: organisation at the level of politics and ideology to resist the threat. Effective action in this area crucially involves working to undermine the unstable relationship between disparate elements on the right – for example, between authoritarians and libertarians, fascists and conservatives, Christians and neo-pagans.

To resist the growth of tyranny, particularly that of the right, an important principle is divide and conquer. It is vital to expose the inherent, unstable contradictions within potentially tyrannical movements, even if that may be at an unconscious level.

The second front involves the development of a kind of crossover politics – one which emphasises and strengthens the libertarian impulse and finds common ground between libertarians on the right and left (for example, opposition to drug laws, bank bailouts and foreign military intervention, and favour toward the defence of civil liberties, including freedom of speech). This is not to obscure unavoidable left–right differences, which may be multitudinous and intractable. Nevertheless, it is up to libertarians on both left and right to look for tactical alliances, across the traditional political spectrum, against authoritarianism of whatever variety.

Thirdly, and relatedly, the left should stop behaving in ways that make them an easy target for the right. This involves the necessity of forsaking the censorious tyranny of the good, otherwise known as political correctness or cant culture. In the not-entirely-inaccurate terms of the opposition, this is also described as the culture of virtue signalling. In more traditional terms, it is a flagrant example of self-righteousness. We need to remove the plank from our own eye before trying to deal with the speck of dust in someone else's.

Tzvetan Todorov points out the difference between a moral person and a moraliser: a moral person tries to live a good life; a moraliser focuses on the lives of others, implicitly comparing them (to the others' disadvantage) with his or her own.[1]

On the left, opposition to the phenomenon of political self-righteousness would involve reinstating currently marginalised issues. Class politics and the struggle for equal economic opportunity, therefore, would have to be restored to their appropriate place alongside, for example, racial and gender issues.

Fourthly, there is a need for the left to signal, if only in general terms, the kind of society they want to build. This would go beyond the traditional historicism that regards socialism as both desirable and inevitable. If state socialism doesn't work, then what vision do leftists have to take us beyond the Scandinavian model of social democracy or the oxymoron of compassionate capitalism (though the last-mentioned may be the least harmful alternative in existence)?[2] It needs to be spelled out.

TRUTH, SECULARISATION AND RELATED ISSUES

A further need is for secularisation. This necessity exists at a number of different levels. Weakening the links between church and state (or the equivalent in the context of non-Christian cultures) would expand the realm of social and political freedom. At the same time, it would allow religion to flourish (or decline) of its own accord, untrammelled either by state establishment or repression.[3]

Breaking the link between church and state has often been the goal of liberals and progressives. In parallel, severing the links between mosque and state, and synagogue and state, would deprive racists (and sectarians) of important ammunition.

Given such a development towards a secular state, Islamophobes could no longer excuse their bigotry by citing a need to resist the imposition of religious (Sharia) law on society as a whole. Similarly, anti-Semites could no longer point to the political privilege of those who, in an Israeli context, identify as Jews in a religious sense.

The university is another venue where secularisation is required. Here, there is an urgent need to distinguish the search for truth from the priorities of racial, sexual and – indeed – class-based justice. This would help to take the sting out of the right-wing jibe of political correctness and deprive anti-woke right-wing culture of much of its energy.

In the current situation, an overemphasis on identity politics tends to undermine the impetus towards social-economic equality; it also deflates opposition to potentially catastrophic threats, such as that of global warming, deforestation and the loss of biodiversity.

Politics may grow out of theory, but its pursuit is independent of the search for truth. A person may engage in academic discussion during the day and political activity in the evening – or indeed vice versa. They may be linked, in that political action may grow out of theory, but the two activities are in essence dissimilar. Consequently, for practical purposes, they belong in separate boxes.

The fact that a particular theory may induce comfort or discomfort, social harmony or disturbance, is entirely separate from the question of whether it is true or not.

Perhaps what is needed, particularly in universities, is a new slogan that reverses Marx's well-worn maxim. The new slogan would be something like 'Politicians have only attempted to change the world in various ways. The point, however, is to understand it.' Once you've understood it, you can then try to change it as appropriate. But theory and practice are two distinct activities, and do not necessarily go comfortably together. The unhappy history of Social Darwinism provides an example here.[4]

How to deal with the negative consequences that the search for truth sometimes involves is an important question, though not one that necessarily has an easy answer. But the search for truth and the search for social harmony are two distinct enterprises that may not always be consonant with each other. The fact that the search for truth may open up difficult political issues is a political problem, not a scientific or philosophical one.

The concept of truth needs vigorous defence. There may or may not be such a thing as truth in some ultimate sense, but it is probably appropriate to behave as if there were.[5] Otherwise rational attempts at discourse – which make an implicit appeal to the concept of truth – have no validity. In the era of biopolitics, the need for balanced and critical thought is, perhaps, more pressing than ever before.

In the context of the pandemic and associated issues of biopolitics, responses should surely include acknowledgement of the fact that medical science is in a continual process of finding its way. As with any other field of activity, science may be affected negatively by issues of power, status and money. These often conflict with the motivations of altruism, social concern and the unbiased search to uncover the nature of reality.

AN ALTERNATIVE SOCIETY

What would an alternative to our current society, with its fragile and fracturing veneer of freedom and democracy, look like? Utopianism is always risky, and historically has been one of the factors feeding into totalitarianism. That said, at the present juncture the lack of a utopian vision may feed into societal and environmental collapse. So it is perhaps worth the risk to try, tentatively, to sketch out what a desirable society might look like.

I suggest something like an eco-social model. 'Eco-social' is perhaps a more politically useful term than 'eco-socialist', since the latter has unfortunate connotations of centralised state control, and of a tendency towards dictatorship – however supposedly temporary such an envisaged form of control might be.

An eco-social society is one that is 'Green' in two ways: (1) in the ecological sense, whereby people and planet take precedence over economic growth; and (2) in the sense of grass-roots control, where decisions are made at the lowest effective level, from the ground up rather than from the top down.

Such a society is not Luddite and does not reject technology; it judges technology not on its profit-maximising capabilities but in terms of its social and ecological contribution to society. Certainly, it rejects technological inevitabilism, whereby a technology-dominated society is seen as both desirable and unavoidable.

A desirable eco-social society would be the antithesis of traditional state socialism, and consequently those favouring it could escape the barbs thrown – often justly – at the proposal of top-down state control. An eco-social society would go some way towards fostering a sense of identity and community, the lack of which in our capitalist democracies allows fascism to offer a bogus substitute.

Here, there is only space to briefly sketch out what an eco-social society might look like. In such a system, small-scale business and worker co-operatives are facilitated and encouraged, while large-scale corporations are broken up into smaller-scale entities. Ethical investment, worker management, profit-sharing, a strong (renewed) role for trade unions, collective wage bargaining, social partnership and economic democracy function to water down the role of profit-making in the economy, and to foreground social and ecological values. Alternative systems of money creation are explored and implemented as appropriate. The corporate influence on government and media is strictly curtailed, and individual freedom – and specifically privacy – are to the fore as values to be defended, and indeed expanded where they have been curtailed.

Advertising is strongly regulated, and in some cases eliminated. For example, a ban on alcohol and tobacco advertising might be counterbalanced by removing the ban on the use and availability of recreational drugs – a win for individual freedom compensates for the loss of corporate freedom.

Decisions in such an eco-social society are made at the lowest effective level, whether local, regional, national, supranational or international. State involvement is appropriate insofar as it benefits areas like basic industry, finance, transport, health, housing and education. Otherwise, economic and social activities are left to small-scale business and co-operatives.

In either case, there is maximum provision for popular involvement in the ownership and control of resources (which could feed into a universal monetary dividend as appropriate). Such ownership and control is, to the greatest extent possible, from the ground up rather than from the top down. Ecology would replace economics as the dominant driving force, both at a practical and an academic level.

The urgent need is for more democracy in both the economic and political spheres. In specific terms, this would involve public control over finance, along with a restructuring of economic goals – away from the dominant demand for an increase of GDP, towards humane and ecological objectives (insofar as these can be quantified).

More immediately, there is an urgent need for a crash course in political literacy for the population as a whole. This might start with an overhaul of the educational system at all levels; however, it would not be confined to such an overhaul – the situation is too urgent for that.

Such aims as those outlined above may come across as utopian, and indeed they are. Nonetheless, the alternative to utopia is not normality – it is a new, unknown and potentially terrifying form of dystopia, where freedom has been effectively abolished.

It remains to be seen whether, or to what extent, such a roughly sketched scenario would interface with the technological scenario outlined by futuristic thinkers (such as Klaus Schwab). The latter scenario includes implantable technologies, wearable internet, ubiquitous computing, the internet of things, smart cities, driverless cars, the enhanced role of artificial intelligence in decision-making, robotics, the blockchain, 3D printing and neurotechnologies.[6]

Technological development is neither bad nor good in itself – the issue is whether or not it is employed for the good of humanity and the planet. Such decisions need to be made on a case-by-case basis, rather than on the basis of either technophilia or technophobia.

The political answer to the challenge posed by technology is not some form of neo-Luddism: technology has its place. The answer is informed consent and participation by the populace as a whole, independently of the various forms of media mind-control and manipulation that predominate at present.

In a post-pandemic world, some version of the Great Reset may be inevitable and, to a degree, desirable. The key issue lies in the extent to which such a reset is under democratic control – a control that, in turn, is influenced by a public consciousness where issues of civil liberties are to the forefront.

Such control would require the weakening, and ultimate elimination, of the corporate domination and financing of politics, along with a massive increase in public participation in decision-making. This would greatly expand our current, somewhat gestural democratic system, which involves ticking a box every few years. In a society that wants to defend and expand freedom, such a system is simply not adequate.

Alternative forms of taxation, such as land tax, would, in this scenario, be implemented at the expense of income tax. Consequently, the burden of personal taxation would be lifted from the population as a whole, and shifted to its appropriate place: the desks of public servants who are paid to deal with bureaucratic affairs – as distinct from the citizenry, who are not.

De-bureaucratisation is crucial to public well-being, even as the NHS is currently under attack from the right. Contrary to the stereotype, privatisation may involve an increase in bureaucracy rather than its diminution – an example being the clunky and often unworkable system of health insurance in the United States, as compared to the NHS in the United Kingdom. It is bad enough to be sick, but to be worried about form-filling – not to mention possible bankruptcy – at the same time is surely an unacceptable, and unnecessary, addition to the burden.

In our proposed example of a new kind of society, social, ethical and ecological concerns would replace the pressure of wealth creation; company laws would mandate such priorities, rather than simply the need to make money for shareholders.

In such a society, prosperity is no longer measured in terms of economic growth, but – insofar as measurements in this area have any meaning – factors such as security, happiness, sustainability, personal fulfilment, health and education would prevail as markers of a desirable society.

A universal basic income would provide the basis for social security, encourage individual and co-operative entrepreneurship, and compensate those engaged in currently unrewarded, or under-rewarded, activities such as caring and child-rearing.

Since radical redistribution of wealth would take the form of a social dividend from which everyone – not just the poor – would benefit, the arguments against such redistribution would be weakened. Once implemented, such a system of direct wealth distribution would be politically difficult, if not impossible, to abolish, and could indeed function as an impetus towards further wealth-sharing and a more equitable society.

A shortening of the current working day, week and year would help to put an end to the dehumanising work ethic (or rather labour ethic) that currently blights our society. The recent turn to working from home has shown the advantages of cutting down on wasteful commuting, but the advantages should not be forgotten when, or rather if, we return to a pandemic-free society. Such a return is predicated on the radical reorganisation of our unsustainable socioeconomic system, with its depredations on nature.

A reemphasis on military defence (as distinct from offence and consequent global destabilisation) would lessen the problems of global terrorism and political instability.

In an eco-social society, corporations – to the extent that they continue to exist – are more tightly controlled, small-scale and monitored than at present, as well as being politically impelled towards democratisation and social and ecological goals.

The issue with the kind of alternative politics outlined here is that it is 'populist' in the sense that it trusts the instincts of ordinary people to form and maintain it. In that sense, it may be open to the same kinds of arguments directed against current and former kinds of populism: that the people as a whole may have a less than optimal political consciousness.

The answer lies in a combination of education, enhanced political debate, an end to corporate control of politics and the mass media, and a cessation of media censorship (whether in terms of digital and social media, or mainstream media). There is certainly an element of trust involved in the sanguine notion that, in the long term, people will act not only in their own interests but also in those of society as a whole.

The basic priority is the enhancement of democracy and freedom, as distinct from their current erosion.

In particular, the pursuit of truth – independently of pressures from left and right, science and religion, blind conformity and wild conspiracies – is crucial to the maintenance of liberty, and to its reestablishment where it has been lost.

Historically, totalitarianism – particularly in its right-wing form – had a love–hate relationship with modernity, pushing the development of technology while harking back to premodern values and ideals. Finding an alternative to the renewed threat of totalitarianism involves a different kind of love–hate relationship – this time, with the state. We need to find ways of consolidating the positive role of the state while simultaneously negating its downside and developing economic and social alternatives. It is a difficult but essential task.

Afterword

THE PUTIN PERPLEX[1]

This book was at an advanced editorial stage when Vladimir Putin decided to throw a spanner in the works by invading Ukraine.

This world-shaking development has far-reaching implications for global security and raises anew the question of the authoritarian (or totalitarian) threat to the West. Given time constraints, the response will have to be confined to the addition of this afterword. In any event, things change so fast on the contemporary world stage that any update runs the risk of being outdated by the time of publication. And who knows what new, or renewed, panic may prevail at that time?

On the face of it, the situation is surreal: a Jewish man in command of Ukrainian forces faces down an ex-KGB officer, reputedly the richest man in the world, who is holed up in the Kremlin with the backing of the Russian Orthodox Church. It sounds like a comic strip, or a bad knock-off of a Quentin Tarantino film. Indeed, it is difficult to imagine a pitch for such an outlandish plot succeeding in Hollywood.

Nonetheless, had it been an actual film proposal, the plot device of making life imitate art would have added an intriguing postmodern perspective. The Ukrainian president, Volodymyr Zelenskyy, first achieved a fictional electoral victory in a television series before his 'real' victory. The recent transformation of a reality television star (Trump) into President of the United States, echoing that of his predecessor, former actor Ronald Reagan, seems to indicate the blurring of the distinction between media and reality, if not the actual takeover of the latter by the former. Are we all simply actors, and extras, in a poorly written film or television show?

Matrix-inspired speculations about the world-as-simulation will have to remain in the realm of speculation, and the outrages that have been perpetrated by Russian forces since the invasion, as well as the threat to freedom and security, make such armchair philosophical exercises seem indecent. What does emerge clearly is the dominance of media in shaping reality, specifically that of the relatively old medium of television. Indeed, the weakness of the penetration of digital media in Russia compared to the dominance of state-controlled television was a major factor in shoring up Putin's aggressive politics by giving him a captive audience. The extent to which reactionary politics seems to rely on 'old' media is noteworthy: television in Russia, Brexit-supporting newspapers in the United Kingdom.[2]

In the fog of war, it can be difficult to steer a middle course through the competing accusations and justifications. Groupthink, digging in further to an entrenched position, is an unfortunate though widespread propensity, and one to be resisted as much as possible. Suspicion of large-scale media manipulation is hard to avoid; it is as if the cosmic scriptwriter has a permanent need for a new terror. Covid suddenly vanished off the headlines to be replaced by the equally dreadful image of the gremlin in the Kremlin, with his finger on the nuclear button.

Comparable outrages to the invasion, such as the war on Iraq and the suffering in Yemen, have received nothing like the same unified response, raising questions about the racial component of Western antipathy to the Russian assault on white Europeans who share our values and aspirations.

Censorship takes place on both fronts. This has notoriously been the case in Russia itself, where the state controls television: it was made a criminal offence to describe the invasion in accurate terms ('don't mention the war' as a sinister reprise of the catchphrase from the UK television series *Fawlty Towers*). Groupthink, though, has also been found in the West, where there has been a tendency to suppress any questioning of the dominant narrative, in the case of Ukraine as much as in that of Covid: the sidelining of the Russian television channel RT is a case in point. It is important to try to find one's way through the partial truths of competing narratives; censorship makes this difficult or impossible.[3]

That said, the voices of dissenting figures like realist political theorist John Mearsheimer,[4] filmmaker Oliver Stone, UK politician George Galloway, and Irish politicians Clare Daly and Mick Wallace are still permitted in the West, unlike those of their anti-establishment counterparts in Russia, where the justice system has been turned into a means of suppressing dissident views. The latter situation raises the spectre of the rejection of liberal social values in Russia and the development of extreme authoritarianism, if not of totalitarianism itself.

The extent to which the Putin regime is authoritarian or totalitarian in nature is a matter of ongoing debate. Catherine Belton writes that Putin's early economic reforms were aimed at bringing about an Augusto Pinochet type of regime, with the 'totalitarian force' of the state driving them.[5] Anton Shekhovtsov sees Putin's Russia as authoritarian rather than totalitarian, in part because of the lack of an all-embracing ideology and the existence of ideological diversity.[6]

Shekhovtsov traces the complicated and convoluted relationship between Putin's Russia and the Western far right, centred on the goal of developing an illiberal alternative to Western democratic society and values, and ideologically undermining the West. It should be stressed that historically, there has not been as strict a dichotomy between Soviet Russia and the far right as might seem to be the case – this is evidenced by the phenomenon of 'National Bolshevism' between the wars, and by the writings of right-wing ideologues such as Francis Parker Yockey and

Jean Thiriart.[7] In Shekhovtsov's terms, 'the Russian political establishment increasingly perceived the European far right as Russia's legitimate allies.'[8]

Putin's strategy to win support includes a defence of traditional religious values and a critique of multiculturalism.[9] Shekhovtsov defines Putin's Russia as 'an authoritarian kleptocracy'.[10] Fear of Ukraine involves fear of the example it might set for Russia, in terms of democratisation.[11] Nonetheless, the question as to whether or not Putin's regime conforms to the definition of 'fascism' is a matter of debate and disagreement.[12] Shekhovtsov argues that Putin's overriding aim is 'the preservation of the existing patrimonial regime at any cost'.[13] To this end, Putin embraces tradition against the despised liberal values of the West.[14]

There are defensible counternarratives to the dominant Western perspective – narratives on which the repressive system in Russia relies for popular support. There was, no doubt, mistreatment of Russians by Ukrainians, though certainly not on a scale that would justify Russia's invasion of a neighbouring sovereign state. With the collapse of the Soviet Union, NATO's eastward expansion took place in bad faith and with the primary aim of preserving NATO at a time, after the collapse of the USSR, when there was no real need for NATO any more: the emphasis could, and should, have been on integrating Russia with Europe.[15] The extent to which Ukrainian resistance politics was spontaneous or Western-fomented has been a matter of contention.[16] It is difficult to believe that everything about Ukraine is, or has been, entirely clean. Wars are not usually fought between the forces of absolute good and absolute evil; it is more often a case of the bad against the worse, as when Communism and capitalist democracy squared off against fascism in the Second World War.

That said, it is somewhat difficult for a Westerner to understand the Russian paranoia that has developed over recent decades about the (real or perceived) encroachment of NATO and the EU, unless such paranoia is essentially rooted in an endemic fear of freedom. It may be the case that a renewed Russian imperialism is threatened by Western democracy, which operates as a major reason for the former to try to undermine the latter.[17] Timothy Snyder cites the influential Russian (Hegelian) philosopher Ivan Ilyin as an important source of antipathy to Western values such as individualism, succession, truth and equality.[18]

Why Russia, with its transformation from market to state capitalism dominated by the secret service and the Kremlin,[19] should view NATO as an existential threat is the key question. In the aftermath of Communism, the antipathy to the West seems to be based on a combination of the rejection of Western values of freedom, democracy and the rule of law, as well as a hankering after the glory days of the Soviet Union and the previous Russian empire. Crucially, the presence of freedom and associated values in Western countries may have the effect of showing up their lack in Russia.

None of these viewpoints – unlike suspicion of the Western arms industry – appears defensible. Russians may, admittedly, have a point when they criticise Western materialism, consumerism and cultural shallowness,[20] though their views in this regard have led to a disastrous underestimation of Ukraine's will to resist, and the will of the West to support Ukraine.

The United States may have its own (questionable) reasons for supporting the continued separation of Ukraine from Russia,[21] but the fact that the United States wants something does not mean that the goal is necessarily bad. The desire to spread freedom and democracy is not to be condemned; the problem is the disastrously bungling way in which it is often done, and the underestimation of the intransigent nature of anti-Western values and ideologies. Consequently, through meddling in the affairs of other countries, the West often makes things worse for everyone, with the exception of the arms industry. The best way to spread the values of freedom and democracy is by example: by practising them at home.

The Western dismissal of Russia after the collapse of the Soviet Union was both arrogant and, perhaps, characterised by a covetous eye on Russian natural resources. Nonetheless, this does not negate the argument, uncomfortable though it may be, that NATO's presence may now be needed to curb the Russian monster that NATO, with US backing, itself helped to create.

Indeed, Putin may have unwittingly blundered into the trap of contributing to NATO's greatly increasing power and influence. Chomsky questions why, since Russia has so clearly shown itself to be a paper tiger in military terms, neutral states like Sweden and Finland should feel the need to run towards NATO for protection.[22] This position, though, ignores the extremity of the current situation: a possibly irrational Kremlin leader, living in a delusional echo chamber, with his finger on the nuclear button.

The arms manufacturers must be delighted – not to mention the Western fossil fuel industry, which will receive a renewed impetus given the pressure on Russian sources of oil and gas. Putin's strategic mistakes could hardly have been graver, even from a Russian point of view. The main winner looks as if it will be China, though the United States has also won in the short term at least, since it will now – as Chomsky points out[23] – exert much greater control over Europe.

Ukraine's role in the Second World War involved undeniable links with Nazism – links that may be understood, though not condoned, in the context of Stalinist depredations on Ukraine. The presence of some extreme nationalist elements in the Ukrainian defence forces, particularly given the minimal electoral support for the far right in Ukraine, should not undermine support for the defence of Ukraine.[24] If your house is on fire, you don't really care about the politics of the fire-fighters. It may be an issue, but it's an issue for another day. Your main priority, at this point in time, is to put out the fire.

There were no doubt some radical right elements involved in the Ukrainian national resistance,[25] though as noted already, the success of the far right at the electoral level has been minimal. Nevertheless, in a familiar process of projection, the Putin regime sees Nazism everywhere in Ukraine, when it would be a more fruitful exercise to look within, to its own values and practices, based on the same urge to imperial domination and will to power that motivated Hitler and his acolytes. The Russian state has become a toxic stew of corruption, rotten within and infecting the politics of everything it touches outside.[26]

The invasion of Ukraine has brought into sharp relief some of the major themes of this book. These include the rise of authoritarianism – most recently in Russia – and the danger of its turning into totalitarianism. This is particularly so with the control of language and the suppression of free speech, and the use of the legal system as a political weapon by the government. The question as to whether Russia is actually a totalitarian state is a matter of ongoing debate, but there is no doubt of the toxicity of the system, however one may define it in academic terms.

The problem of the entwinement of religion with politics, already familiar from Islamism, seems to have taken on a new urgency. Repressed for a century, Orthodox Christianity, or a version of it, has rebounded with vigour, and now threatens freedom and liberal values.[27] Ironically, these threats display an alarming similarity to their Communist predecessors. (Communism, in turn, with its sexual repressiveness, displayed some continuity with its religious predecessor.) Though nominally atheistic, Communism embodies a quasi-religious element in its (implicitly moral) demand for political commitment to the Communist ideal. In the contemporary situation, accounting for the erosion of freedom, Snyder lists the blurring of the church–state separation, the enhancement of the powers of the security services, and a crackdown on the dissemination of information and political activity.[28]

The power-hungry in Russia, realising that an appeal to the socioeconomic interests of the workers and peasants on whom socialism once relied is a lost cause, now embrace 'traditional' Russian values, including religion, with enthusiasm. Desecularisation has arrived with a vengeance. Authoritarian religion is achieving a new lease of life under Putin, with the assistance of the writings of philosopher-theologian Ilyin.[29] In Ilyin's terms, a person who is 'spiritually healthy' is obliged to quash forceful evil.[30] Putin seems to have taken this philosophy to heart: a Christian version of Islamist jihad, perhaps.

The clerico-fascist thinker Ilyin has apparently been a major influence on Putin. Ilyin is a weird figure, who comes across as a combination of Danish philosopher Søren Kierkegaard and the film character Dirty Harry. Indeed, it may be the case that current events in Russia trace their political lineage not so much to Hitler or Mussolini but to the Christian fascism of (for example) Spain and Slovakia. If Western (and Eastern) Christians wish to resist this new Behemoth, they will urgently need to challenge this interpretation of Christian teaching.[31]

Under the influence of resurgent religious and cultural ideologies, Russia has turned into a kind of mafia state, where feudal values, repressed since the overthrow of the aristocracy in the Russian Revolution, become all-important and supplant the values of democracy and the rule of law. If, in Carl Clausewitz's terms, war is politics by other means, perhaps crime is business by other means. The Russian experience certainly suggests that is the case.

Combined with this has been the toxic stew of complex relations between Russia and the Western far right. This has fed into the project of undermining the US political system through Russian shoring up of the politics of Trump. Russia has tried to undermine the EU through its support for Brexit, and support of far-right politics in Europe.[32] The aim is 'Eurasia',[33] a Russian empire 'from Dublin to Vladivostok'.[34] The lack of a succession principle in Russia means that Russia must undermine democracy abroad, which embodies the principle of succession.[35]

Communism was spectacularly unsuccessful in generating an altruistic ideology that might have countered the rise of a new feudalism, perhaps due to its own 'ends justify the means' mindset, together with its (related) materialist notion that social being determines consciousness. Oligarchy, organised crime and the secret service combine in Russia to reinstate feudal values, a veneer for kleptocracy and corruption.

Disinformation, assassination and support for terrorism were the *modus operandi* of the 'securocracy' that emerged in Russia, where a symbiosis existed between organised crime and the security services.[36] The tail of the security services wags the dog of the state.

It appears that the Bolshevik attempt to institute socialism in Russia, far from leap-frogging over capitalism into utopia, merely led to the repression of Russian feudalism and the eventual return of the repressed. We are now faced with a top-down state capitalism[37] that may be seen as a reversal of the inverted totalitarianism of the West. At the time of writing, it seems as if the Russian state now controls the oligarchs, rather than vice versa as in the West, though it is conceivable that the oligarchs might once more achieve dominance, perhaps through a palace coup against Putin. Belton cites a source close to Putin as referring to the dictator's rule as being based on three essential elements: autocracy (a strong ruler), territory (the fatherland) and the Church.[38]

A dysfunctional (top-down) military structure,[39] inherited from Soviet times, has hampered Russian military successes in Ukraine, while the (predictable) dictator's practice of surrounding oneself with sycophants means that Putin has tended to operate in a bubble, or echo chamber. This has hindered his military aspirations, offering him a distortedly positive view of the Ukraine invasion's progress.

In terms of dealing with the Russian threat, comparisons to the rise of Hitler, with his invasion of Czechoslovakia and Poland, are of limited value. Charges of 'appeasement' ignore the fact that Hitler did not have nuclear weapons, while Putin does. At the time of writing, the question has arisen as to whether Putin is to be treated as a schoolyard bully (stand up to him and he'll run away) or a cornered rat (stand up to him and he'll attack you in desperation). Nuclear weapons complicate what would otherwise be a fairly straightforward issue: the rejection of the strategy of appeasement, given its historical failure in the context of the Second World War.

The Western solidarity with Ukraine may be heartening, but it raises some questions as well. The astonishing facility – particularly in Ireland, where I live – in accommodating Ukrainian refugees is in shining comparison to the fate of less-fortunate refugees from non-Europeans countries, not to mention the desperate plight of native Irish people who cannot afford accommodation in their home country. This is not to denigrate the laudable goal of helping refugees from Ukraine and elsewhere, but – as with the Covid crisis – it does call in question how solutions, hitherto apparently unachievable, can be found so quickly and easily under the pressure of global circumstances. This in turn seems to flag the workings of invisible, transnational, media-manipulating and self-interested power systems, normally somewhat opaque but occasionally giving fleeting indications of their presence, and their ability to override the normal socioeconomic constraints by which most of us are bound.

Beneath the surface, the question becomes ever more urgent: how to strengthen the positive core values of the West, crucially including those of freedom and democracy, against the incursions of those who neither understand nor accept them.[40] The interconnected grotesqueries of Putinism in Russia, Brexit in the United Kingdom, Trumpism in the United States and the far right in Europe challenge us to defend democracy, freedom and world peace against those who would undermine them.

NOTES

Introduction

1   ACLU, 'Surveillance under the Patriot Act', https://www.aclu.org/issues/national-security/privacy-and-surveillance/surveillance-under-patriot-act (accessed 1 March 2021). According to the information given on this site, the result in terms of catching terrorists has been minimal. However, there seem to have been spectacular scores in terms of the so-called war on drugs. For the complete legal text, see https://epic.org/privacy/terrorism/hr3162.html (accessed 1 March 2021).

2   ACLU, 'Indefinite Detention, Endless Worldwide War and the 2012 National Defense Authorization Act', https://www.aclu.org/issues/national-security/detention/indefinite-detention-endless-worldwide-war-and-2012-national (accessed 1 March 2021). For the act itself, see https://www.govinfo.gov/content/pkg/BILLS-112hr1540enr/pdf/BILLS-112hr1540enr.pdf (accessed 1 March 2021).

3   BBC News, 'Double Jeopardy Law Ushered Out', 3 April 2005, http://news.bbc.co.uk/2/hi/uk_news/4406129.stm (accessed 1 March 2005).

4   Owen Bowcroft, 'Secret Court Proposals Threaten Habeas Corpus Safeguards, Charity Warns', *The Guardian*, 13 July 2012, https://www.theguardian.com/law/2012/jul/13/secret-court-habeas-corpus-reprieve (accessed 21 March 2021).

5   Citizens Information [Ireland], 'Right to Silence in Criminal Cases', https://www.citizensinformation.ie/en/justice/arrests/right_to_silence_in_criminal_cases.html (accessed 1 March 2021).

6   Irish Council for Civil Liberties, 'ICCL Welcomes Proposal to Outlaw Hate Crime, Sounds Note of Caution re Free Speech', 17 Dec. 2020, https://www.iccl.ie/news/iccl-welcomes-proposal-to-outlaw-hate-crime-sounds-note-of-caution-re-free-speech/ (accessed 1 March 2021). See also BBC News, 'Why is Scotland's Hate Crime Bill So Controversial?' 15 Dec. 2020, https://www.bbc.com/news/uk-scotland-scotland-politics-53580326 (accessed 1 March 2021).

7   Portugal has taken some steps towards a more rational approach in this area,

though they fall far short of full legalisation. See Drug Policy Alliance, 'Drug Decriminalization in Portugal: A Health-Centred Approach', 15 Feb. 2021, https://drugpolicy.org/sites/default/files/DPA_Fact_Sheet_Portugal_Decriminalization_Feb2015.pdf (accessed 2 March 2021).

8   On the reactionary role of police and prison officer unions, see Shawn Gude, 'The Bad Kind of Unionism', *Jacobin,* 12 Jan. 2014, https://www.jacobinmag.com/2014/01/the-bad-kind-of-unionism/ (accessed 2 March 2021).

9   Zygmunt Bauman, *Modernity and the Holocaust* (Cambridge, UK: Polity), p. 86.

10 The term 'neoliberal' is extremely problematic and amorphous. See, for example, Philop Morowski, 'Neoliberalism: The Movement That Dare Not Speak Its Name', *American Affairs*, vol. 2, no. 1 (Spring 2018), https://americanaffairsjournal.org/2018/02/neoliberalism-movement-dare-not-speak-name/ (accessed 27 April 2021).

11 Robert Brenner, 'Escalating Plunder', *New Left Review*, no. 123 (May/June 2020), pp. 5–22, https://newleftreview.org/issues/ii123/articles/robert-brenner-escalating-plunder (accessed 9 March 2021).

12 Rajeev Syal and Libby Brooks, 'Covid Travel Rule-Breakers Could Face 10-year Jail Terms, says Hancock', *The Guardian*, 9 Feb. 2021, https://www.theguardian.com/world/2021/feb/09/covid-travel-rule-breakers-could-face-10-year-jail-term-says-hancock (accessed 1 March 2021). For a useful resource regarding legal issues

around the current pandemic, see Barrie Sander and Jason Rudall (eds), *COVID-19 and International Law:* Opinio Juris *Symposium (March–April 2020)*, https://www.academia.edu/42655495/Symposium_COVID_19_and_International_Law?email_work_card=view-paper (accessed 13 April 2021). The symposium covers relevant issues, including human rights, criminal sanctions, nationality, state protection, the economy, globalisation, surveillance and the environment.

13 For a right-libertarian critique of the income tax system in the United States, see Frank Chodorov, *The Income Tax: Root of All Evil*, (Alabama: Mises Institute, 2019).

14 Daniel Murray, 'Deforestation, the Wildlife Trade and Intensive Farming: A Recipe for Lethal Virus Outbreaks', *Business Post*, 28 Feb. 2021, p. 12.

15 Rose Evelith, 'Academics Write Papers Arguing over How Many People Read (and Cite) Their Papers', *Smithsonian Magazine*, 25 March 2014, https://www.smithsonianmag.com/smart-news/half-academic-studies-are-never-read-more-three-people-180950222/ (accessed 2 March 2021).

16 See Edward S. Herman and Noam Chomsky, *Manufacturing Consent: The Political Economy of the Mass Media* (London: Vintage, 1994).

17 See Casey Chalk, 'Amusing Ourselves to Death: Revisiting the Prophetic Work of Neil Postman', *Public Discourse*, 19 Oct. 2020, https://www.thepublicdiscourse.

com/2020/10/72174 (accessed 27 April 2021).

Chapter 1

1 See http://www.irishstatutebook.ie/ pdf/2020/en.act.2020.0001.pdf; see also Irish Council for Civil Liberties, 'Covid-19 Emergency Legislation: We've Got This', https://www.iccl.ie/ human-rights/covid-19-emergency-leg-islation-everything-you-need-to-know/ (accessed 4 Feb. 2021). See also Jack Horgan-Jones, 'Covid-19 Restrictions "Raise Human Rights and Equality Concerns"', *The Irish Times*, 25 Feb. 2021, https://www.irishtimes.com/ news/politics/covid-19-restrictions-raise-human-rights-and-equality-concerns-1.4494196 (accessed 26 April 2021).

2 Colin Hay and Michael Lister, 'Introduction: Theories of the State', in Colin Hay, Michael Lister and David Marsh, eds, *The State: Theories and Issues* (London: Macmillan/ Red Globe Press, 2006), pp. 14, 18. This useful compendium offers a breakdown of state theory in terms of such categories as Pluralism, Elitism, Marxist State Theory, Public Choice, Insitutionalism, Feminism, Green Theory, Poststructuralism and Globalisation.

3 Alan Finlayson and James Martin, 'Poststructuralism', in Colin Hay *et al*, eds, *The State*, p. 155.

4 Angelique Crisafis, 'The Nation State is Back: Front National's Marine Le Pen Rides on Global Mood', *The Guardian*, 18 Sep. 2016, https://www. theguardian.com/world/2016/sep/18/

nation-state-marine-le-pen-global-mood-france-brexit-trump-front-na-tional (accessed 6 Feb. 2021).

5 For an illuminating account of the struggles within Marxist theory of the state, see Colin Hay, '(What's Marxist about) Marxist State Theory?', in Colin Hay *et al*, eds, *The State,* pp. 59–78.

6 See Robert Nozick, *Anarchy, State and Utopia* (New York: Basic Books, 1977).

7 See Ralph Nader, *Unstoppable: The Emerging Left-Right Alliance to Dismantle the Corporate State* (New York: Nation Books, 2014).

8 The nation state, linked to the process of modernisation, involves a sense of identification that both transcends and includes local forms of community and identification. Michael Lister and David Marsh, 'Conclusion', in Colin Hay *et al*, eds, *The State*, p. 260.

9 For an account of an intriguing cultural clash on the issue, involving the interface of Irish and European politics with art history, see Tony Canavan, 'A Papist Painting for a Protestant Parliament', *History Ireland*, 16/1 (Jan./Feb. 2008), https:// www.historyireland.com/18th-19th-century-history/a-papist-painting-for-a-protestant-parliament/ (accessed 3 Feb. 2021). The support, by Pope Innocent XI, may have included financial aid. See Paddy Agnew, 'New Book Claims Pope Bankrolled King Billy', *The Irish Times,* 7 May 2008, https://www.irishtimes.com/ news/new-book-claims-pope-bank-rolled-king-billy-1.921042 (accessed 3 February 2021). The book in question, described by Agnew as a 'thriller/

historical novel', is written by two Italian academics: Rita Monaldi and Francesco Sorti, *Imprimatur* (Edinburgh: Polygon, 2008).

10 Montesquieu, *The Spirit of the Laws*, trans. and ed. Anne M. Cohler, Basia C. Miller and Harold S. Stone (Cambridge: Cambridge University Press, 1989), p. 463.

11 The concept of freedom in a political sense is widely discussed in philosophy. See, for example, 'Positive and Negative Liberty', *Stanford Encyclopedia of Philosophy*, https://plato.stanford.edu/entries/liberty-positive-negative/ (accessed 10 March 2021).

12 The key text on the right to privacy is Samuel D. Warren and Louis D. Brandeis, 'The Right to Privacy', *Harvard Law Review*, vol. 4, no. 5 (15 Dec. 1890), pp. 193–220, https://www.jstor.org/stable/1321160?seq=1#metadata_info_tab_contents (accessed 10 March 2021). The authors seek to derive a right to privacy from related areas of legal deliberation, such as copyright. Technological developments in the time since then have given the issue additional urgency, and have added massive complexity.

13 Haroon Siddique, 'Is the EU Referendum Legally Binding?' *The Guardian*, 23 June 2016, https://www.theguardian.com/politics/2016/jun/23/eu-referendum-legally-binding-brexit-lisbon-cameron-sovereign-parliament (accessed 6 Feb. 2021).

14 Alexis de Tocqueville, *Democracy in America*, trans. Henry Reeve (Hertfordshire: Wordsworth, 1998), p. 30.

15 Tocqueville famously pointed out the tendency towards the tyranny of the majority, with its propensity to erode mental independence and liberty of discussion. Nonetheless, he also noted the existence of countervailing forces, such as the legal profession and the jury system. See Tocqueville, *Democracy in America*, pp. 101–12.

16 Martin Ruhs and Carlos Vargas-Silva, 'The Labour Market Effects of Immigration', *The Migration Observatory at the University of Oxford*, 18 Feb. 2020, https://migrationobservatory.ox.ac.uk/resources/briefings/the-labour-market-effects-of-immigration/ (accessed 3 Feb. 2021).

17 For a left-wing anti-EU argument, see John King, 'The Left-Wing Case for Leaving the EU', *New Statesman*, 15 June 2015, https://www.newstatesman.com/politics/2015/06/john-king-left-wing-case-leaving-eu (accessed 5 Feb. 2021). See also Alan Johnson, 'Why Brexit Is Best for Britain: The Left-Wing Case', *The New York Times*, 28 March 2017, https://www.nytimes.com/2017/03/28/opinion/why-brexit-is-best-for-britain-the-left-wing-case.html (accessed 5 Feb. 2021). For a left-wing rebuttal of pro-Brexit positions, see Ben Chu, 'The European Union Is Not a "Neoliberal Conspiracy" – and It's Disturbing that Some in the Labour Party Apparently Believe this Nonsense', *Independent*, https://www.independent.co.uk/voices/european-union-neoliberal-conspiracy-labour-party-brexit-jeremy-corbyn-a8349316.html (accessed 5 Feb. 2021). The most persuasive political argument I have come across in regard

to this issue is the 'critical support' for the EU of Yanis Varoufakis, as outlined in his book *Adults in the Room: My Battle with Europe's Deep Establishment* (London: Vintage, 2018).

18 Klaus Schwab and Thierry Malleret cite the 'trilemma' noted by Dani Rodrik that globalisation, democracy and the nation state cannot be reconciled; you can have two of them, but not all three. See Schwab and Malleret, *Covid-19: The Great Reset* (Geneva: Forum Publishing, 2020), p. 107, and Dani Rodrik, *The Globalization Paradox: Why Global Markets, States, and Democracy Can't Coexist* (Oxford: Oxford University Press, 2012).

19 The Offences Against the State Act is an example of emergency legislation in Ireland. In place for decades, it is renewed every year. Originally aimed at political subversives, it is now directed at gangland crime as well. Harry McGee, 'Government Considers Review of Offences Against the State Act', *The Irish Times*, 24 June 2020, https://www. irishtimes.com/news/politics/ government-considers-review-of-of-fences-against-the-state-act-1.4286768 (accessed 3 Feb. 2021). The most significant contribution to the (local and global) power of organised crime – and to related repressive measures – is, arguably, the criminalisation of recreational drugs.

20 A drop in Irish support for the EU was measured in 2020. However, the drop was to a current 84 per cent from a previous 93 per cent. Tony Connelly, 'Irish Support for EU Drops from Peak Hit During Brexit Talks', RTÉ

News, 28 April 2020, https://www. rte.ie/news/2020/0428/1135186-euro-pean-union/ (accessed 3 Feb. 2021). With the Brexit debacle functioning as a salutary warning, support for EU membership in 2019 was above 80 per cent in most member states. See Jon Stone, 'Support for EU Membership Above 80% in Most Member States Amid Brexit Mess', *Independent*, 26 April 2019, https://www.inde-pendent.co.uk/news/world/europe/ brexit-eu-survey-italy-ireland-portu-gal-eurosceptic-poll-a8888126.html (accessed 4 Feb. 2021).

21 According to the CIA World Factbook, the population of Ireland (Republic) is currently (2021) estimated at 5,224,884, while that of England is currently estimated at 55,483,744, https://www.cia.gov/the-world-factbook/ (accessed 3 Feb. 2021). *The Encyclopedia of the Nations* gives the area of England as 130,373 square kilometres, and of Ireland as 70,280 square kilometres, https://www. nationsencyclopedia.com/economies/ Europe/index.html (accessed 3 Feb. 2021).

22 See Bryan Fanning and David Farrell, 'Ireland Cannot be Complacent about Populism', *The Irish Times*, 17 Aug. 2018, https://www.irishtimes.com/ opinion/ireland-cannot-be-com-placent-about-populism-1.3598461 (accessed 6 Feb. 2021). The authors point out that even in the midst of serious economic dislocation, there was negligible antipathy to immigrants in Ireland. They speculate that this was a result of a historical Irish memory of

the perils of sectarian conflict and of extreme nationalism.

23 Vaughne Miller, '"Ever-Closer Union" in the EU Treaties and Court of Justice Case Law', *UK Parliament, House of Commons Library,* Research Briefing, 16 Nov. 2015, https://commonslibrary. parliament.uk/research-briefings/cbp-7230/ (accessed 6 Feb. 2021).

24 Lili Bayer, 'Hungary Replaces Rule by Decree with "State of Medical Crisis"', *Politico,* 18 June 2020, https://www.politico.eu/article/ hungary-replaces-rule-by-decree-con-troversial-state-of-medical-crisis/ (accessed 4 Feb. 2021).

25 Karan Bilimoria, 'Britain Doesn't Need to "Take Back Control" of Immigration. We Already Have it', *The Guardian,* 31 July 2017, https://www. theguardian.com/commentisfree/2017/ jul/31/britain-take-back-control-immi-gration-eu-directive-brexit (accessed 3 Feb. 2021). The author points out that the United Kingdom could have taken back control of its borders under European Parliament and Council Directive 2004/38/EC. This permits EU member states to repat-riate EU nationals, without jobs or means of support, after three months.

26 For recent figures, see Carl O'Brien, 'Irish Universities Climb Up Latest Global Rankings', *The Irish Times,* 10 June 2020, https://www. irishtimes.com/news/education/ irish-universities-climb-up-latest-glob-al-rankings-1.4274986 (accessed 4 Feb. 2021). The highest-scoring Irish university, Trinity College Dublin, scores just outside the top hundred in world terms. By contrast, the United

Kingdom has four universities in the top ten.

27 The northern European states are often described as 'socialist' in US parlance, but they are actually social democ-racies – or more accurately, social capitalist states. The United States, by contrast, while in formal terms a cap-italist democracy, might at this stage be more appropriately described as embodying a form of state corporatism or plutosocialism, or indeed neo-feu-dalism (or, in Sheldon Wolin's terms, managed democracy or 'inverted total-itarianism'). China, on the other hand, seems to have developed a kind of cap-italist socialism, or socialist capitalism, perhaps on the road to an aspirational pure socialism or communism. On the rather bizarre relationship between neoliberalism and socialism in China, see Christopher Connery, 'Coase in Beijing', *New Left Review,* no. 115 (Jan–Feb 2019), pp. 29–57.

28 See Denis Staunton, '"An Independent Spirit of Mind": The March Towards Welsh Independence', *The Irish Times,* 24 April 2021, https://www.irishtimes. com/news/world/uk/an-independ-ent-spirit-of-mind-the-march-to-wards-welsh-independence-1.4545872 (accessed 26 April 2021).

29 Quoted in Jean Davidson, 'UCI Scientists Told Moscow's Aim Is to Deprive U.S. of Foe', *Los Angeles Times,* 12 Dec. 1988, https://www. latimes.com/archives/la-xpm-1988-12-12-me-14-story.html (accessed 3 March 2021).

30 The oddly named 'neoliberalism', a term used by leftists to denote extreme forms of capitalism, is another matter

– the entity it attempts to characterise is neither new nor liberal, and the positive connotations of the term 'liberalism' tend to undercut the attempt at critique. 'Hypercapitalism' may be a happier, or perhaps unhappier, descriptor.

31 Aristotle, *The Politics*, trans. T.A. Sinclair (London: Penguin, 1992), p. 334.

32 *Ibid.*, p. 346.

33 Plato, *Republic*, Book VIII, trans. G.M.A. Grube, revised by C.D.C. Reeve, in Plato, *Complete Works*, ed. John M. Cooper (Indianapolis/Cambridge: Hackett,1997), pp. 1174–7.

34 Plato writes that, in the interest of success in war, we should practice control over others and submission to them in return: freedom from control, in his view, should be eradicated from life. Plato, *Laws*, Book XII, trans. Trevor J. Saunders, in Plato, *Complete Works*, p. 1592. Here and elsewhere may be observed Plato's (destructive) influence on the development of education, and its historical outcome in imperialism.

35 See Noel Ignatiev, *How the Irish Became White* (London: Routledge, 1995).

36 Nicholas Carnes and Noam Lupu, 'It's Time to Bust the Myth: Most Trump Voters Were Not Working Class', *Washington Post*, 5 June 2017, https://www.washingtonpost.com/news/monkey-cage/wp/2017/06/05/its-time-to-bust-the-myth-most-trump-voters-were-not-working-class/ (accessed 4 Feb. 2021).

37 Tocqueville, *Democracy in America*, p. 212.

38 *Macrotrends*, 'US Military Spending/Defense Budget 1961–2021', https://www.macrotrends.net/countries/USA/united-states/military-spending-defense-budget (accessed 4 Feb. 2021). According to this source, the budget increased from the previous year by 7.22 per cent in 2019, by 5.53 per cent in 2018, and by 1.08 per cent in 2017.

39 Robert Reich, 'How Trump Has Betrayed the Working Class', *The Guardian*, 22 Dec. 2019, https://www.theguardian.com/commentisfree/2019/dec/22/trump-wants-to-be-champion-of-the-working-class-but-with-tax-cuts-for-the-rich-it-doesnt-add-up (accessed 14 Oct. 2021).

40 In a comparable way in Ireland, the civil service, with the supposedly cushy lifestyle of its employees, was the target of misdirected, media-generated ire among the population at the time of the economic crash and the resultant bank bailout and intervention by the IMF.

41 Jessica Murphy, 'Toronto Professor Jordan Peterson Takes On Gender-Neutral Pronouns', BBC News, 4 Nov. 2016, https://www.bbc.com/news/world-us-canada-37875695 (accessed 26 Nov. 2020).

42 See Dustin Guastella, 'We Need a Class War, not a Culture War', *Jacobin*, 25 May 2020, https://www.jacobinmag.com/2020/05/we-need-a-class-war-not-a-cultural-war (accessed 26 Nov. 2020).

43 Lee Drutman, 'America is Now the Divided Republic the Framers Feared', *The Atlantic*, 2 Jan. 2020, https://www.theatlantic.com/ideas/archive/2020/01/two-party-sys-

tem-broke-constitution/604213/ (accessed 3 March 2021).

44 Cato Institute, 'Living with Guns: A Liberal's Case for the Second Amendment', video, 1.31.35, 9 Jan. 2013, https://www.cato.org/ events/living-guns-liberals-case-second-amendment (accessed 3 March 2021).

45 See Stephen C. Webster, 'Chomsky: Ron Paul Is Right about Al Qaeda', *Raw Story*, 13 Sep. 2011, https://www. rawstory.com/2011/09/chomsky-ron-paul-is-right-about-al-qaeda/ (accessed 6 Feb. 2021).

46 Ellen Brown, 'Why Qaddafi Had To Go: African Gold, Oil and the Challenge to Monetary Imperialism', *Ecologist*, 14 March 2016, https://theecologist.org/2016/ mar/14/why-qaddafi-had-go-african-gold-oil-and-challenge-monetary-imperialism (accessed 28 Nov. 2020).

47 Tocqueville, *Democracy in America*, p. 68.

48 Commissioner for Human Rights, *Council of Europe: OpenDemocracy*, 17 July 2017, https://www.coe.int/en/ web/commissioner/-/poland-has-a-duty-to-preserve-judicial-independence (accessed 28 Nov. 2020).

49 This did not prevent Hitler from making common cause with the non-Aryan Finns and Japanese, as well as the Hungarians, or from persecuting the Aryan Roma and Slavs – his racism was, to some extent, a means to satisfying his will to power.

50 See Tony Judt, *The Burden of Responsibility: Blum, Camus, Aron and the French Twentieth Century* (Chicago: The University of Chicago Press, 1998).

51 Emmanuelle Reungoat and Colin Kinniburgh, 'The Roots of the French Far Right's Rise', *Dissent*, 4 June 2019, https://www.dissentmagazine. org/online_articles/the-roots-of-the-french-far-rights-rise (accessed 10 March 2021).

52 Albert Speer, *Inside the Third Reich*, trans. Richard and Clara Winston, introd. Eugene Davidson (New York: Simon and Schuster, 1970). Speer (p. 98) quotes Hitler, 'You see, it's been our misfortune to have the wrong religion. Why didn't we have the religion of the Japanese, who regard sacrifice for the Fatherland as the highest good? The Mohammedan religion too would have been much more compatible to us than Christianity. Why did it have to be Christianity with its meekness and flabbiness?' According to Speer (p. 98), Hitler speculated that if the Arabs had won the Battle of Tours in the eighth century, the modern world would be Muslim. (However, in Hitler's view, due to what he regarded as the racial inferiority of the Arabs, Islamised Germans would dominate.)

53 'Anti-Semitism: In the Arab/Muslim World', AICE, Jewish Virtual Library, https://www.jewishvirtuallibrary.org/ anti-semitism-in-the-arab-muslim-world (accessed 6 Feb. 2021).

54 See Jean Jacques Rousseau, *The Social Contract*, ed. and introd. Charles Frankel (New York: Hafner, 1947).

55 Aristotle, *Politics*, p. 187.

56 *Ibid.*, pp. 60–1.

57 Montesquieu, *The Spirit of the Laws*, trans. and ed. Anne M. Cohler,

Basia C. Miller and Harold S. Stone (Cambridge: Cambridge University Press), p. 114.

58 Tocqueville, *Democracy in America*, p. 136.

59 Thomas Hobbes, *Leviathan*, ed. and introd. C.B. MacPherson (London: Penguin, 1985), pp. 185, 186.

60 *Ibid.*, p. 227.

61 *Ibid.*, p. 272.

62 *Ibid.*, p. 315. For an entertaining deconstruction of conventional approaches to the history of the state and inequality, and a dismissal of prejudices against the viability of participatory democracy, see David Graeber and David Wengrow, 'How to Change the Course of Human History (At Least, the Part That's Already Happened)', *Eurozine*, 2 March 2018, https://eurozine.com/change-course-human-history (accessed 14 April 2021).

63 John Locke, 'An Essay Concerning Toleration', in Locke, *Political Writings*, ed. and introd. David Wooton (London: Penguin, 1993), p. 200.

64 John Locke, 'The Second Treatise of Government', in Locke, *Political Writings*, p. 289.

65 John Stuart Mill, *On Liberty*, in John Stuart Mill, *Utilitarianism, Liberty, Representative Government,* ed. H.B. Acton (London: J.M. Dent, 1972). In a key passage, with devastating implications for modern anti-drug laws, Mill writes (p. 73), 'the only purpose for which power can be rightfully exercised over any member of a civilised community, against his will, is to prevent harm to others. His own good, either

physical or moral, is not a sufficient warrant. He cannot rightfully be compelled to do or forbear because it will be better for him to do so, because it will make him happier, because, in the opinions of others, to do so would be wise, or even right [...] The only part of the conduct of any one, for which he is amenable to society, is that which concerns others.' The distinction between sin (moral evil) and crime is here clearly delineated by Mill.

66 Montesquieu, *The Spirit of the Laws*, p. 197.

67 *Ibid.*, p. 199.

68 See Rutger Bregman, *Utopia for Realists: The Case for Universal Basic Income, Open Borders, and a 15-Hour Workweek*, trans. Elizabeth Manton (Netherlands: The Correspondent, 2016).

69 See Scott Shane and Jo Becker, 'The Libya Gamble: A New Libya, With "Very Little Time Left"', *The New York Times*, 27 Feb. 2016, https://www.nytimes.com/2016/02/28/us/politics/libya-isis-hillary-clinton.html (accessed 4 Feb. 2021).

70 Matthew Paterson, Peter Doran and John Barry, 'Green Theory', in Colin Hay *et al*, eds, *The State*, p. 138.

71 Michael Lister and David Marsh, 'Conclusion', in Colin Hay *et al*, eds, *The State*, p. 258.

72 Matthew Paterson, Peter Doran and John Barry, 'Green Theory', in Colin Hay *et al*, eds, *The State*, pp. 139–40.

73 *Ibid.*, p. 141.

74 See Paul O'Brien, *Universal Basic Income: Pennies from Heaven* (UK: The History Press, 2017).

75 See Matthew Paterson, Peter Doran and John Barry, 'Green Theory', in Colin Hay *et al*, eds, *The State*, pp. 135–54.

76 Yevgeny Zemyatin, *We*, trans. Bernard Guilbert Guerney, introd. Michael Glenny (London: Penguin, 1987).

77 George Orwell, *Nineteen Eighty-Four* (London: Penguin, 2013).

78 Karl Popper coined the term 'Oedipus Effect' for a theory that has the effect of changing the object it theorises about: Popper, *The Poverty of Historicism* (London: Routledge, 2002), pp. 11–12. The term might be applied to *Nineteen Eighty-Four*, though its effects (both positive, in terms of a defence of freedom, and negative, as contributing to the suspicion of socialism) can only be suggested rather than quantified in any meaningful way.

79 See Jaclyn Peiser, 'The Rise of the Robot Reporter', *The New York Times*, 5 Feb. 2019, https://www.nytimes.com/2019/02/05/business/media/artificial-intelligence-journalism-robots.html (accessed 6 Feb. 2021).

Chapter 2

1 It is estimated that, as a result of the pandemic, an extra 40 billion euros will be added to the Irish national debt over a period of two years. See Jack Horgan-Jones, 'State to Outline Plans to Tackle National Debt Caused by Covid-19 Next Year', *The Irish Times*, 13 Oct. 2020, https://www.irishtimes.com/news/politics/state-to-outline-plans-to-tackle-national-debt-caused-by-covid-19-next-year-1.4380155 (accessed 3 Dec. 2020).

2 Rob Wallace, interview by Yaak Pabst, 'Capitalist Agriculture and COVID: a Deadly Combination', Climate & Capitalism, 11 March 2020, https://climateandcapitalism.com/2020/03/11/capitalist-agriculture-and-covid-19-a-deadly-combination/. The interview is also available in *Marx21* (English version) https://www.marx21.de/coronavirus-agribusiness-would-risk-millions-of-deaths/ (accessed 3 Dec. 2020). See also Jonathan Safran Foer and Aaron S. Gross, 'We Have to Wake Up: Factory Farms are Breeding Grounds for Pandemics', *The Guardian*, 20 April 2020, https://www.theguardian.com/commentisfree/2020/apr/20/factory-farms-pandemic-risk-covid-animal-human-health (accessed 14 Feb. 2021). For a comprehensive overview from a left perspective of the socioeconomic background to the pandemic, see Rob Wallace, Alex Liebman, Luis Fernando Chaves and Rodrick Wallace, 'Covid-19 and Circuits of Capital', *Monthly Review*, 1 May 2020 https://monthlyreview.org/2020/05/01/covid-19-and-circuits-of-capital/ (accessed 7 Dec. 2020).

3 Nonetheless, Biden's corporate tax plans may also add to the economic storm clouds already on the horizon for Ireland in terms of threats to its tax arrangements, including the celebrated 12.5 per cent corporate tax rate: see Aiden Regan, 'Biden's Historic Plan for America and What It Means for Ireland Inc', *Business Post*, 4 April 2021. See also Editorial, 'Biden's Plan Puts Irish Corporate Tax Regime Back into Focus Again', *Business Post*, 4 April

2021. The editorial notes that 'The most objectionable aspect of Ireland's corporate tax regime in the eyes of its critics is not the 12.5 per cent tax rate, but the jungle of loopholes and special arrangements that flourish beneath and around it.' At the time of writing it looks as if the (almost sacred) 12.5 per cent tax rate will be sacrificed.

4   At the time of writing, a 'pilot' UBI scheme for artists, one of the worst-hit groups of the pandemic, is being implemented in Ireland.

5   See, for example, Daniel Romer and Kathleen Hall Jamieson, 'Conspiracy Theories as Barriers to Controlling the Spread of COVID-19 in the U.S.', *Social Science and Medicine*, vol. 263 (Oct. 2020), https://www.sciencedirect.com/science/article/pii/S027795362030575X (accessed 3 Dec. 2020).

6   Schwab and Malleret, *Covid-19: The Great Reset.*

7   *Ibid.*, pp. 18–19.

8   *Ibid.*, p. 92.

9   *Ibid.*, p. 101.

10 *Ibid.*, pp. 153, 160–6.

11 *Ibid.*, pp. 165–6.

12 *Ibid.*, p. 106.

13 *Ibid.*, p. 195.

14 *Ibid.*, pp. 201–4.

15 *Ibid.*, pp. 137–8.

16 *Ibid.*, pp. 139–40.

17 Naomi Klein, 'How Big Tech Plans to Profit from the Pandemic', *The Guardian*, 13 May 2020, https://www.theguardian.com/news/2020/may/13/naomi-klein-how-big-tech-plans-to-profit-from-coronavirus-pandemic (accessed 7 Dec. 2020).

18 *Ibid.*

19 For an interesting discussion touching on the issue of 'life years' lost or potentially lost, and the moral choices that the pandemic forces on us, see Emily Bazelon, 'Restarting America Means People Will Die. So When Do We Do It? Five Thinkers Weigh Moral Choices in a Crisis', *The New York Times Magazine*, 15 June 2020, https://www.nytimes.com/2020/04/10/magazine/coronavirus-economy-debate.html (accessed 6 April 2021).

20 In practice, totalitarianism, at least of the Nazi variety, reverses traditional notions of good and evil, turning Judeo-Christian moral distinctions on their head and substituting racial-aesthetic values for conventional notions of morality.

21 The statement may be too sweeping, as some non-theists believe in life after death, perhaps with associated beliefs in karma, reincarnation, etc.

22 Ernst Nolte, *Three Faces of Fascism*, trans. Leila Vennewiz (New York: Mentor, 1969), p. 36.

23 For discussions of this area, see https://diresomnet.files.wordpress.com/2020/05/law-religion-and-covid-19-emergency_diresom-papers-1-2.pdf (accessed 26 April 2021). See also Breda O'Brien, 'Government Treats Religion As Whimsical Hobby', *The Irish Times*, 24 April 2021, https://www.irishtimes.com/opinion/breda-o-brien-government-treats-religion-as-whimsical-hobby-1.4545772 (accessed 26 April 2021).

24 Carl Schmitt, *The Concept of the Political*, trans. and introd. George Schwab (Chicago: The University of Chicago Press), p. 22.

25 *Ibid.*, p. 25. The relationship between the concept of the total state and totalitarianism in Schmitt's thought is rather complicated and unclear (see *ibid.*, pp. 38–9). I use the two terms interchangeably. Schmitt attacks liberalism in particular for its critical attitude – in the interest of preserving the freedom of the individual as well as private property – to politics and the state (*ibid.*, p. 70).

26 Roger Eatwell and Matthew Goodwin, *National Populism: The Revolt against Liberal Democracy* (London: Pelican, 2018), p. 63. The authors refer to the following: Juan Linz, *Authoritarian and Totalitarian Regimes* (Boulder, CO: Lynne Riener, 2000); Roger Eatwell, 'The Nature of "Generic Fascism": Complexity and Reflective Hybridity', in António Costa Pinto and Aristotle Kallis, eds, *Rethinking Fascism and Dictatorship in Europe* (Basingstoke: Palgrave Macmillan, 2014); Robert Gellately, *Backing Hitler: Consent and Coercion in Nazi Germany* (Oxford: Oxford University Press 2001); and Ian Kershaw, *The Hitler Myth: Image and Reality in the Third Reich* (Oxford: Oxford University Press, 1987).

27 Richard Shorten, *Modernism and Totalitarianism* (London: Palgrave Macmillan, 2012), p. 4.

28 *Ibid.*, p. 59.

29 *Ibid.*, p. 60. See also p. 254, n. 46.

30 *Ibid.*, p. 240.

31 *Ibid.*, p. 72.

32 *Ibid.*, p. 208.

33 *Ibid.*, p. 166.

34 *Ibid.*, pp. 237–9.

35 Tzvetan Todorov, *Hope and Memory: Reflections on the Twentieth Century*, trans. David Bellos (London: Atlantic Books, 2014), p. 14.

36 *Ibid.*, p. 312.

37 *Ibid.*, p. 77.

38 *Ibid.*, pp. 314–18.

39 Hannah Arendt, *The Origins of Totalitarianism* (New York/London: Harcourt Brace Jovanovitch, 1973). The book first appeared in 1951, though an edition with an added section was published in 1958. Roberts, in *Totalitarianism* (p. 152, n. 7), observes that the added part was originally a 1950 lecture – therefore from the same time as the original book.

40 *Ibid.*, pp. 287–9. For an informative discussion of statelessness in the light of Arendt's thought, see Caylee Hong, 'The Citizen as Mere Human: Litigating Denationalization in Post-9/11 UK', *Anthropological Theory*, https://www.academia.edu/43568782/The_Citizen_as_Mere_Human_Litigating_Denationalization_in_Post_9_11_UK (accessed 12 Feb. 2021).

41 See John Podesta, 'The Climate Crisis, Migration and Refugees', *Brookings: Brookings Blum Roundtable on Global Poverty*, 25 July 2019, https://www.brookings.edu/research/the-climate-crisis-migration-and-refugees/ (accessed 8 Feb. 2021).

42 For a useful discussion of the philosophical background to Arendt's thought in this area – particularly regarding her responses to the philosophers Augustine, Martin Heidegger and Carl Schmitt – see John Wolfe Ackerman, 'The Memory of Politics: Hannah Arendt, Carl Schmitt

and the Possibility of Encounter',
in G. Pollock and M. Silverman,
eds, *Concentrationary Memories:
Totalitarian Terror and Cultural
Resistance* (London/New York: I.B.
Tauris), 2013, pp. 31–43, https://
tinyurl.com/or7os1es (accessed 4 Dec.
2020).

43 See John Lukacs, 'Intellectual
Opportunism and the Arteriosclerosis
of the American Intelligentsia',
Vital Works Reconsidered, 3, *The New
Oxford Review* [Archives], April 1990,
https://www.newoxfordreview.org/
documents/intellectual-opportun-
ism-the-arteriosclerosis-of-the-ameri-
can-intelligentsia/ (accessed 4 March
2021). Lukacs here also criticises
Arendt in regard to her status as a
political theorist rather than a historian.

44 See, for example, Strobe Talbott,
'Stalin, Hitler and the Temptations of
Totalitarianism', *The New York Times*,
18 Oct. 2017, https://www.nytimes.
com/2017/10/18/books/review/
stalin-hitler-totalitarianism.html
(accessed 8 Feb. 2021).

45 Arendt, *The Origins of Totalitarianism*,
p. 301.

46 *Ibid.*, p. 456.

47 *Ibid.*, p. 457.

48 *Ibid.*, p. 323.

49 *Ibid.*, p. 460.

50 *Ibid.*, pp. 461–2.

51 *Ibid.*, p. 466.

52 This is currently a hot topic in India,
with its traditional caste system. See
for example Shambhavi Naik, 'The
Scientific Argument for Marrying
Outside Your Caste', *The Print,* 8 Feb.
2020, https://theprint.in/science/

the-scientific-argument-for-mar-
rying-outside-your-caste/360975/
(accessed 8 Feb. 2021).

53 Even before the war, Hitler remarked
that the healthy lives of the Slavs made
them, ultimately, superior in biological
terms to the Germans: quoted in
Albert Speer, *Inside the Third Reich*, p.
96.

54 Arendt, *The Origins of Totalitarianism*,
p. 382.

55 *Ibid.*, p. 474. Whether such an ideal
subject actually exists is a moot point,
though approximation to such a state
of being seems as conceivable in our
own day as it did in hers.

56 For a left-realist discussion of the issue,
see Michiko Kakutani, 'The Death
of Truth: How We Gave Up on Facts
and Ended Up with Trump', *The
Guardian*, 14 July 2018, https://www.
theguardian.com/books/2018/jul/14/
the-death-of-truth-how-we-gave-up-
on-facts-and-ended-up-with-trump
(accessed 8 Feb. 2021). Kakutani
notes issues such as the erosion of
the distinction between news and
entertainment, and the appropriation
from the academy, by the right, of the
philosophical perspective of relativism.

57 Arendt, *The Origins of Totalitarianism*,
p. 325. Indeed, in Orwell's *Nineteen
Eighty-Four* there is a question as to
whether the leader, 'Big Brother', even
exists in the first place.

58 Arendt, *The Origins of Totalitarianism*,
p. 327.

59 *Ibid.*, p. 339.

60 Jonathan R. Cole, 'Ignorance
Does Not Lead to Election Bliss',
The Atlantic, 8 Nov. 2018, https://
www.theatlantic.com/education/

archive/2016/11/ignorance-does-not-lead-to-election-bliss/506894/ (accessed 8 Feb. 2021).

61 Shawn Rosenberg, 'Opinion: We'll Find Out After the 2020 Presidential Election if Americans Were Just too Angry and Fed Up with Democracy to Save It', *Market Watch*, 12 Sep. 2020, https://www.marketwatch.com/story/americas-elites-are-failing-in-the-covid-19-pandemic-and-thats-pushing-us-voters-towards-right-wing-populism-2020-09-09 (accessed 14 Oct. 2021). See also Shawn Rosenberg, 'Democracy Devouring Itself: The Rise of the Incompetent Citizen and the Appeal of Right Wing Populism', in *Psychology of Political and Everyday Extremism* (UC Irvine, 2019), retrieved from https://escholarship.org/uc/item/8806z01m.

62 Arendt, *The Origins of Totalitarianism*, p. 395.

63 Quoted in *ibid.*, p. 394. The dictum is from Hitler's 'warning' to the jurists in 1933, quoted in Hans Frank, *Nationalsozialistische Leitsätze für ein neues deutsches Strafrecht*, Zweiter Teil, (1936), p. 8.

64 Arendt, *The Origins of Totalitarianism*, p. 394.

65 *Ibid.*, p. 400. Far from being mono-lithic, totalitarianism in Arendt's terms involves not only competition between state and party but also within the party itself and its various organs. In a description that could have come straight from Kafka, Arendt describes how the Central Committee and the Politburo dealt with the reports of the varying Soviet police agencies. Here, a decision was made between the reports and the associated police measures. Arendt notes that no one knew which decision would be made as to who would be chosen to carry out the will of the leadership, except that ultimately one of them would be. Competition is actively fostered by totalitarianism – a process that under-mines the possibility of opposition from within (*ibid.*, pp. 403–4).

66 See, for example, Andy Beckett, 'PPE: The Oxford Degree that Runs Britain', *The Guardian*, 27 Feb. 2017, https://www.the-guardian.com/education/2017/feb/23/ppe-oxford-university-de-gree-that-rules-britain (accessed 8 Feb. 2021).

67 Arendt, *The Origins of Totalitarianism*, p. 358. See Adolf Hitler, *Reden*, ed. Ernst Boepple (Munich: 1933), p. 125; and Josef Stalin, *Leninism* (1933), Vol. II, chapter iii.

68 Arendt, *The Origins of Totalitarianism*, p. 430.

69 *Ibid.*, p. 433.

70 *Ibid.*, p. 411.

71 *Ibid.*, p. 434.

72 *Ibid.*, p. 438.

73 *Ibid.*, p. 452.

74 *Ibid.*, p. 455.

75 *Ibid.*, p. 465.

76 Bauman, *Modernity and the Holocaust*, p. xiii.

77 *Ibid.*, p. 18.

78 *Ibid.*, p. 46.

79 *Ibid.*, p. 93.

80 *Ibid.*, p. 95.

81 *Ibid.*, pp. 108–9.

82 *Ibid.*, p. 219.

83 *Ibid.*, pp. 219–20.

84 David D. Roberts, *Totalitarianism* (Cambridge, UK: Polity, 2020), p. 28.

85 *Ibid.*, p. 31.

86 *Ibid.*, p. 72.

87 Roberts, *Totalitarianism*, pp. 32–3. For further discussion in the area of totalitarianism over the last couple of decades, see for example, Bauman, *Modernity and the Holocaust*; Richard Shorten, *Modernism and Totalitarianism*; Tzvetan Todorov, *Hope and Memory*; and Slavoj Žižek, *Did Somebody Say Totalitarianism? Five Interventions in the (Mis)Use of a Notion* (London: Verso, 2001).

88 Carl J. Friedrich and Zbigniew Brzezinski, *Totalitarian Dictatorship and Democracy*, 2nd ed. (New York: Praeger, 1965 [1956]).

89 Roberts, pp. 33–4.

90 *Ibid.*, p. 34.

91 Žižek, *Did Somebody Say Totalitarianism?*, pp. 3, 5.

92 Daniel Defoe, *Journal of the Plague Year* (London: 1722), https://www.gutenberg.org/files/376/376-h/376-h.htm (accessed 11 March 2021).

93 Michel Foucault, *Discipline and Punish: The Birth of the Prison*, trans. Alan Sheridan (New York: Vintage/Random House), p. 195.

94 Binoy Kampmark, 'The Pandemic Surveillance State: An Enduring Legacy of COVID-19', *Journal of Global Faultlines*, vol. 7, no. 1 (June–Aug. 2020), p. 67, https://www.jstor.org/stable/pdf/10.13169/jglobfaul.7.1.0059.pdf?refreqid=excelsior%3A87fb482bf-0e40c7ab2fe24a3971e099c (accessed 9 Feb. 2021). The article as a whole is a valuable source of information on the topic.

95 The Left in the European Parliament, 'Covid-19 Exposes the Destructive Legacy of Neoliberalism', 22 April 2020, https://www.guengl.eu/covid-19-exposes-the-destructive-legacy-of-neoliberalism/ (accessed 9 Feb. 2021).

96 *Ibid.*

97 Giorgio Agamben, *Homo Sacer: Sovereign Power and Bare Life,* trans. Daniel Heller-Roazen (Stanford: Stanford University Press, 1998), p. 105.

98 Christopher Caldwell, 'Meet the Philosopher Who Is Trying to Explain the Pandemic', *The New York Times*, 21 Aug. 2020, https://www.nytimes.com/2020/08/21/opinion/sunday/giorgio-agamben-philosophy-coronavirus.html (accessed 7 Dec. 2020).

99 Giorgio Agamben, 'Biosicurezza e politica', *Quodlibet*, 11 May 2020, https://www.quodlibet.it/giorgio-agamben-biosicurezza (accessed 9 Dec. 2020). For a translation, see Giorgio Abamben, 'Biosecurity and Politics', *Autonomies*, posted by Julius Gavroche, 13 May 2020, https://autonomies.org/2020/05/giorgio-agamben-biosecurity-and-politics/ (accessed 14 Oct. 2021). See Patrick Sylberman, *Tempêtes microbiennes* (Gallimard, 2013).

100 Agamben, *ibid.*

101 Giorgio Agamben, *State of Exception*, trans. Kevin Attell (Chicago: University of Chicago Press, 2005), p. 1.

102 *Ibid.*, p. 2.

103 *Ibid.*, p.15.

104 Robert Paxton, *The Anatomy of Fascism* (London: Penguin, 2004), p. 107.

105 *Ibid.*, pp. 107–8. Catholic political support for Nazism was mixed with opposition, as for example with the papal document of 1937, *Mit Brennender Sorge*. See Nolte, *Three Faces of Fascism*, p. 37.

106 Carl Schmitt, *Staat, Grossraum, Nomos* (Berlin: Duncker & Humblot, 1995), p. 25, quoted in Agamben, *State of Exception*, p. 15.

107 Agamben, *State of Exception*, p. 15.

108 *Ibid.*, p. 2.

109 *Ibid.*, pp. 3–4.

110 *Ibid.*, p. 5.

111 Carl J. Friedrich, *Constitutional Government and Democracy*, 2nd ed. (Boston: Ginn, [1941] 1950), p. 584, quoted in Agamben, *State of Exception*, p. 8.

112 Agamben, *State of Exception*, p. 22.

113 'Watch: Why is the US Always at War?' *University of California Press, UC Press Blog*, https://www.ucpress.edu/blog/52585/watch-why-is-the-u-s-always-at-war/ (accessed 9 Feb. 2021).

114 Agamben, *State of Exception*, pp. 15–22.

115 *Ibid.*, p. 17. Agamben gives historical examples of the erosion of liberty in England (p. 19), the United States (pp. 20–1) and contemporary Italy (p. 18).

116 For a useful discussion of these issues in the context of state surveillance, see Kristine Eck and Sophia Hatz, 'State Surveillance and the COVID-19 Crisis', *Journal of Human Rights*, 19/5 (2020), pp. 603–12, https://www.tandfonline.com/doi/full/10.1080/14754835.2020.1816163 (accessed 20 April 2020).

117 Agamben, *State of Exception*, p. 24.

118 *Ibid.*, p. 48.

119 *Ibid.*, p. 50.

120 See Nedra Pickler, 'Group Says Body Scanners an "Unreasonable Search"', *Washington Post*, 10 March 2011, https://www.washingtonpost.com/wp-dyn/content/article/2011/03/10/AR2011031003628.html (accessed 12 Feb. 2021).

121 Agamben, *State of Exception*, pp. 86–7.

122 Agamben, *Homo Sacer*, p. 3. See Michel Foucault, *History of Sexuality*, Volume 1: An Introduction, trans. Robert Hurley (New York: Random House, 1978).

123 Agamben, *State of Exception*, p. 119. Foucault's book *The Birth of Biopolitics*, comprising a collection of his lectures from 1978–9, gives the historical context for the rise of biopolitics, but actually says little about biopolitics per se. See Michel Foucault, *The Birth of Biopolitics*, ed. Michel Senellart, trans. Graham Burchell (New York: Picador, 1978).

124 Agamben, *Homo Sacer*, p. 8.

125 See 'Bare life', Oxford Reference, https://www.oxfordreference.com/view/10.1093/oi/authority.20110803095446660 (accessed 11 March 2021).

126 Agamben, *Homo Sacer*, p. 10.

127 *Ibid.*, p. 20.

128 *Ibid.*, p. 123.

129 *Ibid.*, p. 147.

130 *Ibid.*, p. 115.

131 James J. Criss, 'COVID-19 and Social Control', *Academicus*, 2021, pp. 34, 35–7, https://www.academia.edu/44917242/COVID_19_and_Social_Control (accessed 10 Feb. 2021).

132 Sarah Repucci and Amy Slipowitz, 'Democracy Under Lockdown: The Impact of COVID-19 on the Global Struggle for Freedom', *Freedom House*, Oct. 2020, https://www.academia.edu/45079713/The_Impact_of_COVID_19_on_the_Global_Struggle_for_Freedom (accessed 10 Feb. 2021).

133 Agamben, *Homo Sacer*, p. 120. See Hannah Arendt, *Essays in Understanding, 1930–1954*, ed. Jerome Kohn (New York: Harcourt & Brace, 1994), p. 240.

134 Agamben, *Homo Sacer,* p. 120.

135 *Ibid.*, pp. 142–3.

136 On developments on assisted dying with an Irish focus, see Jennifer O'Connell, 'Assisted Dying: How Has It Worked in Other Countries?' *The Irish Times*, 15 Feb. 2021, https://www.irishtimes.com/news/social-affairs/assisted-dying-how-has-it-worked-in-other-countries-1.4484734 (accessed 29 April 2021).

137 Agamben, *Homo Sacer*, pp. 166–7.

138 *Ibid.*, p.167.

139 *Ibid.*, p.168.

140 *Ibid.*, pp. 168–9.

141 *Ibid.*, p. 171.

142 *Ibid.*, pp. 174–5.

143 *Ibid.*, p. 175.

144 *Ibid.*, p. 184.

145 Joelle M. Abi-Rached, 'The Covid-19 Caesura and the Post-Pandemic Future', *Biosocieties*, https://www.academia.edu/45058478/The_Covid_19_caesura_and_the_post_pandemic_future (accessed 10 Feb. 2021). This is a very useful review of recent Covid-19 literature – from philosophical, sociological and politi-cal perspectives, published in English and French. The literature covered includes J. Attali, *L'économie de la Vie* (Paris: Fayard, 2020); R. Horton, *The Covid-19 Catastrophe: What's Gone Wrong and How to Stop It Happening Again* (London: Polity, 2020); E. Morin (with the collaboration of S. Abouessalam), *Changeons de Voie: Les Leçons du Coronavirus* (Paris: Denoël, 2020); J-L.Nancy, *Un trop Humain Virus* (Paris: Bayard, 2020); S. Žižek, *Pandemic! Covid-19 Shakes the World* (London: Polity, 2020). The author also refers to G. Agamben, '*The State of Exception Provoked by an Unmotivated Emergency', Positions*, 26 Feb. 2020, http://positionspolitics.org/giorgio-agamben-the-state-of-exception-provoked-by-an-unmotivated-emergency/ (accessed 11 March 2021).

146 For a useful critique of Agamben in relation to Arendt and Foucault, see Claire Blencowe, 'Foucault's and Arendt's "Insider View" of Biopolitics: A Critique of Agamben', *History of the Human Sciences,* 23/5 (Dec. 2010), pp. 113–30, https://www.researchgate.net/publication/49837793_Foucault%27s_and_Arendt%27s_%27insider_view%27_of_biopolitics_A_critique_of_Agamben (accessed 12 Feb. 2021). Blencowe criticises Agamben for what she views as his (overly) abstract, transhistorical and disempowering perspective in regard to biopolitics.

147 Shorten, *Modernism and Totalitarianism*, p. 58.

148 For a fairly recent, mildly optimistic discussion of Agamben vis-à-vis the pandemic, see

Jörn Ahrens, 'Theorising – Praise of Biopolitics? The Covid-19 Pandemic and the Will for Self-Preservation', *The European Sociologist*, 45, Pandemic (Im)possibilities, vol. 1 (2020), *https://www.europeansociologist.org/issue-45-pandemic-impossibilities-vol-1/theorising-praise-biopolitics-cov-id-19-pandemic-and-will* (accessed 9 February 2021).

149 Alexis de Tocqueville, *Democracy in America* (Hertfordshire: Wordsworth, 1998), p. 358.

150 The account of Wolin's ideas in the preceding paragraphs is based on Chris Hedges, 'Sheldon Wolin and Inverted Totalitarianism', Truthdig, 2 Nov. 2015, https://www.truthdig.com/articles/sheldon-wolin-and-inverted-totali-tarianism/ (accessed 4 March 2021). The key texts are Sheldon Wolin, *Democracy Incorporated: Managed Democracy and the Spectre of Inverted Totalitarianism* (Princeton: Princeton University Press, 2017), and Sheldon Wolin, *Politics and Vision: Continuity and Innovation in Western Political Thought* (London: George Allen & Unwin, 1961).

151 Wolin, *Democracy Incorporated*, pp. xxi, 44. Wolin defines 'traditional' totalitarianism as 'the attempt to realize an […] idealized conception of a society as a systematically ordered whole, where the "parts"[…] are premeditatedly […] coordinated to support and further the purposes of the regime. The formulation of those purposes is monopolized by the leadership.' In inverted totalitarianism, by contrast, 'managed' democracy prevails. Wolin, *Democracy Incorporated*,

pp. 46–7. Capitalism, rather than being subordinate to the state – as, for example, in Nazism – is directly involved in government (p. 63).

152 *Ibid.*, p. 185.

153 *Ibid.*, pp. 196–7.

154 *Ibid.*, p. 64.

155 *Ibid.*, p. 68.

156 *Ibid.*, p. 126.

157 *Ibid.*, pp. 127–8.

158 *Ibid.*, p. 135.

159 *Ibid.*, pp. 88, 132.

160 *Ibid.*, p. 93.

161 *Ibid.*, p. 133.

162 *Ibid.*, p. 198.

163 *Ibid.*, p. 107.

164 *Ibid.*, p. 111.

165 *Ibid.*, pp. 110–11.

166 *Ibid.*, p. 155.

167 *Ibid.*, pp. 228–30.

168 *Ibid.*, pp. 235–7.

169 *Ibid.*, pp. 162–3.

170 *Ibid.*, pp. 182–3.

171 *Ibid.*, pp. 239, 242.

172 *Ibid.*, pp. 246–7.

173 *Ibid.*, p. 256.

174 *Ibid.*, p. 257.

175 *Ibid.*, p. 287.

176 The distinction between the capitalised and non-capitalised terms should be noted. I use the initial lower case to denote the broader sense of the term – in other words, it is not confined to the name of a particular political party.

177 *Ibid.*, p. 258.

178 *Ibid.*, pp. 273–4. Wolin's endorsement here of the system of checks and balances, and the separation of powers, seems to run counter to his criticism of the origin of such measures as being to inhibit democratic potential (see p. 155).

179 *Ibid.*, pp. 290–2.

Chapter 3

1 Karl Popper, *The Open Society and Its Enemies* (Routledge: London and New York, [1945] 2011). Other key texts of Popper's include *Conjectures and Refutations: The Growth of Scientific Knowledge* (London: Routledge, 1963), *The Logic of Scientific Discovery* (London: Hutchinson, 1959), and *The Poverty of Historicism* (London: Routledge, 1961).

2 For a controversial outline of post-Covid options, see Schwab and Malleret, *Covid-19: The Great Reset.* See also Klaus Schwab, *The Fourth Industrial Revolution* (UK: Portfolio Penguin, 2017).

3 Popper, *The Open Society*, p. 189.

4 For an illuminating discussion of Green politics in its intellectual and political context, see Anna Bramwell, *Ecology in the Twentieth Century: A History* (New Haven and London: Yale University Press, 1989).

5 See C.P. Snow, *The Two Cultures*, introd. Stefan Collini (Cambridge: Cambridge University Press, 1993). Debates among Greens sometimes come down to a discussion as to whether politics is to be based on scientific facts, on the one hand, or on (non-measurable) values, on the other. Putting it in a nutshell, politics (of whatever kind) is based on values rather than facts. It is predicated on the desirability of a certain kind of society, whether actual or possible, rather than necessarily having reference to a current state of things – a

society that may not even be measurable.

6 Popper, *The Open Society*, pp. 83–4. (In a note, Popper refers to the influence of Plato on Rousseau.)

7 *Ibid.*, p. 102.

8 *Ibid.*, p. 163.

9 *Ibid.*, p. 165.

10 *Ibid.*, pp. 238–9, 241. The correctness of Popper's interpretation of 'the essence of Christianity' as being the opposite of Platonism is outside our scope. Platonic thinking, at least on the metaphysical if not the political side, was common in the early history of Christianity. However, there are some similarities even on the political side: the early Christians, like the inhabitants of Plato's Republic, practised a form of communism (see the Bible, Acts 2: 44; 4: 32–35). Also, the biblical books of Hebrews and Revelation seem to embody implicit Platonic perspectives of a dichotomy between the world of experience and an ideal world beyond it, echoing Jesus' dichotomy between the given world and the Kingdom of Heaven.

11 Lynn White, 'The Historical Roots of Our Ecologic Crisis', in R.J. Berry, ed., *The Care of Creation: Focusing Concern and Action* (London: Inter-Varsity Press, 2000), pp. 37–40. White situates the pre-eminence of progress, dualism, human domination of nature and the emergence of the scientific and technological mindset in Christianity itself – thus neatly turning on its head the prevalent view of Christianity by the 'new atheists' as being anti-scientific in spirit. Nonetheless, this overturning has another, if opposite, kind of nega-

tive result. Christianity in White's view is to blame for the negative ecological consequences of the domination of the scientific and technological mindset that it engendered. From a Christian perspective, White seeks refuge from this deplorable situation in the example of St Francis. See my article 'Religion, Domination and Serial Killing: Western Culture and Murder', in Edia Connole and Gary J. Shipley, eds, *Serial Killing: A Philosophical Anthology* (USA: Schism, 2015) pp. 183–198.

12 Popper, *The Open Society*, pp. 245–6.

13 *Ibid.*, p. 237.

14 *Ibid.*, p. 287 (Popper gives no source for the Schopenhauer quote).

15 *Ibid.*, p. 273.

16 *Ibid.*, pp. 274–84.

17 *Ibid.*, p. 273.

18 *Ibid.*, pp. 317–18.

19 On the other hand, socioeconomic issues may certainly be of relevance in the case of science – for example, by revealing why one line of enquiry has been pursued at the expense of another.

20 *Ibid.*, pp. 317–18.

21 See chapter 'The Autonomy of Sociology', *ibid.*, pp. 301–10.

22 There is a variant position, more recent, which holds that while the economic level may not determine the nature of society at any particular moment, it determines which of the other levels is determinant at that moment; thus, it may be determinant in 'the last instance'. (What exactly that might mean, if anything, is open to debate.)

23 *Ibid.*, pp. 314–15.

24 *Ibid.*, pp. 293–8.

25 *Ibid.*, pp. 327–9.

26 *Ibid.*, pp. 330–2.

27 *Ibid.*, pp. 332–4.

28 *Ibid.*, pp. 334–5. This is dangerous territory, as a key feature of totalitarianism has been the domination of the economy by politics. The exception is the contemporary structure mentioned already, defined by Sheldon Wolin as 'inverted totalitarianism', whereby politics is dominated by economic, corporate interests.

29 *Ibid.*, pp. 334–5.

30 *Ibid.*, pp. 337–41.

31 See Hamilton Nolan, 'Billionaire-Funded Protest Is Rearing its Head in America', *The Guardian*, 27 Nov. 2019, https://www.theguardian.com/commentisfree/2019/nov/27/billion-are-funded-protests-america (accessed 13 Feb. 2021).

32 Popper, *The Open Society*, p. 348.

33 For an informative account of the issue, see Mohamed Elzarka, 'The Role of Religion in the Yugoslav War', *Aisthesis*, vol. 9 (2018), pp. 29–35.

34 Popper, *The Open Society*, pp. 359–60.

35 *Ibid.*, p. 370.

36 *Ibid.*, p. 365.

37 *Ibid.*, pp. 369–72.

38 See John Bellamy Foster, *Marx's Ecology: Materialism and Nature* (New York: Monthly Review Press, 2000); John Bellamy Foster, Brett Clark and Richard York, *The Ecological Rift: Capitalism's War on the Earth* (New York: Monthly Review Press, 2010); John Bellamy Foster, *The Return of Nature: Socialism and Ecology* (New York: Monthly Review Press, 2020).

39 On ecosocialism, see Joel Kovel, *The Enemy of Nature: The End of Capitalism or the End of the World?* (London/New York: Zed Books, 2007), https://www.greanvillepost.com/special/Kovel,%20Enemy%20of%20Nature%20(2007).pdf (accessed 17 Dec. 2020).

Chapter 4

1   Juan J. Linz, 'Comparative Study of Fascism', in Walter Laqueur, *Fascism: A Reader's Guide* (Berkeley and Los Angeles: University of California Press, 1978), p. 36.

2   For an illuminating account of the development of the 'Cold War liberal' ideology, with roots in the pessimistic 'Christian Realism' of the theologian Reinhold Niebuhr, see Wolin, *Democracy Incorporated*, p. 27.

3   On the national security state, see Gore Vidal's observations, still relevant more than thirty years later: 'Proposals to Improve U.S. Government', video, 58.57, C-Span, 19 March 1988, https://www.c-span.org/video/?1708-1/proposals-improve-us-government (accessed 31 Dec. 2020).

4   Gottfried refers to a 'crude didacticism' found in German anti-fascism as 'the tyranny of the Good'. Paul A. Gottfried, *Fascism: The Career of a Concept* (Illinois: NIU Press/Dekalb: 2017), p. 71. The form of dogmatic groupthink Gottfried describes seems to have spread widely in the interim, taking on the forms of political correctness, cant culture, cancel culture and the more extreme forms of wokeness.

5   See Christopher Norris, *Against Relativism: Philosophy of Science, Deconstruction and Critical Theory* (Oxford: Blackwell, 1997).

6   Raju Das, 'Identity Politics: A Marxist View', *Class, Race and Corporate Power*, 8/1, Article 5 (2020), https://digital-commons.fiu.edu/cgi/viewcontent.cgi?article=1155&context=classracecorporatepower (accessed 1 Jan. 2021).

7   See Nader, *Unstoppable: The Emerging Left-Right Alliance to Dismantle the Corporate State*.

8   See Russell Brand, 'The Great Reset: Conspiracy or Fact?', video, 16.42, https://www.facebook.com/RussellBrand/videos/849745872485739 (accessed 19 March 2021).

9   Degrowth is shorthand for a set of ideas that question the dominance of the ideology of economic growth, as measured by GDP, or Gross Domestic Product. Degrowth would replace the predominance of economic measurements with an emphasis on alternative values – pertaining, for example, to the environment and the quality of life. See William Reville, 'GDP Measures Economic Activity and Nothing Else', *The Irish Times*, 18 March 2021, p. 8.

10 See Gottfried, *Fascism: The Career of a Concept*, p. 21. Gottfried cites Nolte, *Der Faschismus: Von Mussolini zu Hitler* (Schnellroda: Antaios, 2003), p. 368.

11 This brings up the dual implications of the term 'nationalism': benign in the sense of resistance to foreign colonial oppression, malign in the sense of intensifying state domination or oppression (as in the case of Germany in the 1930s). Both Italian Fascism and German National Socialism may be seen as subsets of fascism in the broader sense, though the extent to

which they overlap in specific aspects is complicated and contested, as with so much in this area.

12   Paxton, *The Anatomy of Fascism*, p. 211, notes the coining of the adjective 'totalitaria' by Giovanni Amendola, an opponent of Fascism: Mussolini subsequently took up the term and twisted it in a positive direction. Paxton concedes that Mussolini's regime fell short of total control (*ibid.*, p 147). There is a good deal of scholarly debate on the extent to which fascist regimes were totalitarian (or not). See, for example, Adrian Lyttleton, 'Italian Fascism', in Walter Laqueur, ed., *Fascism: A Reader's Guide* (Berkeley and Los Angeles: University of California Press, 1978), pp. 136–38; Hans Mommsen, *National Socialism: Continuity and Change*, in Laqueur, ed., *Fascism*, pp. 180–2, and see in particular note 11; Mommsen, *National Socialism: Continuity and Change*, pp. 190, 198; Zeev Sternhell, 'Fascist Ideology', in Laqueur, ed., *Fascism*, pp. 337, 355–60; Paxton, *The Anatomy of Fascism*, pp. 211–13. Paxton notes the phenomenon of 'parallel structures' used by fascist parties, with the replication of government agencies – in particular, the party police. In this they differed from Communist parties, who eclipsed the state structures when in power (*ibid.*, p. 85). The maintenance of a police force on traditional bureaucratic lines, rather than as the instrument of unlimited state power, was the main distinction between Italian Fascism and Nazi practice. Mussolini's stated objective of a 'totalitarian' state was, in practice, considerably watered down (*ibid.*, p. 152). While Italian Fascism endorsed the concept of totalitarianism, the Nazi regime defined itself as a racial state rather than a totalitarian state – see Enzo Traverso, *The New Faces of Fascism: Populism and the Far Right* (London: Verso, 2019), p. 154. Traverso here notes the transition from the vision of 'total' to 'racial' state, as described in Ernst Forsthoff, *Der Totale Staat* (Hamburg: Hanseatische Verlagsanstalt, 1933). Traverso (*ibid.*, p. 155) points out the difference between Italian Fascism, focussing on the state, and Nazism, focussing on race. In terms of the history of the concept of totalitarianism, Traverso (*ibid.*, pp. 155–6) notes its birth in Italy in the 1920s, its spread in the 1930s among both proponents and opponents, its recognition by scholars after the German–Soviet pact, the alliance between opponents of fascism and totalitarianism after 1941, the post-war political equation of communism and totalitarianism, the decline of the concept from the 1960s to the 1980s, its rebirth in the 1990s, and its use after 9/11 against Islamic fundamentalism. Traverso (*ibid.*, p. 131) notes the 'tortuous' development of the concept of totalitarianism through recent political history, tracing this in the chapter 'The Uses of Totalitarianism' (*ibid.*, pp. 151–82). In terms of the applicability of the concept of totalitarianism, Traverso (*ibid.*, pp. 159–60) highlights the definition by Carl J. Friedrich and Zbigniew Brzezinski of totalitarianism as suppression of democracy and the rule of law, single-party rule with a charismatic leader, the installation

of an official ideology through the control of media, government as institutional violence, and the establishment of a planned economy – see particularly Chapter 2 of Carl J. Friedrich and Zbigniew Brzezinski, *Totalitarian Dictatorship* and *Autocracy* (Cambridge, MA: Harvard University Press, 1956), pp. 15–26. To this view, Traverso (*ibid.*, p. 160) contrasts Franz Neumann's analysis of the Nazi state as anarchic, in Neumann's *Behemoth: The Structure and Practice of National Socialism, 1933–1944* (New York: Harper & Row, 1966), p. xii, and the further influence of that analysis on the 'polycratic' model of the Nazi state, with Hans Mommsen going so far as to characterise Hitler as a 'weak dictator' (Traverso, *ibid.*, p. 160). Traverso contrasts Nazism and the Soviet Union in terms of ideology: the former involved a synthesis of mythology, counter-Enlightenment thought, technology and biology; the latter claimed to be a universalist heir of the Enlightenment. Nazism came to power legally, while Soviet power came from a revolution. In addition, Stalin's personal power was more 'distant' than that of the fascist leaders (*ibid.*, pp. 161–2). While Stalinism and Nazism were both murderous, their 'internal logic' was quite different: the former was focused on forced modernisation; the latter, on the destruction of human lives (*ibid.*, pp. 165–6).

13 See Gottfried, *Fascism: The Career of a Concept*, p. 87.

14 Erich Fromm, *The Fear of Freedom* (London: Ark/Routledge & Kegan Paul, 1984), p. 183.

15 *Ibid.*, p. 185.

16 *Ibid.*, p. 187.

17 *Ibid.*, p. 190.

18 *Ibid.*, p. 191.

19 William Stroud, 'Wilhelm Reich's *The Mass Psychology of Fascism*', *The Brooklyn Rail*, Dec. 2020–Jan. 2021, https://brooklynrail.org/2020/12/books/Wilhelm-Reichs-The-Mass-Psychology-of-Fascism (accessed 27 April 2021). Stroud draws parallels with contemporary politics in the United States – particularly in terms of class politics, authoritarianism, the subvention of the rich and the capitalist control of media.

20 Juan J. Linz defines fascism, *inter alia*, as 'a hypernationalist, often pan-nationalist, anti-parliamentary, anti-liberal, anti-communist, populist and therefore anti-proletarian, partly anti-capitalist and anti-bourgeois […] movement', the goal of fascism being social integration and totalitarianism through a combination of legality and violence. Juan J. Linz, 'Some Notes Toward a Comparative Study of Fascism in Sociological Historical Perspective', in Laqueur, ed., *Fascism*, pp. 12–13. Sternhell cites Giovanni Gentile's notion of fascism as a 'revolt against positivism' and against industrial culture (Zeev Sternhell, 'Fascist Ideology', in Laqueur, ed., *Fascism*, p. 322), and see Giovanni Gentile, 'The Philosophic Basis of Fascism', *Foreign Affairs*, VI, 1927–28, pp. 295–6. On idealism, feudalism, emotionalism and the cult of the outdoors, see Sternhell, 'Fascist Ideology', p. 339. On fascism as environmentalism, and the return to nature, see Sternhell, 'Fascist Ideology',

p. 341. On fascism and anti-capitalism, see Alan S. Milward, 'Fascism and the Economy', in Laqueur, ed., *Fascism*, p. 384. On fascism against privacy, see Paxton, *The Anatomy of Fascism*, p. 11. Paxton refers to fascism, in its Nazi form, as an attempt to form a more 'natural' type of community (*Volksgemeinschaft*) in a reaction against impersonal modern society (*Gesellschaft*): see *ibid.*, p. 35. Paxton argues that fascism has historically manifested in weak liberal states and damaged capitalist systems (*ibid.*, p. 81). He notes the tension within fascist countries between party and state, drawing on Ernst Fraenkel's notion of a 'dual state', whereby the traditional 'normative state' elbowed for power with a 'prerogative state' of the organisations of the party. Mussolini, however, conceded much more power to the normative state than did Hitler (*ibid.*, pp. 121–2). Here, Paxton references Ernst Fraenkel, *The Dual State* (New York: Oxford, 1941) and Emilio Gentile, 'The Problem of the State in Italian Fascism', *Journal of Contemporary History*, 19/2 (April 1984), pp. 251–74. Paxton also notes the concept of polyocracy, or rule by multiple rival party elements (Paxton, *The Anatomy of Fascism*, p. 127).

21 Paxton, however, notes the attempt of the rump Fascist state (the 'Italian Social Republic') to implement radical socialist measures, including the socialisation of basic sectors of the economy encompassing energy and raw materials, worker participation in public sector management, and government by an assembly chosen by unions and other groups. *Ibid.*, p. 168.

22 Nicholas Goodrick-Clarke, *The Occult Roots of Nazism: Secret Aryan Cults and their Influence on Nazi Ideology* (London/New York: I.B. Tauris, 1992).

23 Paul A. Gottfried, *Fascism: The Career of a Concept*, p. 4. For the authoritarian–totalitarian distinction, Gottfried (p. 5) cites Juan J. Linz, *Totalitarian and Authoritarian Regimes* (Boulder, Co: Lynne Rienner), pp. 159–263.

24 See A. James Gregor, *The Ideology of Fascism: The Rationality of Totalitarianism*, (New York/London: Free Press, 1969), pp. 365–74, cited in Gottfried, *Fascism: The Career of a Concept*, p. 19.

25 Gottfried, *Fascism: The Career of a Concept*, pp. 45–6.

26 *Ibid.*, pp. 25–6, 31.

27 *Ibid.*, p. 151.

28 'How the Nazi Capital Would Have Looked', *The Irish Times*, 5 April 2008, https://www.irishtimes.com/news/how-the-nazi-capital-would-have-looked-1.910286 (accessed 15 Feb. 2021).

29 For some images, see 'Fascist Architecture in Italy', *New York Architecture*, http://www.nyc-architecture.com/ARCH/Notes-Fascist-IT.htm (accessed 1 Jan. 2021).

30 See Houston Stuart Chamberlain, *Foundations of the Nineteenth Century*, introd. George L. Mosse (New York: Howard Fertig, 1968); Arthur de Gobineau, *The Inequality of Human Races*, trans. Adrian Collins (New York: Howard Fertig, 1999); Madison Grant, *The Passing of the Great Race or The Racial Basis of European History*

(New York: Charles Scribner's Sons, 1918); Hans F.K. Günther, *The Racial Elements of European History* (Ostara Publications, 2012); Hans F.K. Günther, *Rassenkunde des Deutschen Volkes* (J.S. Lehmann, Munich, 1922). (The only copy I have been able to obtain of the last-mentioned is printed in the old German script and may consequently be difficult to decipher for the modern reader.) See also Alfred Rosenberg, *The Myth of the Twentieth Century: An Evaluation of the Spiritual–Intellectual Confrontations of Our Age*, trans. Vivian Bird (UK: Historical Review Press, 2004).

31 Grant, *The Passing of the Great Race*, p. 229.

32 *Ibid.*, p. 137.

33 *Ibid.*, p. 153.

34 Günther, *The Racial Elements of European History*, p. 195.

35 *Ibid.*, pp. 49–53

36 *Ibid.*, p. 123. See also pp. 145, 207.

37 *Ibid.*, p. 225.

38 *Ibid.*, pp. 184, 220, 223.

39 *Ibid.*, p. 235.

40 Grant, *The Passing of the Great Race*, p. 231.

41 Günther, *The Racial Elements of European History*, pp. 169–70.

42 Grant, *The Passing of the Great Race*, p. 55.

43 Günther, *The Racial Elements of European History*, p. 54.

44 *Ibid.*, pp. 123–4.

45 *Ibid.*, pp. 166–7. This was to play out later in a political sense, with Catholic resistance to Hitler's implementation of euthanasia.

46 Nietzsche blamed Christianity for substituting the values of equality and compassion for those of strength and domination. He wrote that 'In Christianity, the instincts of the subjugated and oppressed come into the foreground: it is the lowest classes who seek their salvation in it.' Friedrich Nietzsche, *The Anti-Christ*, in *Twilight of the Idols and The Anti-Christ,* trans. and introd. R. J. Hollingdale (London: Penguin, 1978), p. 131. The extent of Nietzsche's influence on the development of Nazism is contentious.

47 Grant, *The Passing of the Great Race*, p. 109.

48 On the issue of intellectual context, see Shorten, 'The Problem of Intellectual Antecedents', in *Modernism and Totalitarianism*, pp. 73–106.

49 Günther, *The Racial Elements of European History*, pp. 182, 209.

50 *Ibid.*, p. 172.

51 Grant, *The Passing of the Great Race*, pp. 52–3.

52 Günther, *The Racial Elements of European History*, pp. 216–20.

53 Adolf Hitler, *Mein Kampf,* introd. D. Cameron Watt, trans. Ralph Manheim (London: Pimlico, 2019), p. 258.

54 Hitler, *Mein Kampf,* 258–9.

55 Günther, *The Racial Elements of European History,* p. 204. Ironically, this edition of Günther's book features on the cover a bronze statue of a young female from the first century AD. She has European features and straight (braided) hair, but she is in fact black – or that is how she comes out in the reproduction at least. While this may simply have been an attempt to illustrate Günther's ideas, its practical effect is subtly to undermine them. Sculpture is colour blind.

56 The best analysis of anti-Semitism and its outcome in the Holocaust that I have come across is Zygmunt Bauman, *Modernity and the Holocaust* (Cambridge, UK: Polity, 2000).

57 *Ibid.*, pp. 67–8.

58 *Ibid.*, p. 72.

59 Hitler, *Mein Kampf,* pp. 272–9.

60 Only in the last few years did the Bank of England finally clarify the process of money-creation as fundamentally involving the creation of loans by commercial banks making loans – a situation that had hitherto remained largely hidden from the public at large and, less explicably, many mainstream economists. See Michael McLeay, Amar Radia and Ryland Thomas, 'Money Creation in the Modern Economy', *Quarterly Bulletin*, 2014 Q1, pp. 14–27, https://www.bankofengland.co.uk/-/media/boe/files/quarterly-bulletin/2014/money-creation-in-the-modern-economy (accessed 22 April 2021).

61 There is perhaps room for a study that compares the quasi-incestuous aspects of Hitler's background and personal life with the quasi-incestuous Nazi search for a pure-blooded racial elite.

62 Arnold Zweig, *Insulted and Exiled: The Truth About the German Jews*, trans. Eden and Cedar Paul (London: John Miles, 1937), p. 223.

63 A distinction should be drawn between religious values on the one hand, and theological beliefs on the other. The countries of northern Europe, characterised by a pervasive secularism, manifest in socioeconomic terms what might be seen as an advanced form of Christian social and economic practice. The southern states of the United States, by contrast, combine widespread theological literalism and fundamentalism on the one hand, with extreme economic inequity and indeed deprivation on the other. Somewhat perplexingly, adherents of fundamentalism often regard judgementalism and self-righteousness as core Christian values.

64 Opposition to people of a particular religious profession, purely on the basis of their beliefs, might more accurately be described as sectarianism than racism. The example that is nearest at hand (to me anyway) is that of Northern Ireland. That said, historical Protestant–Catholic antipathy may embody an element of (repressed) racism as well, on the part of the (Protestant) Lowland Scots towards the (Catholic) Irish Gaels. At the moment, this is a tentative hypothesis, but one that may be worthy of further exploration.

65 For an overview of this complex area, see Florence Gaub, 'Islamism and Islamists: A Very Short Introduction', *European Union Institute for Security Studies*, Oct. 2014, https://www.iss.europa.eu/sites/default/files/EUISSFiles/Brief_28_Islamism.pdf (accessed 2 Jan. 2021).

66 The widespread perception of a decline in the Jewish population may actually be incorrect. Figures for the number of Jews in Dublin, and Ireland in general, are unclear for a variety of reasons, including the coming and going of Jewish families helping to set up high tech industries in recent times, the presence of non-practising Jews,

and the fact that it is not compulsory to declare one's religion in the Irish census. Contrary to popular perception, Ireland's Jewish population may actually have grown over the last three decades. See Patsy McGarry, 'Census Figures for Ireland's Jewish Population in 2016 Not What They Seem', *The Irish Times*, 14 Nov. 2017, https://tinyurl.com/y6djvyux (accessed 2 Jan. 2021).

67 Bauman, *Modernity and the Holocaust*, p. 237 (italics in original).

68 *Ibid.*, Bauman, p. 239.

69 The historical oppression of the Irish may, indeed, be understood in the context of an aim to deter the political resurgence of Roman Catholicism in Ireland – a goal which itself may be seen in the light of the experience of the British themselves under the horrific reign of the Catholic Queen Mary in the sixteenth century – not to mention the threat posed by the Spanish Armada. There are (at least) two sides to every story.

70 Enzo Traverso, *The New Faces of Fascism,* pp. 45–55.

71 See Sayyid Qutb, 'Religion and Society in Christianity and in Islam', in *The Sayyid Qutb Reader: Selected Writings on Politics, Religion and Society*, Albert J. Bergesen, ed., (London: Routledge, 2008). On the relationship between Islamism and totalitarianism, see David D. Roberts, *Totalitarianism* (Cambridge, UK: Polity, 2020), pp. 92–111.

72 Annalisa Merelli, 'Marxist Philosopher Slavoj Žižek Explains Why We Shouldn't Pity or Romanticize Refugees', *Quartz*, 9 Sep. 2016, https://qz.com/767751/marxist-philosopher-slavoj-zizek-on-europes-refugee-crisis-the-left-is-wrong-to-pity-and-romanticize-migrants/ (accessed 4 Jan. 2021).

73 Deborah Lipstadt, *Antisemitism Here and Now* (London: Scribe, 2019), p. 179.

74 Lipstadt (*ibid.*, p. 23) points out that there is no such thing as a Semitic people.

75 For a slightly nuanced endorsement of this position, see Gary Lee, 'Did Early Native Americans Live in Harmony with Nature?' *Washington Post*, 5 Dec. 1994, https://www.washingtonpost.com/archive/politics/1994/12/05/did-early-native-americans-live-in-harmony-with-nature/2981bdb7-3466-42a7-9e16-30cc75c06761/ (accessed 4 Jan. 2021).

76 Similarly, the spectre of Islamification of the United Kingdom is a direct result of former British colonialism and imperialism, particularly in regard to Muslim-majority countries.

77 For some background on this, see 'Fourteen Words', ADL, https://www.adl.org/education/references/hate-symbols/14-words (accessed 4 Jan. 2021).

78 Grant, *The Passing of the Great Race*, p. 222.

79 For an interesting perspective on racism in non-Western countries, and its socioeconomic dimensions, see Martin Jacques, 'The Power of the Ethnic Minority', review of Amy Chua, *World on Fire*, *The Guardian*, 21 Feb. 2004, https://www.theguardian.com/books/2004/feb/21/highereducation.news (accessed 27 April 2021).

80 For some background on this, see
    Marek Kohn, *The Race Gallery: The
    Return of Racial Science* (London:
    Vintage, 1995), and Adam Rutherford,
    *How to Argue with a Racist: History,
    Science, Race and Reality* (London:
    Weidenfeld and Nicholson, 2020).

81 These questions feature in Susan
    Sontag, *Under the Sign of Saturn*
    (London: Penguin, 2013).

82 There is also, it should be said, an
    implicit or explicit commitment to
    the well-being of future generations,
    which surely involves a moral or
    ethical dimension, if only at an uncon-
    scious level.

83 See Anders Nygren, *Agape and Eros*,
    trans. Philip S. Watson (London:
    SPCK, 1982), and C.S. Lewis, *The Four
    Loves* (London: HarperCollins, 2012).

84 For a key discussion of the rela-
    tionship between aesthetics,
    sexuality and reproduction, see Arthur
    Schopenhauer, 'On the Metaphysics of
    the Love of the Sexes', Chapter XLIV
    of Schopenhauer, *The World as Will
    and Idea*, trans. R.B. Haldane and J.
    Kemp (London: Kegan Paul, Trench,
    Truebner, 1909), https://www.guten-
    berg.org/files/40868/40868-h/40868-h.
    html (accessed 5 Jan. 2021).

85 See Nicole Kobie, 'The Complicated
    Truth about China's Social Credit
    System', *Wired*, 7 June 2019, https://
    www.wired.co.uk/article/china-so-
    cial-credit-system-explained (accessed
    4 Jan. 2021).

86 Outside of Europe, Paxton notes the
    increased potential of the development
    of fascism due to the proliferation of
    failed experiments in representative
    democracy. Paxton, *The Anatomy of
    Fascism*, p. 205.

87 Paxton, *The Anatomy of Fascism*,
    p. 202. Paxton (p. 205) does see a real
    danger in a combination of political
    gridlock and conservatives with their
    backs to the wall, looking for mass
    support in the stirring up of nationalist
    and racist feelings in the population.

Chapter 5

1   Anthony DiMaggio, 'Why is Anyone
    Surprised by Trump's Fascist Politics?'
    CounterPunch, 7 Jan. 2021, https://
    www.counterpunch.org/2021/01/07/
    the-coup-in-washington-why-is-any-
    one-surprised-by-trumps-fascist-poli-
    tics/ (accessed 11 Jan. 2021)

2   Whether the event is best described
    as an attempted fascist takeover or a
    kind of 'self-coup' will no doubt be
    debated for a long time. See Fiona
    Hill, 'Yes, It Was a Coup Attempt.
    Here's Why', *Politico*, 11 Jan. 2021,
    https://www.politico.com/news/
    magazine/2021/01/11/capitol-riot-
    self-coup-trump-fiona-hill-457549
    (accessed 15 Oct. 2021).

3   Oxford English Dictionary, 'fascism',
    https://oed.com/view/Entry/
    68376?redirectedFrom=Fascism#eid
    (accessed 19 March 2021).

4   Roger Griffin, 'General Introduction',
    in Roger Griffin, ed., *Fascism* (Oxford:
    Oxford University Press), 1995, p. 2.
    The Third Reich theorist Carl Schmitt
    argued that, in fact, 'there is no normal
    state which is not a total State', as
    the state needs to avoid the dangers
    of becoming fragmented and falling
    apart. For Schmitt, the strength of the
    Nazi state is that the Führer principle

permeates it. Carl Schmitt, 'The Legal Basis of the Total State', trans. Roger Griffin, in Roger Griffin, ed., *Fascism*, pp. 138–9.

5   Oxford English Dictionary, 'totalitarian', https://oed.com/view/Entry/203795?redirectedFrom=totalitarian#eid (accessed 19 March 2021).

6   Gottfried Benn described 'The Total State' as embodying the complete 'identity of power and spirit, individuality and the collective', Gottfried Benn, 'The New Breed of German', trans. Roger Griffin, in Roger Griffin, *Fascism*, p. 135.

7   See 'The Discobolus: Greeks, Nazis and the Body Beautiful', in BBC Culture, https://www.bbc.com/culture/article/20150324-hitlers-idea-of-the-perfect-body (accessed 16 Feb. 2021); Frederick Spotts, *Hitler and the Power of Aesthetics* (New York: Harry N. Abrams, 2004); Helen Roche, 'Mussolini's "Third Rome", Hitler's Third Reich and the Allure of Antiquity: Classicizing Chronopolitics as a Remedy for Unstable National Identity?' *Brill*, vol. 8, no. 2 (17 Dec. 2019), pp. 127–52, https://brill.com/view/journals/fasc/8/2/article-p127_127.xml?language=en (accessed 16 Feb. 2021).

8   Oxford English Dictionary, 'populism', https://oed.com/view/Entry/147930?redirectedFrom=populism#eid (accessed 19 March 2021).

9   See Gregory Stanton, 'QAnon is a Nazi Cult, Rebranded', *Just Security*, 29 Sep. 2020, https://tinyurl.com/y22nxxpg (accessed 8 Jan. 2021).

10 Eatwell and Goodwin, *National Populism*, pp. xxi–xxiv. The authors argue (p. 32) that the 'sense of relative deprivation' is a crucial element of national populism.

11 *Ibid.*, pp. 4–6. The authors cite Nate Silver, 'The Mythology of Trump's "Working Class Support"', *FiveThirtyEight*, 3 May 2016, https://fivethirtyeight.com/features/the-mythology-of-trumps-working-class-support/ (accessed 15 Oct. 2021), and Emma Green, 'It Was Cultural Anxiety that Drove White, Working-class Voters to Trump', *The Atlantic*, 9 May 2017, https://www.theatlantic.com/politics/archive/2017/05/white-working-class-trump-cultural-anxiety/525771/ (accessed 12 Jan. 2021).

12 Eatwell and Goodwin, *National Populism*, p. 6.

13 *Ibid.*, pp. 9–14. The authors cite James Tilley and Geoffrey Evans, 'Ageing and Generational Effects on Vote Choice: Combining Cross-sectional and Panel Data to Estimate APC Effects', *Electoral Studies*, vol. 33, no. 1 (2014), pp. 19–27, https://www.sciencedirect.com/science/article/abs/pii/S0261379413000875 (accessed 28 April 2021).

14 Eatwell and Goodwin, *National Populism*, pp. 166–7.

15 *Ibid.*, pp. 172–5.

16 *Ibid.*, p.18.

17 *Ibid.*, p. 27. Educational attainment is not of course synonymous with intelligence. I am not aware of systematic attempts to estimate the connection between IQ and political preference;

it would be an interesting project, though perhaps a fraught one.

18 *Ibid.*, pp. 30, 39.

19 *Ibid.*, p. 54.

20 Marco Respinti, 'Marine le Pen Succeeded by "Breaching into the Left"', *Acton Institute*, 24 April 2017, https://www.acton.org/publications/transatlantic/2017/04/24/marine-le-pen-succeeded-breaching-left (accessed 12 Jan. 2021).

21 Eatwell and Goodwin, *National Populism*, p. 65.

22 *Ibid.*, p. 66.

23 See Katrin Bennhold, 'Trump Emerges as Inspiration for Germany's Far Right', *The New York Times,* 7 Sep. 2020 (updated 15 Oct. 2020), https://www.nytimes.com/2020/09/07/world/europe/germany-trump-far-right.html (accessed 6 Jan. 2021).

24 Eatwell and Goodwin, *National Populism*, p. 69.

25 *Ibid.*, pp. 71–2.

26 *Ibid.*, pp. 85–6.

27 *Ibid.*, p. 278.

28 Eatwell and Goodwin (*ibid.*, p. 116) point to a finding of the Pew Research Centre in 2017 that, on average, only one in ten people across the United States and Europe rejected democracy. This should be tempered with the more sobering finding that, while more than two-thirds of older people in the United States think it is essential to live in a democracy, less than one-third of millennials do. David Frum, 'If America's Democracy Fails, Can Other Ones Survive?', *The Atlantic*, March 2018, cited in Peter Geoghegan, *Democracy for Sale: Dark Money and Dirty Politics* (London: Apollo/Head of Zeus, 2020), p. 305.

29 Eatwell and Goodwin, *National Populism*, p. 120.

30 Rachael Pells, 'UK Schools Falling Behind Leading Countries, New Global Rankings Reveal', *Independent,* 6 Dec. 2016, https://www.independent.co.uk/news/education/education-news/pisa-oecd-rankings-uk-schools-falling-behind-leading-countries-global-international-singapore-a7458751.html (accessed 6 Jan. 2021); Marc Tucker, 'Why Have American Education Standards Collapsed?' *EducationWeek*, 23 April, 2015, https://www.edweek.org/teaching-learning/opinion-why-have-american-education-standards-collapsed/2015/04 (accessed 6 Jan. 2021).

31 E.M. Forster, speaking on 'Liberty in England' at the International Congress of Writers in Paris, 1935, from E.M. Forster, *Abinger Harvest* (London: Edward Arnold & Co, 1953), p. 64, as quoted in Anthony Lester, *Five Ideas to Fight for* (London: Oneworld, 2016), pp. 48–9.

32 Eric Kaufmann, *Whiteshift: Populism, Immigration and the Future of White Majorities* (London: Penguin Random House, 2018), p. 212.

33 Geoghegen, *Democracy for Sale*, p. 257.

34 *Ibid.*, 'Making Europe Great Again', pp. 255–90.

35 Tímea Drinóczi and Agnieszka Bień-Kacała, 'Illiberal Constitutionalism: The Case of Hungary and Poland', *German Law Journal*, vol. 20, no. 8, published online by Cambridge University Press (2 Dec. 2019), https://

tinyurl.com/y6ajktpn (accessed 11 Jan. 2021).

36 Jonathan Watts, 'Our Planet Can't Take Many More Populists like Brazil's Bolsonaro', *The Guardian*, 24 Oct. 2018, https://www.theguardian.com/commentisfree/2018/oct/24/planet-populists-brazil-jair-bolsonaro-environment (accessed 12 Jan. 2021).

37 See, for example, Alexander Dugin, *The Fourth Political Theory* (London: Arktos, 2012).

38 However, the often-cool response of western feminists to the brutal oppression of women in some Islamic countries seems to detract from such a hope.

39 Enzo Traverso, *The New Faces of Fascism: Populism and the Far Right*, trans. David Broder (London: Verso, 2019), p. 9. The phrase 'extreme centre' is quoted from Tariq Ali, *The Extreme Centre: A Warning* (London: Verso, 2015).

40 Traverso, *The New Faces of Fascism*, pp. 184–5.

41 See Desmond Morris, 'The Human Zoo', *Macleans*, 1 Oct. 1969, https://archive.macleans.ca/article/1969/10/1/the-human-zoo (accessed 8 Jan. 2021).

42 For an illuminating discussion of the relationship between cultural signifiers and social class, see Pierre Bourdieu, *Distinction: A Social Critique of the Judgement of Taste* (London: Routledge, 2010).

43 On goth subculture, see Lauren M.E. Goodlad and Michael Bibby, *Goth: Undead Subculture* (Durham, North Carolina: Duke University Press, 2007).

44 See for example Ronald Hall, 'Black America's Bleaching Syndrome', *The Conversation*, 2 Feb. 2018, https://theconversation.com/black-americas-bleaching-syndrome-82200 (accessed 7 Jan. 2021).

45 Kaufmann, *Whiteshift*, p. 7. Kaufmann's argument, it should be noted, does not apply to countries like Japan and Korea, where cultural and immigration policies militate against the growth of cosmopolitan liberalism, and consequently mitigate the rise of populist reaction (*ibid.*, pp. 16–17).

46 *Ibid.*, p. 28.

47 *Ibid.*, p. 12.

48 *Ibid.*, p. 431.

49 *Ibid.*, p. 422. Kaufmann cites W. Easterly and R. Levine, 'Africa's Growth Tragedy: Policies and Ethnic Divisions', *Quarterly Journal of Economics*, vol. 111, no. 4 (1997), pp. 1203–50. It should be noted here that 'growth' is itself questionable as a measure of social well-being, particularly in the era of deforestation, agribusiness, loss of biodiversity, global warming and pandemics.

50 Kaufmann, *Whiteshift*, p. 451.

51 *Ibid.*, pp. 17–18.

52 *Ibid.*, p. 27.

53 *Ibid.*, p. 136. See Noel Ignatiev, *How the Irish Became White* (London and New York: Routledge, 2009).

54 Kaufmann, *Whiteshift*, pp. 442–3.

55 *Ibid.*, pp. 159–61.

56 *Ibid.*, p. 228.

57 *Ibid.* pp. 233–4.

58 *Ibid.*, p. 337.

59 See Derek Scally, 'How Ireland Failed Refugees from Nazi Germany', *The Irish Times*, 4 Feb. 2017, https://www.

irishtimes.com/culture/heritage/ how-ireland-failed-refugees-from-nazi-germany-1.2961062 (accessed 13 Jan. 2021). The article makes reference to Gisela Holfter and Horst Dickel, *An Irish Sanctuary: German-Speaking Refugees in Ireland 1933–1945* (Berlin: De Gruyter Oldenbourg, 2017).

60 Bregman, *Utopia for Realists*.

61 Kaufmann, *Whiteshift*, p. 260. See Eric Kaufmann, *Shall the Religious Inherit the Earth?: Demography and Politics in the Twenty-First Century* (London: Profile, 2010), p. 169.

62 Kaufmann, *Whiteshift*, pp. 260–2.

63 *Ibid.*, p. 440. Kaufmann cites the likelihood of the ethnic assimilation of non-British whites (*ibid.*, p. 457).

64 *Ibid.*, p. 448. Kaufmann cites P. Schrag, *Decline of the WASP* (New York: Simon and Schuster, 1973), p. 37.

65 See for example Diana Darke, *Stealing from the Saracens: How Islamic Architecture Shaped Europe* (London: Hurst, 2020). The book describes the underestimation of the influence of Islamic architecture on that of the West.

66 To take a cynical perspective, it might even seem that establishment of religion is a means of sapping and neutralising its energy, rather than installing it in power. A militant atheist of a particularly Machiavellian disposition might even be led to support religious establishment, while opposing the separation of church and state, on the grounds that establishment is bad for religion and thereby favours secularism.

67 Kaufmann, *Whiteshift*, p. 482.

68 This, however, is not certain in Kaufmann's view, and whites may instead opt to become a tight-knit minority. Such a result would represent a multicultural society. *Ibid.*, p. 510.

69 *Ibid.*, p. 513.

70 See for example Alan Barrett, Adele Bergin and Elish Kelly, 'Estimating the Impact of Immigration on Wages in Ireland', Discussion Paper No. 4472, *IZA*, Oct. 2009, https://www. tcd.ie/Economics/assets/pdf/dp4472. pdf (accessed 7 Jan. 2019), and Alan de Brauw, 'Does Immigration Reduce Wages?' *Cato Journal*, Fall 2017, https://www.cato.org/cato-journal/fall-2017/does-immigration-reduce-wages (accessed 7 Jan. 2021).

71 For a libertarian perspective, see Jeffrey Miron and Erin Partin, 'Police Violence and the Racist Drug War', *Cato at Liberty*, 3 June 2020, https:// www.cato.org/blog/police-violence-racist-drug-war (accessed 11 Jan. 2021).

Chapter 6

1 For a fascinating account of this area, see John Harvey, *Men in Black* (London: Reaktion, 1995).

2 Mark Fisher, 'Exiting the Vampire Castle', openDemocracy, 24 Nov. 2013, https://www.opendemocracy.net/ en/opendemocracyuk/exiting-vampire-castle/ (accessed 6 March 2021).

3 Anthony Lester, *Five Ideas to Fight for*, p. 102. Lester cites Lee Lewis, 'Cameras Spy on Chinese Academics', *The Times*, 4 Dec. 2014.

4 Lester, *Five Ideas to Fight for*, p. 102. Lester cites Ian Black, 'Global Outrage at Saudi Arabia as Jailed

Blogger Receives Public Flogging', *The Guardian*, 11 Jan. 2015.

5   Lester, p. 128.

6   Lester, p. 131. Lester (pp. 131–2) claims credit for the watering-down of the final act, thereby reducing some of its negative potential.

7   Emma Graham-Harrison, 'Ireland Votes to Oust "Medieval" Blasphemy Law', *The Guardian*, 27 Oct. 2018, https://www.the-guardian.com/world/2018/oct/27/ireland-votes-to-oust-blasphemy-ban-from-constitution (accessed 23 Jan. 2021).

8   'How the Islamic States at the United Nations Use the Irish Blasphemy Laws to Justify Their Own Laws', *Atheist Ireland*, 19 Oct. 2018, https://atheist.ie/2018/10/islamic-states-irish-blasphe-my-law/ (accessed 17 Feb. 2021).

9   A notable exception is the article by Patrick Wintour, 'Persecution of Christians "Coming Close to Genocide" in Middle East – Report', *The Guardian*, 2 May 2019, https://www.theguardian.com/world/2019/may/02/persecution-driving-chris-tians-out-of-middle-east-report (accessed 19 Jan. 2021).

10   Mackinac Center For Public Policy, 'The Overton Window', https://www.mackinac.org/OvertonWindow (accessed 14 Jan. 2021).

11   Carol Hunt, 'Why is Feminism so Silent about Muslim Women Who Refuse to Wear the Hijab?' *The Irish Times*, 21 Aug. 2017, https://www.irishtimes.com/life-and-style/people/why-is-feminism-so-quiet-about-mus-lim-women-who-refuse-to-wear-the-hijab-1.3189620 (accessed 14 Jan. 2021).

12   See F. Brinley Bruton, 'Saudi School Textbooks Teach Violence, Anti-Semitism, ADL Report Says', *NBC News,* 20 Nov. 2018, https://www.nbcnews.com/news/world/saudi-school-textbooks-violence-an-ti-semitism-adl-report-says-n938316 (accessed 19 Jan. 2021). See ADL, 'ADL Analysis Finds Saudi School Textbooks Still Teach Anti-Semitic Incitement and Hatred', https://www.adl.org/news/press-releases/adl-analysis-finds-saudi-school-textbooks-still-teach-an-ti-semitic-incitement (accessed 19 Jan. 2021).

13   Günther Jikeli, 'Antisemitic Attitudes among Muslims in Europe: A Survey Review', *ISGAP Occasional Paper Series*, no. 1 (May 2015), https://www.researchgate.net/publication/288986435_Antisemitic_Attitudes_among_Muslims_in_Europe_A_Survey_Review (accessed 19 Jan. 2021).

14   *Ibid.*, pp. 337–8.

15   *Abrams v. United States* 250 US 616 (1919), quoted in Lester, p. 143.

16   As distinct from the outdated, gender-exclusive language in the preceding quote.

17   See 'Man Complains of "Orwellian Police" after Tweet Investigation', BBC News, 25 Jan. 2019, https://www.bbc.com/news/uk-england-hum-ber-47005937 (accessed 11 April 2021). The relevant legal judgement is available here: https://www.judiciary.uk/wp-content/uploads/2020/02/miller-v-college-of-police-judgment.pdf (accessed 17 Feb. 2021).

18   See for example, 'Money, Managerialism and the University',

Dublin Review of Books, no. 129 (Jan. 2021), https://drb.ie/money-manage-rialism-and-the-university/ (accessed 15 Oct. 2021); on the influence on higher education of neoliberalism with its 'managerialist philistinism', see 'Learning My Lesson: Marina Warner on the Disfiguring of Higher Education', *London Review of Books*, vol. 37, no. 6 (19 March 2015), https://www.lrb.co.uk/the-paper/v37/n06/marina-warner/learning-my-lesson (accessed 14 Jan. 2021).

19 William Reville, 'Academic Freedom Is Under Pressure in Irish Universities', *The Irish Times*, 4 June 2021, https://www.irishtimes.com/news/science/academic-freedom-is-under-pres-sure-in-irish-universities-1.4263886 (accessed 14 Jan. 2021).

20 Today, radicals attempting to highlight apartheid in Israel may themselves come under pressure, this time from the right.

21 Kaufmann, *Whiteshift*, p. 367.

22 For an interesting debate on these issues in which Jordan Peterson participates, see 'Munk Debate on Political Correctness', https://www.youtube.com/watch?v=MNjYSnsoopo (accessed 21 Jan. 2021). For a critical yet fair-minded account of Peterson's ideas as elaborated in his book *12 Steps for Life: An Antidote for Chaos* (London: Allen Lane, 2018), see Bryan Fanning, 'Crossing Jordan', *Dublin Review of Books*, no. 129 (2021), https://www.drb.ie/essays/crossing-jordan (accessed 21 Jan. 2021). For a much more negative take on Peterson's ideas, see Nathan J. Robinson, "The Intellectual We Deserve,' *Current*

Affairs, 14 March 2018, https://www.currentaffairs.org/2018/03/the-intel-lectual-we-deserve (accessed 21 Jan. 2021). In an otherwise scathing article, Robinson concedes that 'Peterson is popular partly because he criticizes social justice activists in a way many people find satisfying, and some of those criticisms have merit. And he is popular partly because academia and the left have failed spectacularly at helping to make the world intelligible to ordinary people, and giving them a clear and compelling political vision.'

23 Kaufmann, *Whiteshift*, p. 305.

24 *Ibid.*, p. 311. Kaufmann cites R. Brubaker, 'The Dolezal Affair: Race, Gender and the Micropolitics of Identity,' *Ethnic and Racial Studies*, 39/3 (2016), pp. 414–48. See also Jesse Singal, 'This is What a Modern-Day Witch Hunt Looks Like', *New York Magazine, Intelligencer*, 2 May 2017, https://nymag.com/intelligencer/2017/05/transracial-ism-article-controversy.html (accessed 15 Jan. 2021). For a thoughtful aca-demic response to the controversy, see Trysh Travis, 'Teaching Moments from the "Hypatia" Controversy', *Inside Higher Ed*, 30 June 2017, https://www.insidehighered.com/views/2017/06/30/instructor-analyzes-how-discuss-hypa-tia-controversy-her-grad-students-essay (accessed 28 April 2021).

25 See Maya Wei Haas, 'Controversial New Study Pinpoints Where All Modern Humans Arose', *National Geographic*, 28 Oct. 2019, https://www.nationalge-ographic.com/science/2019/10/controversial-study-pinpoints-birth-

place-modern-humans/ (accessed 16 Jan. 2021).

26   See for example Harry Cockburn, 'Man, 69 Applies to Legally Change Age Because He "Identifies as 20 Years Younger"', *Independent*, 8 Nov. 2018, https://www.independent.co.uk/news/world/europe/man-change-age-netherlands-emile-ratelband-court-arnhmen-gelderland-a8623421.html (accessed 19 Jan. 2021).

27   Zoë Corbyn, 'Live for Ever: Scientists Say They'll Soon Expand Life "Well Beyond 120"', *The Guardian*, 11 Jan. 2015, https://www.theguardian.com/science/2015/jan/11/-sp-live-forever-extend-life-calico-google-longevity (accessed 11 April 2021).

28   The terror of nuclear war in which the post-war generation grew up seems to have been erased from the collective consciousness.

29   For a science-fictional account of this issue, see the novel *Holy Fire* by Bruce Sterling.

30   See my review: Paul O'Brien, 'Embodied Time: Art Video, 1970 to the Present', *Circa*, 120 (Summer 2007), pp. 61–63, Circa Archive, http://circaartmagazine.website/backissues/circa-art-magazine-circa-120-review-embodied-time-art-video-1970-to-the-present/ (accessed 23 Jan. 2021).

31   Eric Kaufmann, *Whiteshift*, p. 329.

32   There is a specific issue in regard to trans rights, in terms of the fact that gender dysphoria is a recognised condition. There are no comparable equivalents in terms of age or race – or at least ones that are recognised.

33   If there is no knowable world outside of thought, perception or language, there is arguably no rationale for class struggle or indeed for socialism.

34   *Ibid.*, p. 303. Kaufmann cites Sean Stevens, 'Campus Speaker Disinvitations: Part 2', *Heterodox Academy*, 7 Feb. 2017.

35   Helen Pluckrose and James Lindsay, *Cynical Theories: How Activist Scholarship Made Everything about Race, Gender and Identity – and Why This Harms Everybody* (Durham, NC: Pitchstone Publishing, 2020).

36   The issue is actually more complicated, since it could be argued that interpretation itself involves a value judgement, based on the premise that understanding is inherently preferable to lack of understanding.

37   *Ibid.*, p. 48.

38   *Ibid.*, p. 99.

39   The term 'liberal' is, through no fault of the authors, a somewhat unfortunate one due to its dual meaning on different sides of the Atlantic. In North America, it has the connotations of economic leftism, statism and secularism. In the United Kingdom, by contrast, it means adherence to the free market, anti-statism and social freedom. The term 'neoliberalism' further muddies the water, being normally used by leftists to denote extreme post-Keynesian forms of capitalism that tended to dominate, at least until fairly recently. Those, like the author, who wish to avoid the various pitfalls of identifying as liberals, may use the term 'libertarian' instead. That term has its own drawbacks, however, as it can tend to identify one as a

person who is not only suspicious of the state but also friendly to a 'purified' form of capitalism. 'Left-libertarian' is about the best I've been able to come up with.

40 Pluckrose and Lindsay, *Cynical Theories*, p. 82.

41 See for example Val Plumwood, *Environmental Culture: The Ecological Crisis of Reason* (London/New York: Routledge, 2002), and Carolyn Merchant, *The Death of Nature: Women, Ecology and the Scientific Revolution* (San Francisco: Harper & Row, 1983).

42 For a discussion of the issues around this area, see Thomas Kuhn, *The Structure of Scientific Revolutions* (Chicago: The University of Chicago Press, 1962), and Paul Feyerabend, *Against Method* (New Left Books: 1975).

43 Pluckrose and Lindsay, *Cynical Theories*, pp. 86–7.

44 Iliana Magra, 'Iran Rights Lawyer Sentenced to 38 Years in Prison and 148 Lashes, Husband Says', *The New York Times*, 13 March 2019, https://www.nytimes.com/2019/03/13/world/middleeast/nasrin-sotoudeh-iran-lawyer-lashes.html (accessed 16 Jan. 2021).

45 Mona Eltahawi, 'They Died for Lack of a Head Scarf", *Washington Post*, 19 March, 2002, https://www.washingtonpost.com/archive/opinions/2002/03/19/they-died-for-lack-of-a-head-scarf/86cbcc5a-6cef-49e5-b758-167527e6eed0/ (accessed 16 Jan. 2021).

46 Or at least of a supposedly secular society: Marxism, as we have seen, has its own unconscious quasi-religious motivations.

47 Pluckrose and Lindsay, *Cynical Theories,* pp. 117–19.

48 *Ibid.*, p. 129. See Arwa Mahdawi, 'It's Not a Hate Crime for a Woman to Feel Uncomfortable Waxing Male Genitalia', *The Guardian*, 27 July 2019, https://www.theguardian.com/commentisfree/2019/jul/27/male-genitalia-week-in-patriarchy-women (accessed 15 Oct. 2021). The author bemoans the use of the story by the right-wing media, who are normally no supporters of human rights.

49 Pluckrose and Lindsay, *Cynical Theories*, p. 145.

50 *Ibid.*, p. 152.

51 *Ibid.*, p. 153.

52 *Ibid.*, p. 185.

53 *Ibid.*, p. 190.

54 *Ibid.*, p. 192.

55 *Ibid.*, p. 201.

56 *Ibid.*, p. 204.

57 *Ibid.*, pp. 210–11.

58 *Ibid.*, pp. 215–18.

59 *Ibid.*, pp. 221–3.

60 *Ibid.*, p. 219.

61 Ronan McGreevy, 'Shelbourne Hotel Statues to be Restored to their Plinths', *The Irish Times*, 24 Sep. 2020, https://www.irishtimes.com/news/ireland/irish-news/shelbourne-hotel-statues-to-be-restored-to-their-plinths-1.4362766 (accessed 28 Sep. 2020).

62 Pluckrose and Lindsay, *Cynical Theories*, p. 221.

63 Eoghan Moloney, 'Trinity College Historical Society Rescind Richard Dawkins Invitation Over Author's Stance on Islam and Sexual Assault',

Independent.ie, 29 Sep. 2020, https:// www.independent.ie/irish-news/ trinity-college-historical-socie- ty-rescind-richard-dawkins-invi- tation-over-authors-stance-on-is- lam-and-sexual-assault-39568028. html (accessed 22 Jan. 2021). In a US context, see Michael Powell, 'A Black Marxist Scholar Wanted to Talk About Race. It Ignited a Fury', *The New York Times*, 4 Aug. 2020, https://www.nytimes.com/2020/08/14/ us/adolph-reed-controversy.html (accessed 13 March 2021).

64 Pluckrose and Lindsay, *Cynical Theories*, p. 230.

65 *Ibid.*, p. 204.

66 See Plumwood, *Environmental Culture*.

67 See Merchant, *The Death of Nature*.

68 Lynn White, 'The Historical Roots of Our Ecologic Crisis', in R.J. Berry, ed., *The Care of Creation: Focusing Concern and Action* (London: Inter-Varsity Press, 2000).

69 Theodor Adorno and Max Horkheimer, *Dialectic of Enlightenment*, trans. John Cumming (London: Verso, 1997), p. 6.

70 *Ibid.*, p. 9.

71 *Ibid.*, p. 32.

72 *Ibid.*, p. 24.

73 *Ibid.*, p. 54.

74 David Hart, 'Scientists Have Created Embryos That Are Part-Human, Part-Monkey', *Forbes*, 15 April 2021, https://www.forbes. com/sites/roberthart/2021/04/15/ scientists-have-created-embry- os-that-are-part-human-part-mon- key/?sh=5f7c8bcb396c (accessed 28 April 2021).

75 Adorno and Horkheimer, *Dialectic of Enlightenment,* p. 25.

76 *Ibid.*, p. 86.

77 *Ibid.*, p. 118.

78 *Ibid.*, p. 165.

79 *Ibid.*, p. 185.

80 See Patrick Freyne, 'Conspiracy Theories: Why It's Pointless to Argue', *The Irish Times Weekend Review,* 10 April 2020.

81 See Caesar Kalinowski IV, 'A Legal Response to the Sovereign Citizen Movement', *Montana Law Review*, vol. 80, no. 2 (8 Jan. 2019), https://schol- arworks.umt.edu/mlr/vol80/iss2/2/ (accessed 15 Oct. 2021).

82 The Irish author Flann O'Brien, with his mythical sham-intellectual char- acter de Selby – whose worldview was based on surreal nonsense – offers a parallel in the literary sphere.

83 See Tovia Smith, '"Exit Counselors" Strain to Pull Americans Out of a Web of False Conspiracies', NPR, 3 March 2021, https://www. npr.org/2021/03/03/971457702/ exit-counselors-strain-to-pull-ameri- cans-out-of-a-web-of-false-conspiracies (accessed 13 March 2021).

Chapter 7

1 See John W. Whitehead, 'Big Brother is Still Watching', *CounterPunch*, 4 May 2017, https://www.counterpunch. org/2017/05/04/big-brother-is- still-watching/ (accessed 28 Jan. 2021); Cory Doctorow, 'Unchecked Surveillance Technology Is Leading Us Towards Totalitarianism', *International Business Times*, 5 May 2017, https:// www.ibtimes.com/unchecked-sur- veillance-technology-leading-us-to-

wards-totalitarianism-opinion-2535230 (accessed 20 February 2021).

2   Cameron F. Kerry, 'Why Protecting Privacy is a Losing Game Today – and How to Change the Game', *Brookings*, 12 July 2018, https://www.brookings.edu/research/why-protecting-privacy-is-a-losing-game-today-and-how-to-change-the-game/ (accessed 20 Feb. 2021).

3   See for example Geoghegan, *Democracy for Sale*.

4   'Beware the Borg', *The Economist*, 21 Dec. 2019–3 Jan. 2020, pp. 59–64.

5   Brett Scott, 'The Cashless Society is a Con – and Big Finance is Behind It', *The Guardian*, 19 July 2018, https://www.theguardian.com/commentisfree/2018/jul/19/cashless-society-con-big-finance-banks-closing-atms (accessed 20 Feb. 2021).

6   Lizzie Dearden, 'Facial Recognition Technology "Violates Human Rights and Must End", Landmark Court Case Hears', *Independent*, 21 May 2019, https://www.independent.co.uk/news/uk/home-news/facial-recognition-uk-police-wales-london-legal-challenge-human-rights-a8924296.html (accessed 18 Feb. 2021). The article cites the case of a man in London fined for covering his face. This was pre-pandemic; one might now fall foul of the law for leaving one's face uncovered. The issue of compulsory mask-wearing, in certain circumstances, now intriguingly contextualises the attempts of a few years ago to make face-covering illegal. The latter issue had consequences for the behaviour of some Muslim women in particular.

7   See Rob Toews, 'Deep Fakes Are Going to Wreak Havoc on Society. We Are Not Prepared', *Forbes*, https://www.forbes.com/sites/robtoews/2020/05/25/deepfakes-are-going-to-wreak-havoc-on-society-we-are-not-prepared/?sh=32ac62e07494 (accessed 20 Feb. 2021).

8   For a discussion of some of the dangers of AI, see Bernard Marr, 'Is Artificial Intelligence (AI) A Threat To Humans?' *Forbes*, 2 March 2020, https://www.forbes.com/sites/bernardmarr/2020/03/02/is-artificial-intelligence-ai-a-threat-to-humans/?sh=11fe14f6205d (accessed 19 Feb. 2021).

9   Anthony Lester, *Five Ideas to Fight for*, p. 164. See also Kadhim Shubber, 'Edward Snowden: A Simple Guide to GCHQ's Internet Surveillance Programme Tempora', *Wired*, 24 June 2013, https://www.wired.co.uk/article/gchq-tempora-101 (accessed 8 March 2021); Charlie Savage, 'N.S.A. Said to Search Content of Messages to and From U.S.', *The New York Times*, 8 Aug. 2013, https://www.nytimes.com/2013/08/08/us/broader-sifting-of-data-abroad-is-seen-by-nsa.html?pagewanted=all (accessed 8 March 2021), Nick Hopkins and Julian Borger, 'Exclusive: NSA Pays £100m in Secret Funding for GCHQ', *The Guardian*, 1 Aug. 2013, https://www.theguardian.com/uk-news/2013/aug/01/nsa-paid-gchq-spying-edward-snowden (accessed 21 March 2021), Marcel Rosenbach, Laura Poitras and Holger Stark, 'How the NSA Accesses Smartphone Data', *Spiegel International*, 9 Sep. 2013,

(accessed 21 March 2021), https://
www.spiegel.de/international/world/
how-the-nsa-spies-on-smartphones-in-
cluding-the-blackberry-a-921161.html
(accessed 11 Sep. 2021).

10 Ewan Macaskill and Gabriel Dance,
'NSA Files: Decoded', *The Guardian*,
1 Nov. 2013, https://www.theguardian.
com/world/interactive/2013/nov/01/
snowden-nsa-files-surveillance-revela-
tions-decoded#section/3 (accessed 11
Sep. 2021).

11 Barton Gellman and Ashkan Soltani,
'NSA Infiltrates Links to Yahoo,
Google Data Centres Worldwide,
Snowden Documents Say', *Washington
Post*, 30 Oct. 2013, https://tinyurl.
com/4ybbvmw5 (accessed 23 March
2021).

12 Glenn Greenwald, 'XKeyscore: NSA
Tool Collects "Nearly Everything
a User Does on the Internet"', *The
Guardian*, 31 July 2013, https://www.
theguardian.com/world/2013/jul/31/
nsa-top-secret-program-online-data
(accessed 23 March 2021).

13 Edward Snowden, *Permanent Record*
(London: Macmillan, 2019), p. 113.

14 *Ibid.*, p. 164.

15 *Ibid.*, p. 168.

16 *Ibid.*, p. 177.

17 *Ibid.*, p. 180.

18 *Ibid.*, p. 185.

19 *Ibid.*, p. 195.

20 *Ibid.*, p. 207.

21 Raphael Satter, 'U.S. Court: Mass
Surveillance Program Exposed by
Snowden Was Illegal', *Reuters*, 2 Sep.
2020, https://www.reuters.com/article/
us-usa-nsa-spying-idUSKBN25T3CK
(accessed 23 March 2020).

22 Snowden, *Permanent Record*, p. 328.

23 Yasha Levine, *Surveillance Valley: The
Secret Military History of the Internet*
(London: Icon, 2019), p. 268.

24 Sandra A. Garcia, 'US Requiring
Social Media Information from Visa
Applicants', *The New York Times*,
2 June 2019, https://www.nytimes.
com/2019/06/02/us/us-visa-applica-
tion-social-media.html (accessed 28
Jan. 2021).

25 See Gary Grossman, 'Thought-
Detection: AI Has Infiltrated Our Last
Bastion of Privacy', *VB*, 13 Feb. 2021,
https://venturebeat.com/2021/02/13/
thought-detection-ai-has-infiltrated-
our-last-bastion-of-privacy/ (accessed
20 Feb. 2021).

26 Hebrews 4:13.

27 Sarah Bardon, 'Irish Data Law
Amounts to Mass Surveillance,
says Ex-Chief Justice', *The Irish
Times*, 3 Oct. 2017, https://www.
irishtimes.com/news/politics/
irish-data-law-amounts-to-mass-sur-
veillance-says-ex-chief-justice-1.3243354
(accessed 29 Jan. 2021).

28 Karlin Lillington, 'A Dystopian
Nightmare Rebranded as Travel Perk',
*The Irish Times, Business +: Technology
and Innovation*, 15 Aug. 2019, p. 1.

29 See Karlin Lillington, 'Card Debacle
Will Play Out in Court at Taxpayers'
Expense', *The Irish Times, Business +:
Technology & Innovation*, 5 Sep. 2019,
p. 1. See also, for example, Lillington's
articles 'Pervasive Silent Surveillance
of Public Service Websites', *The Irish
Times*, 21 March 2019, and 'Once We
Searched Google, but Now Google
Searches Us', *The Irish Times, Business
+: Technology and Innovation*, 21 Nov.
2019.

30 Karlin Lillington, "Vaccine Passports Far More Complicated than They Might Appear', *The Irish Times*, 22 April 2021, https://www.irish-times.com/business/technology/vaccine-passports-far-more-complicated-than-they-might-appear-1.4543793 (accessed 24 April 2021).

31 Jennifer O'Connell, 'Pandemic Will Pass, but New Data Measures Might Not', *The Irish Times*, 28 March 2020, p. 18.

32 Klaus Schwab and Thierry Malleret, *Covid-19: The Great Reset* (Geneva: World Economic Forum, 2020).

33 *Ibid.*, p. 167.

34 *Ibid.*, pp. 165–6.

35 *Ibid.*, pp. 170–1. See Evgeny Morozov, 'The Tech "Solutions" for Coronavirus Take the Surveillance State to the Next Level', *The Guardian*, 25 April 2020, https://www.theguardian.com/commentisfree/2020/apr/15/tech-coronavirus-surveilance-state-digital-disrupt (accessed 15 March 2021).

36 Yuval Noah Harari, 'The World After Coronavirus', *Financial Times*, 20 March 2020, https://www.ft.com/content/19d90308-6858-11ea-a3c9-1fe6fedcca75 (accessed 16 March 2121). See Malleret and Schwab, *Covid-19: The Great Reset*, pp. 168–70.

37 See for example Alex Hern, 'The Fashion Line Designed to Trick Surveillance Cameras', *The Guardian*, 14 Aug. 2019, https://www.the-guardian.com/world/2019/aug/13/the-fashion-line-designed-to-trick-surveillance-cameras (accessed 19 Feb. 2021). The article describes the work of artist Kate Rose, who produced garments covered with text from the Fourth Amendment to the US Constitution. The text is printed on a garment in the form of licence plates, which will end up being added to the database of the licence plate reader. The Fourth Amendment, a mainstay of civil rights in the United States, states, '[t]he right of the people to be secure in their persons, houses, papers, and effects, against unreasonable searches and seizures, shall not be violated, and no Warrants shall issue, but upon probable cause, supported by Oath or affirmation, and particularly describing the place to be searched, and the persons or things to be seized.' *Legal Information Institute*, https://tinyurl.com/ycxxmrup (accessed 19 Feb. 2021). This practice is in the tradition of the ground-breaking anti-surveillance work of artist Jonah Brucker-Cohen, as described by Jeremy Hight, 'Police State', in 'Interview with Jonah Brucker-Cohen', Feb. 2011, *Re-Drawing Boundaries, LEA: Leonardo Electronic Almanac New Media Exhibition*, https://www.leoalmanac.org/wp-content/uploads/2011/03/Interview_Cohen.pdf (accessed 19 Feb. 2021). See also my article 'New-Media Art: An Irish Context', *Circa Art Magazine*, Circa Archive, 1 June 2007, https://circaartmagazine.website/backissues/circa-art-magazine-circa-120-review-new-media-art-an-irish-context-2/ (accessed 24 April 2021).

38 Nina Schick, *Deep Fakes and the Infocalypse* (London: Octopus/Monoray, 2020).

39 See Chelsea Whyte, 'Uniquely You', *New Scientist*, 2 March 2019, pp. 22–23.

40 See for example Sarah Zhang, 'When a DNA Test Reveals Your Daughter Is Not Your Biological Child', *The Atlantic*, 12 Oct. 2018, https://www.theatlantic.com/science/archive/2018/10/dna-test-divorce/571684/ (accessed 18 Feb. 2021).

41 Killian Woods and Barry J. Whyte, 'Judgment DNA', *Business Post: Post Plus*, 9 Feb. 2020, p. 2. On the harvesting of genetic data in Ireland, see Killian Woods and Barry J. Whyte, 'Genes for sale?' *Business Post: Post Plus*, 1 Oct. 2020, pp. 1–3.

42 In the mid-twentieth century, the opposing positions were represented by Walter Benjamin and Theodor Adorno respectively.

43 Soshana Zuboff, *The Age of Surveillance Capitalism* (London: Profile Books, 2019). For an overview of the ideas in the book, including an interview with the author, see John Naughton, 'The Goal Is to Automate Us: Welcome to the Age of Surveillance Capitalism', *The Guardian*, 20 Jan. 2019, https://www.theguardian.com/technology/2019/jan/20/shoshana-zuboff-age-of-surveillance-capitalism-google-facebook (accessed 28 Jan. 2021). Zuboff points out in the interview that the objective of the book is 'naming' or identification of the problem, a step on the way towards the ultimate goal of 'taming' or resolving the issue in a political sense. See also 'Shoshana Zuboff on Surveillance Capitalism', video, 49.59, VPRO Documentary, 20 Dec. 2019, https://www.youtube.com/watch?v=hIXhnWUmMvw&ab_channel=vprodocumentary (accessed 29 Jan. 2021). See also Karlin Lillington, 'We Deserve Better than Surveillance Capitalism', *The Irish Times*, 2 Jan. 2020, p. 13. For an informative account of the internet's military origin, see Levine, *Surveillance Valley*. A shorter, less formal argument along comparable lines to Zuboff's, together with a drastic proposed remedy, is Jaron Lanier, *Ten Arguments for Deleting Your Social Media Accounts Right Now* (London: Vintage, 2018).

44 See Evgeny Morozov, 'Capitalism's New Clothes', *The Baffler*, 4 Feb. 2019, https://thebaffler.com/latest/capitalisms-new-clothes-morozov (accessed 15 Oct. 2021). Morozov criticises Zuboff for what he sees as her adherence to 'managerial capitalism', her reformism and lack of consideration of alternatives to capitalism, her lack of attention to alternative analyses, and an overemphasis on surveillance capitalism as a phenomenon – as distinct from the overall system of capitalism itself. Morozov's key criticism of Zuboff's argument seems to be that the notion of surveillance capitalism shifts the theoretical and political focus from issues in regard to production and distribution relations within the realm of digital production, to issues of exchange between companies and consumers: "To make the behavioural surplus of *users* [...] so crucial to that theory is to conclude that the extraction of surplus from all the other parts doesn't matter, or perhaps even doesn't exist.' (The final phrase seems an

unnecessary exaggeration of Zuboff's position.) Morozov also notes Zuboff's transition from techno-optimism to techno-pessimism.

45 See Chapters 7–18 of Karl Marx, *Capital: A Critique of Political Economy*, Volume I, Book One, *The Process of Production of Capital*, trans. Samuel Moore and Edward Aveling, ed. Frederick Engels (London: Lawrence & Wishart, 1954), pp. 173–500. (See also references to 'Surplus-labour' and 'Surplus-value' in the subject index to this volume.)

46 Zuboff, *The Age of Surveillance Capitalism*, pp. 8–9.

47 See Morozov, *Capitalism's New Clothes*.

48 Zuboff, *The Age of Surveillance Capitalism*, p. 11.

49 *Ibid.*, p. 99. Zuboff cites Hannah Arendt, *The Origins of Totalitarianism* (New York: Schocken, 2004), p. 198. See Chapters 26–33 of Marx, *Capital*, Volume I, pp. 667–724.

50 Zuboff, *The Age of Surveillance Capitalism*, p. 129.

51 Trevor Timm, 'The Government Just Admitted It Will Use Smart Home Devices for Spying', *The Guardian*, 9 Feb. 2016, https://www.theguardian.com/commentisfree/2016/feb/09/internet-of-things-smart-devices-spying-surveillance-us-government (accessed 18 Feb. 2021).

52 Whitehead, 'Big Brother is Still Watching'.

53 Zuboff, *The Age of Surveillance Capitalism*, pp. 69–70.

54 *Ibid.*, p. 20.

55 *Ibid.*, pp. 84, 87, 88.

56 *Ibid.*, pp. 114–15.

57 *Ibid.*, p. 109.

58 See Anthony Lester, chapters on 'Free Speech' and 'Privacy', in *Five Ideas to Fight for*, pp. 99–193. Lester notes (p. 146) that one difficult problem is that of maintaining the right balance between freedom of the press, individual privacy and national security.

59 Slavoj Žižek, Did *Somebody Say Totalitarianism? Five Interventions in the (Mis)use of a Notion* (London/New York: Verso), p. 256. For a more recent discussion of the struggle for control of cyberspace, see Alexander Klimburg, *The Darkening Web: The War for Cyberspace* (New York: Penguin, 2017).

60 Zuboff, *The Age of Surveillance Capitalism*, p. 179.

61 *Ibid.*, p. 146.

62 *Ibid.*, pp. 139–40.

63 *Ibid.*, p. 192.

64 *Ibid.*, p. 193.

65 A key contemporary text on freedom is Isaiah Berlin, *Liberty* (Oxford: Oxford University Press, 2002).

66 Zuboff, *The Age of Surveillance Capitalism*, p. 202.

67 *Ibid.*, p. 207.

68 *Ibid.*, pp. 213–16.

69 See M.R. O'Connor, 'The Fight for the Right to Drive', *The New Yorker*, 30 April 2019, https://www.newyorker.com/culture/annals-of-inquiry/the-fight-for-the-right-to-drive (accessed 28 Jan. 2021).

70 Chris Stokel-Walker, 'Universities Are Using Surveillance Software to Spy on Students', *Wired*, 15 Oct. 2020, https://www.wired.co.uk/article/university-covid-learning-student-monitoring (accessed 29 Jan. 2020).

71 Zuboff, *The Age of Surveillance Capitalism*, pp. 221–5.

72 Jason Bloomberg, '7 Reasons Why the Internet of Things Is Doomed', *Wired*, n.d., https://www.wired.com/insights/2014/07/7-reasons-internet-things-doomed/ (accessed 19 Feb. 2021). The author lists such issues as security, privacy, digital fatigue, mutually exclusive digital ecosystems (e.g. Apple versus Android), the lack of a 'killer app', the counterweight of legacy technology, and tensions for control between vendors and consumers. (Bloomberg's overall position is somewhat more nuanced than the strongly worded headline suggests.)

73 Zuboff, *The Age of Surveillance Capitalism*, p. 225.

74 *Ibid.*, p. 237. Zuboff cites Jonathan A. Obar and Anne Oeldorf-Hirsch, 'The Biggest Lie on the Internet: Ignoring the Privacy Policies and Terms of Service Policies of Social Networking Services', in *Information, Communication & Society* (TPRC 44: The 44th Research Conference on Communication, Information and Information Policy, Arlington, VA: Social Science Research Network, 2016), https://papers.ssrn.com/abstract=2757465 (accessed 11 Sep. 2021).

75 Zuboff, *The Age of Surveillance Capitalism* p. 239.

76 *Ibid.*, pp. 243–4.

77 *Ibid.*, pp. 246–7.

78 *Ibid.*, p. 252.

79 *Ibid.*, p. 279.

80 *Ibid.*, p. 256. Zuboff cites Hal R. Varian, 'Beyond Big Data', *Business Economics*, vol. 49, no. 1 (2014), pp. 28–9.

81 Zuboff, *The Age of Surveillance Capitalism*, pp. 341–4.

82 *Ibid.*, p. 344.

83 *Ibid.*, p. 347.

84 *Ibid.*, pp. 352–4.

85 Benito Mussolini, *The Doctrine of Fascism* (Hawaii: Haole Church Library, 2015), p. 4, quoted in Zuboff, *The Age of Surveillance Capitalism,* p. 354.

86 Zuboff, *The Age of Surveillance Capitalism*, p. 355.

87 *Ibid.*, p. 360.

88 *Ibid.*, p. 363.

89 *Ibid.*, pp. 364–70.

90 *Ibid.*, pp. 371–2.

91 *Ibid.*, pp. 376–9.

92 *Ibid.*, p. 383.

93 *Ibid.*, p. 387.

94 *Ibid.*, p. 388.

95 *Ibid.*, pp. 388–90.

96 See 'China Invents the Digital Totalitarian State', *The Economist*, 17 Dec. 2016, https://www.economist.com/briefing/2016/12/17/china-invents-the-digital-totalitarian-state. Quoted in Zuboff, *The Age of Surveillance Capitalism*, p. 391.

97 Zuboff, *The Age of Surveillance Capitalism*, p. 394.

98 Allen Carter, 'China is Introducing the World's First Smart AI City', *Kedlist*, 12 Dec. 2020, https://kedlist.com/china-is-introducing-the-worlds-first-smart-ai-city/ (accessed 29 Jan. 2020).

99 Ed Jefferson, 'No, China Isn't Black Mirror: Social Credit Scores Are More Complex and Sinister Than That', *New Statesman*, 27 April 2018, https://www.newstatesman.com/science-tech/2018/04/no-china-isn-t-black-mirror-social-credit-scores-are-

more-complex-and-sinister (accessed 28 Jan. 2021).

100 Rhett Jones, 'Your Credit Score Should Be Based on Your Web History, IMF says', *Gizmodo*, 18 Dec. 2020, https://gizmodo.com/your-credit-score-should-be-based-on-your-web-history-1845912592 (accessed 28 Jan. 2021).

101 Zuboff, *The Age of Surveillance Capitalism*, p. 399.

102 *Ibid.*, p. 395.

103 See Martin Heidegger, *The Question Concerning Technology and Other Essays*, (New York: Harper and Row, 1977) and Carl Schmitt, 'The Age of Neutralizations and Depoliticizations' (1929) in Schmitt, *The Concept of the Political*, trans. and introd. Georg Schwab (Chicago/London: The University of Chicago Press, 2007), pp. 80–96. In the foreword to the Schmitt book, Tracy B. Strong lists five phases of development in terms of how thought was structured in the last five hundred years, according to Schmitt's perspective. These were theology, metaphysics, ethical humanism, economics and (finally, in our own time) technicity (p. xxviii). For a useful survey of the dominance of technology and associated modes of thought, with particular reference to Heidegger, see William Barrett, *The Illusion of Technique* (New York: Anchor Press/Doubleday, 1978).

104 Unlike many on the right, some far-rightists do not reject environmentalism; they use it as fuel for an envisaged future domination. See Jason Wilson, 'Eco-Fascism is Undergoing a Revival in the Fetid

Culture of the Extreme Right', *The Guardian*, 19 March 2019, https://www.theguardian.com/world/commentisfree/2019/mar/20/eco-fascism-is-undergoing-a-revival-in-the-fetid-culture-of-the-extreme-right (accessed 19 Feb. 2021).

105 Zuboff, *The Age of Surveillance Capitalism*, pp. 480–8. The text of the GDPR is available at https://eur-lex.europa.eu/eli/reg/2016/679/oj (accessed 27 Jan. 2021).

106 David Cowan, 'Is Your Digital Assistant Spying on You?', *The Sunday Business Post Magazine*, 21 Feb. 2019, p. 15.

107 Zuboff, *The Age of Surveillance Capitalism*, pp. 488–92. See for example the discussion of the work of artist Adam Harvey in Derrick Broze, 'Artist Creates Fabric That Can Fool Facial Recognition Tech', *Wired*, 14 Jan. 2017, https://www.activistpost.com/2017/01/artist-creates-fabric-that-can-fool-facial-recognition-tech.html (accessed 11 Sep. 2021).

108 See for example Suzanne Lynch, 'Tide Turns on Social Media Giants in US', *The Irish Times*, 8 Aug. 2019, and Cathal Mac Coille, 'Apple Should Face Same Grilling over Privacy as Politicians', *The Sunday Business Post*, 1 Sep. 2019, p. 19.

109 See Lizzie Dearden, 'Facial Recognition Technology "Violates Human Rights and Must End", Landmark Court Case Hears', *Independent*, 21 May 2019, https://www.independent.co.uk/news/uk/home-news/facial-recognition-uk-police-wales-london-legal-challenge-hu-

man-rights-a8924296.html (accessed 28 Jan. 2021).

110 John Gray, 'The New Tech Totalitarianism', review of Shoshana Zuboff, *The Age of Surveillance Capitalism: The Fight for a Human Future at the New Frontier of Power*, *New Statesman*, 8–14 Feb. 2019, p. 38. For some background to Zuboff's thinking, see Mathias Döpfner, interview with Shoshana Zuboff, *Insider*, 24 Nov. 2019, https://www.businessinsider.com/harvard-professor-shoshana-zuboff-on-big-tech-and-democracy-2019-11?r=US&IR=T (accessed 8 March 2021). For an entertaining, if scary, overview of the area of surveillance, see John Naughton, 'Slouching Towards Dystopia', *New Statesman*, 28 Feb.–5 March 2020. For an account of some recent related issues in an Irish context, see T.J. McIntyre, 'Bill Will Give Garda Access to Your Entire Digital Life', *The Irish Times*, 17 June 2021, p. 12.

111 An informative source on this is 'Surveillance Self-Defence: Tips, Tools and How-Tos for Safer Online Communications: A Project of the Electronic Frontier Foundation', https://ssd.eff.org (accessed 21 Feb. 2021). (See also Lanier, *Ten Arguments*.)

112 Edward Snowden, quoted in Damon Wise, 'Edward Snowden on the Dangers of Mass Surveillance and Artificial Intelligence', *Variety*, 26 Nov. 2019, https://variety.com/2019/digital/festivals/idfa-edward-snowden-1203416674/ (accessed 20 Feb. 2021).

Conclusion

1 Tzvetan Todorov, *Hope and Memory: Reflections on the Twentieth Century* (London: Atlantic Books, 2014), p. 189.

2 For a discussion of this area, see Jeffrey Dorfman, 'Sorry Bernie Bros But Nordic Countries Are Not Socialist', *Forbes*, 8 July 2018, https://www.forbes.com/sites/jeffreydorfman/2018/07/08/sorry-bernie-bros-but-nordic-countries-are-not-socialist/?sh=3a5fe10974ad (accessed 30 March 2021). See also Ann Jones, 'After I Lived in Norway, America Felt Backward. Here's Why', *The Nation*, 28 Jan. 2016, https://www.thenation.com/article/archive/after-i-lived-in-norway-america-felt-backward-heres-why/ (accessed 30 March 2021).

3 To take one example close to home, much time is currently spent on teaching religion in Irish primary schools. This not only is unfair to the non-religious (or members of other religions) but also takes up valuable time that might otherwise be spent on European language learning – vital for the future if, under the pressure of Brexit and other threats, Ireland is to consolidate its future position within the EU.

4 To illustrate the point, the teachings of Darwin, or some version of them, may be 'true' (whatever that may mean) but the consequences of the widespread acceptance of Darwinism were not always desirable. To take one obvious example, Hitler undoubtedly misunderstood Darwinism; but without Darwin, Nazism would not have existed, at least in the form it took. For a brief overview of this conten-

tious area, see History.Com Editors, 'Social Darwinism', *History*, original 6 April 2018, updated 21 Aug. 2018, https://www.history.com/topics/early-20th-century-us/social-darwinism (accessed 10 Jan. 2021).

5   Any discourse, outside of the realm of literary fiction, implicitly admits that truth is preferable to falsehood. (Fiction itself is implicitly justified in terms of the extent to which it reveals underlying 'truths' – for example, about society or psychology).

6   Schwab, *The Fourth Industrial Revolution*. See also Klaus Schwab and Thierry Malleret, *Covid-19: The Great Reset* (Geneva: Forum Publishing, 2020).

Afterword

1   This is a play on the title of the book *The Pooh Perplex* by Frederick Crews, involving the satirical application of literary theory to an analysis of the children's book *Winnie-the-Pooh*.

2   By contrast though, Timothy Snyder points out the collapse of local press in the United States and the transformation of news into entertainment. Timothy Snyder, *The Road to Unfreedom: Russia, Europe, America* (UK: Penguin Random House, 2018), p. 247.

3   For a thought-provoking analysis, see Jacques Baud, 'The Military Situation in the Ukraine', *The Postil Magazine*, 1 April 2022, https://www.thepostil.com/the-military-situation-in-the-ukraine/?fbclid=IwAR2Q-oPUbQ4gIBjafEIegBDc9Pox4Th2cs-fTba5Y1Z1_v1-X-dBo9NBfjmDQ (accessed 18 May 2022).

4   See for example 'John Mearsheimer: Great Power Politics on Ukraine', YouTube video, 19.13, *CGTN World Insight*, 16 April 2022, https://www.youtube.com/watch?v=Zmn-llaCMaJw&ab_channel=CGTN (accessed 16 May 2022). For background, see also 'Why is Ukraine the West's Fault? Featuring John Mearsheimer', YouTube video, 1.4.:15, *The University of Chicago,* 25 Sep. 2015, https://www.youtube.com/watch?v=JrMiSQAGOS4&ab_channel=TheUniversityofChicago (accessed 17 May 2022).

5   Catherine Belton, *Putin's People: How the KGB Took Back Russia and then Took on the West* (London: William Collins, 2020), p. 189.

6   Anton Shekhovtsov, *Russia and the Western Far Right* (London and New York: Routledge, 2018), pp. 80–1.

7   *Ibid.*, p. 3.

8   *Ibid.*, p. 61.

9   Vladimir Putin, Meeting of the Valdai International Discussion Club, 2013, http://en.kremlin.ru/events/president/news/19243 (accessed 19 May 2022).

10 Shekhovtsov, *Russia and the Western Far Right*, p. 71.

11 *Ibid.*, p. 76.

12 *Ibid.*, pp. 69–71.

13 *Ibid.*, p. 71.

14 *Ibid.*, p. 93.

15 For Putin's response to the expansion of NATO, see Belton, *Putin's People,* p. 367.

16 David Lane, 'The Orange Revolution: "People's Revolution" or Revolutionary Coup?' https://commonweb.unifr.ch/artsdean/pub/gestens/f/as/

files/4760/39746_174023.pdf (accessed 19 May 2022).

17 Snyder, *The Road to Unfreedom*, p. 5.

18 *Ibid.*, pp. 18, 30.

19 Belton, *Putin's People*, p. 326.

20 These kinds of cultural criticisms span the political divide, from Martin Heidegger on the right to Theodor Adorno on the left.

21 See Belton, *Putin's People*, p. 386.

22 'Noam Chomsky in Conversation with Davor Džalto,' video, 55.50, *global+conversations*, 28 April 2022, https://www.youtube.com/watch?v=OHocgZjbgFM&ab_channel=EnskildaH%C3%B6gskolanStockholm (accessed 17 May 2022).

23 *Ibid.*

24 For a discussion of this complex issue, see Lara Marlowe, 'Putin Says He Wants to "De-Nazify" Ukraine. Is there any Truth in this?' *The Irish Times*, Saturday 22 April 2022.

25 See Belton, *Putin's People*, p. 385.

26 Belton covers this comprehensively throughout her book *Putin's People*.

27 See Belton, *Putin's People*, pp. 419, 421, 431.

28 Snyder, *The Road to Unfreedom*, pp. 56–7.

29 Ivan Alexandrovich Ilyin, *On Resistance to Evil by Force*, trans. K. Benoit (Taxiarch Press, 2018).

30 *Ibid.*, p. 47. See also Snyder, *The Road to Unfreedom*, pp. 15–35.

31 See Pepe Escobar, 'Clash of Christianities: Why Europe Cannot Understand Russia', *The Cradle*, 29 April 2022, https://thecradle.co/Article/columns/9733?fbclid=IwAR1oZcFI-h7zR6Gk7uO6VKc4JQufDpoUAxy-pmBZDhBy6_Y_OqWhSCZicevrM (accessed 16 May 2022).

32 See Shevovstov, *Russia and the Western Far Right*.

33 Snyder, *The Road to Unfreedom,* pp. 67–109.

34 Jaweed Kaleem, 'A Russian Empire "from Dublin to Vladivostok"? The Roots of Putin's Ultranationalism', *Los Angeles Times*, 28 March 2022, https://news.yahoo.com/russian-empire-dublin-vladivostok-roots-100023581.html (accessed 17 May 2022).

35 Snyder, *The Road to Unfreedom*, p. 252.

36 Belton, *Putin's People*, pp. 36, 102.

37 *Ibid.*, p. 326.

38 *Ibid.*, p. 260.

39 'How Rotten is Russia's Army?' *The Economist*, 30 April 2022 (updated 9 May 2022) https://www.economist.com/leaders/2022/04/30/how-rotten-is-russias-army (accessed 16 May 2022).

40 For an interesting discussion, see Peter Savodnik, 'The Brothers Karamazov: The Secret Source of Putin's Evil', *Vanity Fair*, 10 Jan. 2017, https://www.vanityfair.com/news/2017/01/the-secret-source-of-putins-evil (accessed 25 April 2022).